SAVING PR
SARBI

Sandra Lee is an Australian author and journalist with 25 years of experience in the daily newspaper and magazine publishing industry in Australia and the United States. She is the author of three non-fiction books including the best-selling *18 Hours, The True Story of an SAS War Hero*, which a former Chief of the Australian Defence Force, General Peter Cosgrove (RET) called a 'thrilling, fast-paced account of Australian soldiers in a real war against a real terrorist enemy'.

She also wrote the best-selling true crime book *Beyond Bad: The Life And Crimes Of Katherine Knight, Australia's Hannibal* and *The Promise: An Iraqi Mother's Desperate Flight to Freedom*.

Her books have been published in the United States, the United Kingdom and Europe.

Sandra lived in New York City for almost four years where she worked as a foreign correspondent for News Limited's Australian newspapers. She is a former assistant editor and opinion columnist of *The Daily Telegraph*, editor-at-large at Australia's biggest selling women's magazine, *marie claire*, and was the last back-page columnist of *The Sunday Telegraph*.

She now writes regularly for *Madison* and *Vogue* fashion magazines as well as *Sunday magazine*.

For more information or to contact the author, visit
www.sandralee.com.au

SAVING PRIVATE SARBI

SANDRA LEE

ALLEN&UNWIN

Allen & Unwin
Sydney, Melbourne, Auckland, London

83 Alexander Street
Crows Nest NSW 2065
Australia
Phone: (61 2) 8425 0100
Fax: (61 2) 9906 2218
Email: info@allenandunwin.com
Web: www.allenandunwin.com

Cataloguing-in-Publication details are available
from the National Library of Australia
www.trove.nla.gov.au

ISBN 978 1 74237 557 1

Internal design by Darian Causby
Set in 12/16 pt Goudy by Post Pre-press Group, Australia
Printed and bound in Australia by the SOS Print + Media Group.

20 19 18 17 16 15 14 13

For my husband, JP Clemence

And for the doggies, brave and loyal warriors who have
given us their absolute all, yet ask for nought in return

Also, for their handlers, past, present and future

'There is no faith which has never yet been broken,
except that of a truly faithful dog.'
Konrad Lorenz

In Dogs We Trust
Unofficial motto of the soldiers in the Explosive
Detection Dog Section

To Protect
Motto of the Australian Army's Incident
Response Regiment

Ubique (Everywhere)
Motto of the Royal Australian Engineers Corps

Contents

Prologue

A HIGH-RANKING MUTT

Early on 11 November in 2009 Kevin Rudd hunkered over a wooden trestle table in the mess tent of the Australian Army's elite Special Air Service Regiment at Camp Russell, deep in the war-torn province of Uruzgan in southern Afghanistan. Across the table from the twenty-sixth prime minister of Australia sat General Stanley Allen McChrystal, a strikingly lean figure decked out in United States Army standard-issue combat fatigues. Rudd enthusiastically smeared Vegemite over a slice of buttered toast as McChrystal looked on, sipping a mug of instant black coffee, his usual brew. An outspoken and controversial career officer, he had earned his fourth star five months earlier but won a reputation as a 'snake-eating rebel' long before. McChrystal was the top-ranking officer in Afghanistan with a direct pipeline to the recently installed President of the United States, Barack Obama.

The prime minister and general could not have been more unalike. Rudd's pixie-like countenance and moon-shaped face was topped by a flop of greying blond hair that blew when in a moderate wind. He wore R.M. Williams boots and a blue open-necked shirt tucked into dark trousers. At fifty-two, his body had softened with age and resembled the physique of a man not inclined to the disciplines of athletic pursuit. In the company of soldiers his bookishness was replaced by a manufactured matey-ness and his clipped, almost passionless vowels became riddled with the ockerisms and occasional profanities for which he was known.

McChrystal, by contrast, was wiry and muscular, the result of the eleven-to-twelve kilometres he ran daily regardless of location. A hawkish nose and close-set gimlet eyes punctuated a chiselled face road-mapped with crevasses from a life lived hard. The general was a disciplined man, a perfectionist who slept a maximum of five hours a night and limited his food intake to one 'big-ass meal' a day, usually in the evening. If hungry, he snacked on salted Bavarian pretzels. Coffee kept him alert.

The meeting was significant and came at a critical time in President Obama's strategic plans for the long war in Afghanistan, which he had made a priority over Iraq.

Public support had waned and the number of American and coalition soldiers being killed was growing at an alarming rate. Two months earlier McChrystal had warned the new president that the war was at risk of failure, a word he repeated several times in the top-secret 66-page report he had been asked to compile. The general outlined the status quo, which amounted to eight years and little progress, as well as his vision that highlighted 'the urgent need for a significant change to our strategy and the way that we think and operate'.

Australia, like the United Kingdom, was irrevocably wedded to its alliance with America and had a lot of skin in the game. More than 500 coalition personnel had been killed in 2009 alone, making it the deadliest year since the war began in 2001. Australia had suffered 91 casualties and, at that time, eleven fatalities. Seven Diggers had been killed since Rudd became prime minister. In two years he had made too many heart-wrenching condolence calls to grief-stricken families, the last on 18 July following the death of Private Benjamin Ranaudo, who was killed by an improvised explosive device (IED). The crudely made bombs were the enemy's weapon of choice and were lethally effective, placed to cause maximum carnage to the coalition forces and civilians alike.

Back in April Rudd had increased troop numbers on the ground by 450 servicemen and women, taking the number to 1550. But he signed off on the extra troops with a measure of caution, deliberately limiting the soldiers to roles such as providing security and training and mentoring members of the Afghan National Army (ANA) in the dangerous and violent province of Uruzgan. The prime minister did not hold back on conveying his message either. In September, a day before meeting the president at the international G20 meeting in Pittsburgh, Rudd declared during an interview on CNN that Australia's current troop numbers were 'about right'. The unspoken subtext was that there would be no more coming. 'Our commitment, in partnership with our American allies, is to be there for the long haul,' he added reassuringly.

McChrystal already had sent a message to Canberra via Australia's chief commanders, requesting that restrictions on where the Australian soldiers operated be eased. Known as 'red cards', the restrictions were strictly observed by the Army's commanders in Afghanistan. Yet, under McChrystal's highly publicised new counter-insurgency program, the general ostensibly wanted the Australian troops to deploy on routine combat missions with their Afghan partners beyond Uruzgan.

The prime minister had flown in secrecy to Camp Russell to the isolated and heavily fortified joint Dutch-Australian military outpost, travelling in the belly of a C-17 Globemaster III. The Royal Australian Air Force (RAAF) crew collected the prime minister and his entourage in Chennai, on the Bay of Bengal on the east coast of India, and arrived in Afghan airspace as the sun began its descent over the bone dry and barren landscape. Rudd had a barbeque dinner with the Australian soldiers in Poppy's Bar, a recreational mess area named in honour of the slain soldier David Pearce who was killed by an IED (improvised explosive device) in Uruzgan Province in 2007. Rudd, affecting a blokish idiom in an attempt to bond with the soldiers, boasted he was happy to 'yak with youse all' and was still making good on his promise the next morning.

Not since Billy Hughes spent a night at an army headquarters in France in 1916 had a prime minister bivouacked in a war zone. Yet, as biographer L.F. Fitzhardinge implies in his two-volume history *William Morris Hughes*, the prime minister of the Great War was some distance from the front and made only a fleeting visit. Rudd, by contrast, would spend an entire night in an active war zone, constantly under direct threat of enemy attack. He bedded down in accommodations provided by the highly trained and heavily armed troopers of the Special Air Service Regiment (SAS), men who live by the credo 'Who Dares Wins'. His sawn-off bunk bed was located in Camp Russell. It was, arguably, the safest section of the base, if there could be such a thing on a frontline. But even so, the stakes were extraordinarily high. Heads of government are high-value targets to the enemy. Nothing was left to chance.

This was the prime minister's third visit to Afghanistan but the first to coincide with a historically significant day for the military, Armistice Day.

General McChrystal flew in a small military aircraft with his regular entourage of advisers and a security detachment, landing on the former US base as the sun was rising. The two leaders had a tight schedule, micro-managed almost to the minute. They started the day with a casual meet-and-greet with a couple of SAS troopers who joined them for breakfast, witnessed by the small press pack that travelled with the prime minister.

Next up was a private briefing in which McChrystal would give Rudd, the Australian Defence Minister John Faulkner, and the boss of the Australian Defence Force (ADF), Air Chief Marshal Angus Houston, a strategic and tactical overview of the situation in Afghanistan and discuss Australia's continued contribution.

At 1100 hours the dignitaries would attend the annual

Remembrance Day service to commemorate the signing of Armistice in Europe in 1918, which effectively ended the First World War. The service honoured the 330,000 Australians who served and the 60,000 young men whose blood was fatally spilled on foreign soil. McChrystal, aware of the solemnity of the occasion, would lay a wreath during the ceremony.

After that, a tour of the trades school where Australian soldiers from the Second Mentoring and Reconstruction Task Force, or MRTF2, taught Afghan men basic construction and engineering skills.

Every hour was accounted for yet the prime minister had a surprise for the general—a closely guarded secret that would make headlines around the world when revealed. The brass in Afghanistan had been sitting on the secret for fifteen days. Rudd had been briefed on the subject and, keenly aware of the value of good news in a war zone, was eager to share it with McChrystal. After all, a member of the elite US Special Forces had played an integral role in the unprecedented accomplishment and there was nothing like shared success to cement diplomatic relationships.

Besides, this story was too irresistible to ignore, especially for a dog-loving prime minister who was currently writing a children's book about his own adorable pet golden retriever and mischievous cat and their adventures on Australia Day with the help of actor Rhys Muldoon.

With breakfast done, Rudd, beaming boyishly, directed the American general outside the mess tent. There, sitting obediently beside an Australian soldier, was a big, black dog called Sarbi. She was a highly trained member of the

Explosive Detection Dog Section, or Doggies as it is colloquially known, and one of the Army's secret assets.

The soldier was armed with an automatic rifle slung over
his back, a sidearm strapped to his thigh and a well-chewed
tennis ball for the happy-go-lucky mutt. Sarbi bolted after
the ball when he tossed it for the waiting cameras.

'Sit.'

Sarbi dutifully obeyed. The prime minister and the general crouched down next to the dog as Rudd regaled his
guest with the remarkable story of the beautiful mutt with
a white blaze that ran vertically down her broad chest.

Sarbi was born on 11 September in 2002, one year to
the day after the terrorist attacks on American soil that
killed almost 3000 innocent souls, mostly civilians. There
was unspoken significance in the coincidence.

Loyal and smart, Sarbi was like a puppy that never grew
up, eager to please and quick to protect. Not even the most
world-weary and battle-scarred soldier could remain imper-
vious to the huge hound with beautiful big round eyes the
colour of dark chocolate, especially as she tilted her head
to the side and crinkled her forehead as if deep in thought
whenever an instruction was issued or her name called.
The pink tongue lolling out the front of her mouth helped,
too. Sarbi did dangerous work and never once failed her
masters. In fact, she had protected them from death by
using her powerful nose to sniff out IEDs and explosives
and cleverly alert her handler to their presence.

Sarbi had gone missing in action on 2 September 2008,
when the Taliban ambushed her patrol. Nine Diggers,
including Sarbi's handler, who for security reasons can only

be referred to as D, were injured in the closely fought three-hour battle for life and death. It was the largest number of Australian casualties in one incident since the Vietnam War.

Shrapnel hit Sarbi, too.

One of the three Australians to escape unhurt was SAS Corporal Mark Donaldson, who was awarded the Victoria Cross for his gallantry under fire that day.

Sergeant D's American counterpart, Sergeant First Class Gregory Rodriguez, was killed while trying heroically to protect a wounded colleague. His dog Jacko survived the firefight.

In the chaos of the ambush Sarbi was separated from the patrol. When it was over she was gone, lost in the Afghanistan terrain. But the miracle mutt defied the odds. She survived the firefight and for thirteen months somehow managed to live through a brutal winter and scorching summer in wild and dangerous countryside.

The prime minister simply loved the story of the plucky pooch and the day couldn't have been more appropriate for an unofficial homecoming parade for the explosives detection dog.

Gallipoli had Simpson and his donkey. Now Afghanistan had another four-legged star—Sarbi. The cameras clicked and reporters took notes. The fiercely loyal and resourceful Sarbi was about to become the nation's most famous hound.

General McChrystal couldn't have known it, but a heroic soldier with four paws had just upstaged his four stars.

PART ONE

Sarbi the Civilian

Chapter 1

LITTER OF DISAPPOINTMENT

Sarbi didn't start life as a heroic explosive detection dog, nor was she bred to join the Australian Army and serve her country on foreign battlefields. In fact, she started life as an abject disappointment. Not to Ric Einstein, though. Disappointment was the last thing on his mind when a customer walked into his pet shop one spring day in 2002, carrying a pair of fluffy, squeaking pups wriggling with wonderment at the newness of life. They were two of a litter of eight.

The former computer executive knows dogs, loves them, and has done all his life. He quit his fast-paced life and a high-powered job for a tree change in the picturesque town of Mittagong in the Southern Highlands of New South Wales in 1990. Seeking a new business opportunity, he bought a pet shop in a handsome corner building constructed in 1882 on the old Hume Highway, renamed it Animal Magnetism, and hung out his shingle. The shop previously didn't sell pups, but Einstein changed that and by 2002 had a thriving business selling dogs from reputable breeders.

Einstein's customer, the one with the pups, explained that she had a pair of pure-bred black Labrador retrievers that she had wanted to breed. They were show dogs and, as with most hounds that brave the show ring for judgement day, were just magnificent. Show dogs must be as near to the prescribed definition of physical perfection as the breeder is capable of producing. The Australian National Kennel Council (ANKC), one of the overarching bodies that determine all things to do with breeding, nominates seventeen stipulations that, if met, will allow all dogs including the lovable Lab, as they are commonly and affectionately known, to be anointed with the ultimate status of 'pure-bred'.

The list is exhaustive and would test the tenacity of all but the most determined breeders, showers and doggie stage mothers. General appearance, characteristics and temperament are covered. So too, in minutiae, the dimensions and looks required of the head, the shape of the skull, and the positioning of the eyes, ears, mouth and neck. Forequarters, hindquarters, body, feet, tail, gait and movement, coat, colour and size must also be just so.

Labrador tails, for instance, are known as Otter tails and should be medium in length and covered in thick, dense, short fur that grows evenly all the way around. It must be absent of feathering and, here is its intrinsic charm, 'may be carried gaily'. Mind you, though, not so gaily that it curls over the dog's back. It's a Labrador, not a pug! Coats should be short and dense, hard to the touch, and again, without waviness or feathering off into little tufts of errant fur that don't sit flat. Eyes should be medium-sized and express intelligence, although if you've seen enough Labs you've probably seen one or two with a permanently quizzical look that makes them seem, well, somewhat less than intelligent and perhaps a little dopey.

A small white spot on the chest is tolerable, but only just. As the American Kennel Club states, a white mark is permissible but 'not desirable'. Cow hocks, or feet that turn out while the hocks turn in, are 'highly undesirable'. A 'snipey' jaw will win you no favours from the meticulous judging panel, a powerful one will. Dog fanciers are themselves a fastidious breed. The canines' deviations and flaws, which the Nobel Prize–winning Austrian zoologist Konrad Lorenz dismissively described in his book *Man Meets Dog* as 'well-proportioned triumphs of modern hairdressing', are seriously frowned upon. Pity the poor hound that has the temerity to be shown with any, and pity more its owner who will receive a particularly galling humiliation—disqualification of their dog.

Pure breeds are bred and bred and bred to conform to the rigid, some say sclerotic, specifications, often with disastrous consequences. Not so the lesser mutt whose genetic imperfections and physical flaws are taken for what they are—marvellously muttly. They make the dog stronger and less prone to illness. Hybrid vigour, farmers boast.

Most people regard the handsome, blocky Labrador as

the dolphin of the canine world because it, too, appears to perpetually smile. But technically, they are gun dogs bred to help hunters retrieve their felled prey. However, the majority of real working Labs these days are employed as assistance dogs for people with illnesses or disabilities. They are among the most common canines in the Western world because they make for dependable family pets and are routinely included in the top ten breeds in terms of popularity. Nicely tempered, not shy or aggressive, intelligent, keen and biddable all adds up to making the Lab an adaptable and devoted companion, as the ANKC points out. Very keen swimmers, too, a legacy of their original purpose and provenance as retrievers of fishing nets in the cold waters of Newfoundland on the northeast coast of Canada. And there is a bonus for the fashion conscious: Labs come in three colours: jet black, shades of brown, and gold that can range from fox red to light cream.

Ric Einstein knew the kennel club standards and that the pure-bred black Labradors belonging to his customer were faithful to them. There was one problem: the two pups she brought in that spring day were not. Cute they might be but there was no escaping the obvious. They plainly weren't quite Labrador enough. Einstein's customer couldn't have known that when the bitch fell pregnant in early July. It only became evident that the trusty black Lab wasn't so trusty after all when she whelped on 11 September. She was a tearaway who had made a break from the confines of the family backyard during the most crucial days of her three-week in-heat cycle, the time when an indiscreet doggie dalliance may very well result in pups. And it had. Her intended mating and house partner, it turns out, was not the sire. 'It was a mistake mating,' Einstein says now. 'They had absolutely no idea who the father was.' The woman had come to Einstein for help. Labrador pups are easy to identify for those in the know. Not so this lot. Did he have any idea? Einstein took one look at the giant pups, which had the softest, waviest, feathery fur, impossibly wide-set eyes, and snouts nearly as broad as their heads, and knew instantly. The Lab had mated with a Newfoundland. Who that Newfoundland was, however, was another matter, but he had his suspicions—there can't be that many un-neutered dogs in the area.

Einstein backed his call with first-hand field evidence. He checked the paws—'they were massive'—and found the hallmark webbing between the toes, a signature of both the Labrador retriever and the Newfoundland. On top of that, he had raised two Newfoundlands from pups and was more than familiar with their idiosyncratic physiognomy. His first was named Tiny—because he wasn't—and the one he had with him in the shop that day was Goofy, a protective bulk that could sniff friend or foe from ten paces and place himself between danger and his master without causing offence. Einstein's third, Sampson, is a Landseer, a rare sub-breed of Newfoundlands recognised by the large amount of white in its long coat and startlingly pretty blue eyes. 'They are incredible dogs, known as the gentle giant of the dog world,' he says.

Einstein cast his eyes over the pups one more time just to be sure and was certain beyond doubt of the rogue paternity. The genetic fingerprints—*pawprints?*—of the Lab were there . . . but.

'They looked just like Newfie pups. They were big, much bigger than Labs at the same age. The thing about Newfies and Labs and golden retrievers is that they all come down through the same genes,' he says. 'The goldens and Labs were bred from the Newfoundland, that is the predominant gene.'

Breeders breed to order, usually for very prescriptive clients. Einstein's customer explained that those who had been destined to receive the pure-bred black Labrador pups weren't interested in taking any of these mixed-breed mistakes. Theoretically they were mutts and people who spend good money to buy pure breeds don't want dogs of indeterminate pedigree with no papers to brandish, no matter how enchanting their little faces.

Fortune shone on Einstein. The woman offered her litter of disappointment to him. He was happy to take them on, for a price.

'I took the whole litter, which I normally don't do, but I took these because I knew I would have no trouble moving them,' he recalls fondly, eight years down the track. 'They were lovely.'

The dogs were black, all black, except for one thing. Each had a tiny tuft of fur in pristine puppy white on its excitable chest, the telltale blaze of Newfoundlands and Labradors.

One of them was Sarbi. She was not such a disappointment after all.

*

Something strange but indescribably lovely happens to humans when we see a tiny helpless puppy, a coiled-up bundle of fur with oversized paws and over-long ears it has yet to grow into. We coo, we sigh, we tickle, we smile, and we become radiant with a love so pure it could right all the wrongs of the world in a heartbeat. Even if the puppy is not ours it has the power to make us melt into puddles of mush, like ice-cream left in summer's sun; to make the hardest of us soften with a tenderness we might never have known existed.

We are driven by an inexplicable primal urge to pat the soft little upturned head, punctuated to perfection by beautiful beseeching liquid eyes, a tiny wet nose sniffing, sniffing, sniffing, and a panting pink tongue insistently licking with unrestrained pleasure, to taste and to touch, to learn and to know. A little nip from razor-sharp puppy teeth elicits a squeal, a knowing grimace, but rarely a stronger rebuke. Instead, maybe even an affectionate rub around the ears— after all, he's just a puppy, what does he know?

Biologists and sociologists, scientists and anthropologists might debate the many whys—*why are we compelled to react the way we do?* But they would not, no, they could not, dispute the axiomatic truth of this: the flood of emotions that washes over us at the first sight of a pup is instinctive, instant and ever so intoxicating. Addictive.

Pups, simply put, are just plain goodness. They are innocence and joy with a healthy dose of naughtiness and cheekiness to boot. The beauty is in their simpleness of purpose—they intrinsically want to please and love us and we in turn want to be pleased and loved. They want to bond and we need to bond. It is a genetic imperative, a survival drive, and a burning social need. Dogs are pack animals. Humans too. Neither species does well if left to its own devices. And we do so much better in a pack, or family. It can be a human pack or a blended pack of different but equally adoring species that have adopted each other for mutual benefit. We are united in work, play and companionship and have been for 15,000 years, at the very least, and maybe even 100,000 years.

Pick up that puppy you're lovingly cooing at and feel its little puffs of warm breath on your face, like a shower of gossamer kisses. You're guaranteed to feel infinitely better than before. Watch as he nuzzles into the protective crook of your arm or next to your bosom, or rests his fist-sized head over your shoulder, followed by the plop of a paw, and you'll understand unconditional trust and, in response, feel a bloom of warrior protectiveness. Dogs make people better. Puppies make us giants.

And dogs make us *feel* better, too, healthier in body and soul and mind. You don't have to rely on the hocus pocus of psychobabble to explain the magical connection between humans and canines; you really can measure it in scientifically quantifiable ways. Your body chemistry will change. Your hormones will race. The ones that make us feel good, endorphins, serotonin and dopamine, and those related to social attachment and bonding such as oxytocin and prolactin, will go up. True for the dog, too. The stress-related hormones like cortisol, on the other hand, will go down. Like a finely calibrated set of scales. Your blood pressure will ease, your heart rate will relax, and your mood will improve—until, of course, he piddles on you.

Leave the little pup for a day and see what happens. Your welcome home will be as exuberant as it is energetic—*where have you been so long?* And that's even if you were gone mere minutes. Impulsive paws will dance on the floor and your toes, a muzzle will nudge at your ankles, a tail will wag as fast as a bee's wings and an expression-filled face, showing happiness and relief, will make you wish you'd never left. As Edgar Allan Poe once wrote so beautifully, 'there is eloquence in true enthusiasm'. Stress? What stress?

And this will be yours for several thoroughly enriched years, depending on your dog's breed, or if you're really lucky, maybe fifteen, sixteen or, bless, seventeen years. The oldest known dog, a beagle in the United States, reached a very ripe 28, roughly 196 in human years. That's a lot of doggie love.

Chapter 2

THE NEWFOUNDLAND: A BRIEF HISTORY

Ric Einstein was delighted with his litter of disappointment. He trusted his instincts about the eight black Labrador–Newfoundland mutts with their perfectly webbed feet, each with its own personality. He had a particular affinity for the giant Newfoundland. Two years after turning the local pet shop into something more like a bespoke business, Einstein bought his first Newfie, as he affectionately calls the breed. The purchase was no fluke. He'd been asking every customer who came into the shop about the breed of dog they owned and was struck by one thing. While everyone raved with obvious pride about their pedigree or bitza—bits of this, bits of that—those who owned the petite and pretty King Charles Cavalier or the bearish Newfoundland had one thing in common. Clearly, it wasn't size. 'They all had a gleam in their eye,' Einstein recalls.

Being a bit of a bear of a man himself, Einstein was not too keen on the King Charles but the consistent response from customers about the Newfoundland intrigued him. He asked one of his clients to bring her dog by the shop so he could examine it up close. 'His name was Griz, short for Grizzly Bear, and when I saw him I thought, *I want one of those*,' he says.

Bred as a water dog, the Newfoundland is an instinctive lifesaver, as loyal and gentle as—some might argue more loyal and gentle than—the Labrador, which is descended from it. They are physically impressive beasts, exceptionally strong, said to be the strongest of all canines, and built box-like with stout legs. The male stands, at shoulder height, about 75 centimetres above the ground. The female is only slightly smaller. She can weigh, at her slightest, about 50 kilograms, and he can be as heavy as 80 kilograms—although don't be fooled, none of the weight has to do with fat. The Newfoundland is an agile, muscle-bound, massively boned dog capable of swimming for miles in frigid conditions, or pulling loaded carts beyond the capacity of man. If you are in trouble in the water, you want a Newfoundland beside you. As if by some mysterious telepathy, they intuit danger and will haul you out of a pickle before you knew you were in it, and have done countless times over the centuries, rescuing imperilled fishermen and seafarers, and scores of drowning people caught in rips, tides and dangerous waterways.

Their shaggy coats, long, oily and waterproof, are built for their function as water dogs, evidence again of evolution's preference for function over form or, for the more spiritually minded, an example of how Mother Nature knows best. Either a dull black or a rich brown that verges on chocolate or bronze, and sometimes with tinges of both, they often have a white blaze on their chest and occasionally a sprinkle of white fur on their toes. All of which is heritably acceptable.

The Newfoundland is curiously handsome, not pretty so much—though don't tell an owner that—but noble and elegant. Still, to the dog lover's eye, the Newfoundland face is an all-round heartbreaker and reminds us of all things impossibly sweet. It looks poignant and slightly sad with droopy large jowls that hang like curtains from a perfectly square nose, large again, atop which sit dark, deep-set and small eyes that border on soulful and yet betray an acute intelligence and easy disposition, usually one of utter contentment and docility.

The breed has history on its side, too. It was first noted when Newfoundland was colonised in the early 1600s that the fishermen there used two types of big dogs to help them work. The names are self-explanatory, the Greater Newfoundland and the Lesser Newfoundland, or St John's Dog, which became the founding breed of the golden retriever. How they got to the isolated island is a matter of conjecture but it is thought the modern day version is a mix of the island's native dogs cross-bred with the giant black bear dogs imported by the adventurous Vikings around the year 1000. Portuguese fishermen later introduced the mastiff to the breed sometime in the fourteenth century, ensuring they remained big. True or not, the Nordic connection adds enormously to the romance of the dog and explains how it might have got to Newfoundland.

How it left, on the other hand, is a different story. Explorers and fishermen from Ireland and England arrived in the nineteenth century to fish the species-rich waters off the Grand Banks and they too saw the sense in utilising the clever, workaholic dogs. The dogs' tenacious, biddable and protective natures earned the respect of the industrious, hard-working men. When these nineteenth-century interlopers left, they took the Newfies with them, which is how they found their way into polite company in Europe and, later, America. Possibly because of its unparalleled heft, the breed became a status symbol and was paraded like a prize-winning magnificent mobile showpiece.

One of the most famous of the breed belonged to the prolific and controversial German composer, Richard Wilhelm Wagner, he of the epic operas commonly known as the *Ring Cycle*. Wagner owned four Newfies throughout his career, starting with Robber, who adopted the musician and travelled to London by boat with him when Wagner fled Riga, then the capital of Latvia, leaving behind a mountain of debt and a field of angry creditors. The perilous sea journey, on which both Robber and Wagner suffered torturous seasickness, inspired Wagner's opera *The Flying Dutchman*.

Wagner's second Newfoundland, Russ, was even more beloved and upon the dog's death the grief-stricken composer buried him in the grave in which the master would eventually be interred. The headstone read, 'Here Lies and Watches Wagner's Russ'.

A Newfoundland also unwittingly added to the humiliation of the French general and emperor, Napoleon Bonaparte, whose navy was famously defeated by the British fleet in the historic Battle of Trafalgar. Among the lesser-known aspects of the naval encounter is that a Newfie, serving as the mascot on the frigate HMS *Nymph*, was the first member of the triumphal boarding party to reach the deck of the surrendered French warship, *Cleopatra*. 'Dogs! Must I be defeated by them on the battlefield as well as in the bedroom?' the infamous Napoleon thundered when told the doggie detail. To appreciate the gravitas of the personal insult it helps to know that Napoleon's ultimately unfaithful wife, Josephine, let her pug Fortune sleep on their bed on their wedding night, a ritual he found repellent—and more so after the vicious pug attacked him, leaving a scar and instilling in him a contempt for dogs.

Not so incidentally, three of the fine-looking Newfoundland dogs made their home at 1600 Pennsylvania Avenue—otherwise known as the White House—including Faithful, owned by President Ulysses S. Grant's son, Jesse. After watching his heartbroken son deal with the loss of his previous Newfoundland, the president threatened the jobs of the entire White House staff if anything happened to Faithful. Faithful, like Grant, served two terms at the presidential address. No one lost their job.

The most famous White House Newfie, though, was Lara. She belonged to the fifteenth president of the United States, James Buchanan. The only childless bachelor to occupy the office, Buchanan was trailed everywhere by his dog, who became a celebrity in her own right. The devoted Lara was famous for lying motionless for hours on end with one eye closed and the other open and keeping watch over her master. Man should know such fidelity.

By the time Ric Einstein was introduced to his first Newfie in 1992, nothing of note had changed in the breed since the seventeenth century. He liked what he saw and in quick order acquired one of his own, a pup called Tiny.

Tiny became a celebrity at the Animal Magnetism pet shop and helped draw in customers. After Tiny's death, Einstein bought a second Newfoundland, Goofy, who was also a working dog—of sorts. He lumbered around the shop welcoming potential buyers and putting smiles on people's faces, unbidden, as dogs are wont to do. He also read people and sized up their intentions, a skill at which Newfoundlands in particular, and dogs in general, are highly adept. If Goofy detected foul play on the agenda, or sniffed a wayward teen trying to pocket free treats, he presented himself, an unavoidable and potentially dangerous bear of a dog. That was usually enough. Big dogs can be fearsome, especially if you don't know them.

The canine caper helped business and gave potential buyers an idea of the breed's temperament. No surprise then that Goofy was the poster pooch for Newfies when Einstein began selling his rogue litter.

Wendy Upjohn was determined to buy her children a black dog. She has a thing for them. Maybe it's because of the initial bonds formed in childhood, when colour, sense and memory is imprinted in our plastic, sponge-like brains, which absorb information at a rate we can barely fathom. We are infinitely receptive as children, hopelessly honest, fearlessly inquisitive. We are trustworthy, guileless. If something pleases us, we giggle with glee. If it doesn't, we recoil. No poker face for the young and innocent. Ditto a dog.

Wendy Upjohn grew up with a small menagerie including cats, dogs, a horse and even mice, the latter of which she was not particularly fond. Her first dog was a scruffy black and white terrier type named Taffy. A black Labrador, Lena, followed her. Later, Wendy bought a black cocker spaniel named Becky, who was re-housed to a farming family in New Zealand when Wendy and her then husband moved to China with their six-month-old daughter Gemma. She desperately missed having a canine companion and yearned for the time when that would be possible once more. 'Dogs are really, in my mind, angels given to us as a reminder of how much better we could be,' she says.

By October 2002, Wendy, who had remarried, was ready to introduce the species to her three children, aged between fifteen and five. Gemma, the oldest, had been joined by brothers Nic, who was eight, and Marcelo, then three weeks shy of his sixth birthday. The children had been nagging Wendy and the boys' father, Carlos, about adding a dog to the family for years. Wendy thought the time was right. What family is truly complete without man's best friend?

They lived in Bowral, a verdant and historic township 120 kilometres south of the Sydney GPO that was first established in 1823 as a cattle run. The family occupied a stunning block that backed on to 100 acres of scenic bushland and came with a century-old stone cottage. Their acre-sized property had a majestic oak tree in one corner around which they built a new Federation style house. It was idyllic. The neighbours had dams and duck ponds, the children built billycarts, rode their bikes, and lived a life among the great outdoors. All it needed was a dog.

On Wednesday 23 October, with the children at school, Wendy made the seven kilometre drive north to Animal Magnetism in Mittagong. She wanted to surprise the children with the dog they had long wanted. She was smitten as soon as she saw the Labrador–Newfoundland mutts playfully rolling around their box like tumbleweeds. *This is love at first sight*, she thought.

Goofy, ambling around like a barrel of happiness, helped, not that Wendy needed convincing. The Newfie's temperament reminded her of another dog, a soft natured German shepherd that had brought her family nothing but joy. 'I thought Goofy was adorable. He was big and even more boofy than my dad's Rommel and I had always loved him too,' Wendy says now.

People don't choose dogs. Dogs choose people. As Wendy swooned over the mischievous pups, fighting for attention with high-pitched yips and yaps, one crabbed its way to her in that distinct wobbly sideways walk of puppies. It snuggled under her hand, sliding its wet nose against her palm. She picked it up. 'I cuddled him and he was a real sook. He was the one for me—I am a sucker for a sooky animal,' she says. The dog was whimpering, a sure sign of dependency and need.

Wendy paid $375 and walked out with her children's first pup—vaccinated, microchipped and wormed.

But it wasn't Sarbi. She hadn't made the cut.

Eight-year-old Nic burst into tears as soon as he saw the dog. His dream had come true. The pup was small enough for him to hold in his little hands and Nic gently patted the coat, as feathery as that of a newborn cygnet. The pup scampered from person to person, introducing itself and busily gathering intelligence through its nose, breathing in the smells of the established pack to ascertain its position in the hierarchy. The pup's puppiness was infectious and the children giddily raced after him.

The boys named the pup Rafiki after a character in the animated Disney movie, *The Lion King*. The film had been Nic's favourite for the past couple of years and the children had seen it literally dozens of times. They loved the rich cast of funny, adorable and decent animals that roamed the fictional African veldt called the Pride Lands. They also had the soundtrack and knew every song by heart, not surprising for children of musicians.

If you've seen the film you will have been enchanted from the opening scenes, too, captivated long before the title credit appears on the screen. As dawn breaks, a native African voice calls out a haunting song through the darkness and is answered by an unseen chorus. Then, as if choreographed by an ancient ethologist, rhinoceros, meerkats, a cheetah and Marabou storks start to move across the plain, over which towers the breathtaking majesty of Mount Kilimanjaro. Elephants amble, gazelles leap, a mother giraffe and her baby lope in a mass migration of species heading towards a soaring outcrop called Pride Rock, upon which sit a lion, the eponymous king, his lioness and their newborn cub. A veritable United Nations of animals—zebras, guinea fowl, a hornbill named Zazu—merge below in a kaleidoscope of colour, waiting for a sacred ceremony to begin.

Out of the teeming mass emerges Rafiki, a wise and jungle smart old baboon walking on all fours and carrying a walking stick topped with gourds. He straightens up and walks to the lion, King Mufasa, who beams with obvious pleasure as Rafiki throws his arms around him in a hug. As the original script notes, 'these guys go way back'. Mufasa bends down to tenderly nuzzle his lioness, Sarabi, before doing the same to his cub, Simba, nestled safely out of harm's way at the feet of his mother.

The animals have gathered for Simba's anointment as the heir apparent. Rafiki smears the little lion with a substance from his gourd before tossing a sprinkle of dirt over the cub's cherubic, expectant face. As he does, Simba responds with an explosive sneeze and his parents beam adoringly. Rafiki raises Simba high over his head and presents the cub to the animals below. As one, they react with glee. Zebras stomp. Elephants trumpet. Monkeys applaud and do somersaults. A beam of golden sunlight shines down on the future king of the jungle.

As opening scenes go, it is memorable and spectacularly uplifting. What's not to love?

Rafiki wasn't necessarily the children's favourite character but the name had a certain uniqueness and magic to it. When translated into its native Swahili, it means 'friend' and the family reckoned, *What name could be more perfect for a Labrador than 'friend'?* And so the pup was named. When shortened, it became Rafi, which sounds like Taffy.

There was indeed a circularity to it, however unintended, almost as if ordained by the film's signature song, 'The Circle of Life'.

The children fashioned a soft bed out of old blankets and towels in a big cardboard box, and placed it on the floor in the boys' bedroom, puppy central. They added a clock, to simulate the comforting sound of a maternal heartbeat, a trick veterinarians encourage to reduce a pup's anxiety when separated from its mother and littermates. An old teddy bear was found for the pup to curl next to and he immediately adopted it as his own. Too small to escape, Rafi twirled around a few times, looked up at the human faces looking down at him, found a nook and fell into a deep sleep.

Not for long.

Communicating their needs is hugely important for dependent pups, unable to fend for themselves, and it wasn't too long before Rafi's plaintive puppy cries began, manipulative whimpers calling for any number of things— a desire to be held or played with, hunger, a need to be taken outside to go to the toilet.

Yes, dogs speak. Not like humans with our highly articulated and evolved languages and patterns of speech; rather, they communicate through scent, sound and sight, generally in that order.

The music of dogs is a melody of meaning and intent. They are phenomenally and elastically orchestral. When you own a dog you know how they growl, yowl, howl, squeal, squeak and bark. They cry and yelp, sigh and moan, whimper and whine, rumble and snort. An adagio of low range pitches variously signal threat, aggression or anger, and they use higher-pitched sounds to call for help or announce they are safe creatures, not about to attack, and should not be rated a threat. Puppies almost always use a higher pitch for self-preservation.

Rafi was a quick learner and had succeeded in talking, or communicating, with his new pack that first night in Bowral.

Gemma, Nic and Marcelo slept together in puppy central, with the brothers sharing one of the boys' beds while Gemma took the other. Rafi started out in the box on the floor but his persistent high-pitched cries for attention demanded a response. The only thing that silenced the pup was the boys letting him crawl under the blankets between them. Mother warmth dressed up as brotherly love. They giggled and tickled Rafi until his squirming turned to sleep, exhaling warm pillows of air.

The next morning, bursting with excitement, Rafi piddled on Marcelo's bed. No one complained.

Wendy and Carlos had work and appointments to attend and Nic and Marcelo were too young to miss school, to which they went reluctantly. Gemma volunteered to stay at home and puppy-sit. *Well, someone had to!* She spent the day chasing Rafi and being chased by him. 'He'd suddenly conk out,' Gemma says now. 'He perched on my chest and because he was so tiny I could hold him with one hand.'

The second night was just like the first and by day two, fatigue reigned. Rafi was spent—the children, too. Wendy had a plan.

Chapter 3

TWICE AS NICE

Two days after Rafiki galumphed his way into the collective heart of his new family, Wendy and Carlos realised they had to act. The surest way to combat another sleepless night was to get him a permanent playmate. Wendy figured, *In for a penny, in for a pound.* Besides, what could be cuter than a pup? That's right, two pups. They drove back to Animal Magnetism with Rafi snuggled safely in his box, hoping he would help choose his new companion from the pups that had yet to be sold. Rafi was, as Wendy describes him, 'sooky' and physically affectionate, certainly not a dominant animal, and it was important to pick the right mate.

Dogs have personalities and, as with humans, no dog is the same even when from the same litter. Not all pups are equal and some are naturally more dominant than others, just as some are more energetic or more motivated by food or affection or games or mental challenges. Some are preternaturally fearless while others are more timid or nervous—the runts of the litter. Sometimes the dog's manner is a breed distinction and genetic prerequisite. In other words, it is fulfilling the role or roles it has been designed for, through hundreds of years of breeding. But there's another level to the equation, too.

The way a dog acts can also be the result of the dog's unique predisposition or personality. Dog lovers are adamant their dogs have personalities; we can't help ourselves and nor should we, because we see the canine personalities in action every day. The great naturalist Charles Darwin asserted in *The Descent of Man* that many animals and specifically dogs feel pleasure and pain, happiness and memory. He noted with great eloquence that as dogs became more domesticated and less wild, they 'progressed in certain moral qualities, such as affection, trust, worthiness, temper, and probably in general intelligence'. Music to a dog lover's ears.

The bottom line is that a dog's DNA does not necessarily always equal a dog's destiny. Rather, it is an exquisite mix of environment and genes.

Animal experts counsel that when introducing a new dog to the family, it is best to do so on neutral turf and to take the first dog with you when picking out the next one. Back at Animal Magnetism, Wendy placed Rafi in the pen with his littermates, most of whom inspected him with a conga line of sniffs to the rear end—a native canine courtesy—before scurrying off to other puppy action, wrestling, play-biting and sniffing.

But one stood out, a fiery ball of energy that showed a keen and instant interest in the returning arrival. Whether this was out of familial recognition or simple canine curiosity no one can be sure, but Wendy and Carlos noted how playful the pup was and how it interacted with Rafi and how he responded in kind. The canine chemistry was more than appealing.

Wendy picked up the curious puppy, checked the sex—a girl—and was taken by her vitality and exuberance. This one was confident, adventurous and inquisitive and ever so bouncy. She was high-energy and looked like she might just be unstoppable. The little pup was an ideal counterpoint for Rafi's more restrained and babyish traits that had so endeared him to Wendy in the first place.

Another thing. She also looked slightly different to Rafi, enough to easily tell them apart. The pup was smaller than her brother although she too had the white tuft of fur on her chin and chest. Her fur was slightly different as well. Rafi's ears were fluffier, as if they were topped with little patches of freshly combed lambs' wool that stood up at right angles to his floppy, languid lobes. The female's ears were smoother, flatter. His paws were bigger than hers and his snout wider. He stood slightly taller, and his tail reached out longer.

They looked like brother and sister with their big, round, chocolate eyes but they each had their own style. If it could be said that Rafi was a bit more Newfie, then that's how Wendy would sum it up. The female was a bit more, well, Lab-like. Their rogue heredity was naturally on show and you didn't need to look too hard to find it. In the end, it was a simple case of mutual attraction. Puppy love? Rafi and his sister played well and as far as anyone could tell—because how can you really know what's going on inside the minds of eight-week-old pups other than recognise the expected biological and developmental signposts—would be well-suited kennel companions. There was absolutely no reason to suspect otherwise. Neither had shown any aggression to the other nor any dominant behaviour. Rather, they gravitated around each other in a little dance, sidling up together and taking turns with licks to the muzzles and sniffs to not-so-private parts. It was as if the two pups had choreographed their own getting-to-know-you waltz, albeit a clumsy one. *I like you, let's get to know each other a little better.*

Likewise, neither appeared more submissive or nervous and, considering Rafi's likeable sookiness so far, this was considered a bonus. He held his own with his sister and the pair behaved with perfect puppiness.

Pups learn to communicate and play with each other through a process of trial and error—or, perhaps more accurately, through nips and responses. They learn puppy etiquette from their mothers and littermates: what is acceptable and not. Playtime is school time. As Stanley Coren writes in *How to Speak Dog*, 'play is serious business, not just random chaotic behaviour'.

One of the most important things a pup learns from playing is that physical aggression is completely undesirable and intolerable in the pack. If a pup nips a sibling too hard in the rough and tumble of playtime, the hurt pup will yelp loudly and stop the game until it has recovered.

In this way the nipper is taught not to bite too hard. With order restored, the pups will go back to their puppiness and gentler jaw play. Play-fighting teaches pups about dominance and pack hierarchy, as well as self-defence and ways to hunt and escape from danger. Watch a dog wriggle out of a sticky situation—or get out of a wrestling game of mutual take-turns somersaults—and you'll have a mental image of a canine escape artist.

Pups also use their bodies to communicate. They shift their height, wag, stiffen or straighten their tails, alter their stance, stare, avert or drop their eyes, prick up, flatten or curl their ears over to better hear with, or just plain let them flop as a sign that nothing much is going on. Whiskers, snouts and teeth all reveal an act about to be commissioned—or not—or a motivation or mood. Dogs have built an armoury of postures to signal timidity, submission, fear, warning, imminent attack, playfulness, contentedness, relaxation, work, readiness for a mission, picking up a scent, even stubbornness. The list goes on.

Have you ever seen a dog track down a scent undetected by humans, stare at it, sniff it with growing urgency and, before you have a chance to react, roll his shoulder into it and flip over his body and rub it vigorously over the stink? You have? Well, you've seen a dog on a mission. For humans, a sign of canine stubbornness is when your dog puts the paw-brakes on while out on a leash-walk, nearly ripping your arm out of the shoulder socket. He stops suddenly, perfectly balanced on all four paws, then leans back on his hind legs with his rump slightly elevated while pulling his head down into the shoulders and simultaneously straightening his front legs. Your dog has become an immovable object. Good luck moving on. The message? Your dog wants something right there and then, or has seen something he doesn't want to go past or is too afraid to pass.

Canine communication is a wonderful thing to behold and dogs learn it at the earliest age.

Misbehaved, aggressive or overly dominant pups are regularly disciplined by the mother dog that will put her mouth over the offending muzzle, or a paw on their naughty pup's shoulder or head to push it down and into a submissive position. Both are classic canine displays of dominance. The mother dog has just taught her pup two lessons: the first about aggression, the second about respect.

Wild canines are pack animals and need a clear and defined hierarchy to survive. The domestication of dogs makes that hierarchy less critical for survival but no less important socially. After all, the family pet has a pre-ordained social structure in the shape of us humans who house, feed and water the four-legged fur kid from the moment it arrives home. That's not to say that all dogs accept that they are lower ranked than humans and when they don't it is trouble. As cute and lovable as he was, the now world famous Labrador Marley, of the book and film *Marley & Me*, was a terror. Not for nothing did newspaper columnist and author John Grogan give his best-selling book the sub-title *Life and Love with the World's Worst Dog.*

It was too early to really tell how Rafi and his sister would turn out, or if they would grow to be another Marley or, more challenging, a pair of Marleys, but that wasn't an issue right now. Once again, the pups had done the work for the humans and made the difficult choice for them. Just as Rafi chose Wendy, his sister chose him and he reciprocated.

Wendy parted with another $375, scooped up her squirming brood, gently put them in the box and took them home. Their family now truly was complete.

Chapter 4

WHAT'S IN A NAME?

Rafi had a sister who needed a name. Nic and Marcelo had drawn on *The Lion King* to choose Rafiki and the brothers, eight and five, chose to stick with the film. They were methodical in their choice and, with their sister Gemma, ran through the female names of their favourite characters. Nala, who is Simba's mate, was discounted immediately because it sounded too close to the Spanish 'nada', which when translated means 'nothing' and that wouldn't do for their pup. She was the polar opposite of nothing and meant everything to the family, especially Nic, who was overwhelmed when he jumped in the back of his parents' car to discover a second pup en route to its new home.

'We always wanted pets. For a long time we had been talking to Mum and Dad about it and one day we came home and there was Rafi, and that was amazing, and then two days later we had another,' Nic says now. 'That's why it was so emotional. It was already a big thing having one dog and now we had two.'

The family moved through the animated cast, ticking off this name and that. Shenzi was sweet but she was a hyena. Enough said. Sarafina? Almost, but not quite right. Finally, they found the one they all agreed was absolutely the prettiest, Sarabi.

It was perfect for their pup. The name belonged to Simba's mother, the lion queen who, like Rafiki, was no one's favourite character in particular but, when translated, it means 'mirage' and as we know, every mirage is beautiful. Sarabi fitted their delectable dog to perfection. As the children had done with Rafi, they shortened Sarabi to Sabi and pronounced it Sah-bee*.

Now happily named, the pups trotted around and the house pulsed with excitement as the dogs clumsily explored their new environment, stopping to sniff everything and piddle at the same time. They crab-waddled from one side of the room to another, bumped and slid into objects, skating along on their oversized paws, which reminded Wendy to go on a puppy-proofing mission. Rafi and Sarbi were inseparable, a canine comedy team. Gemma says they were 'partners in crime' who egged each other on and grew in confidence with each new move.

Sarbi forged ahead of Rafi, poking her head around each corner before stopping suddenly to wait for her sibling to

---

* Sabi ultimately would be spelled phonetically as Sarbi by the Australian Army, which is the spelling I will use.

catch up with a little *hey, this way*, flick of her head. Rafi charged on bouncily. Buoyed by Sarbi's adventurous spirit the sooky boy had morphed into a fearless hound in search of who knew what and the vague promise of a scent on the wind. Back and forth they went, *you go, no, you go*. No matter where they went, Rafi and Sarbi went together.

Sarbi climbed over Rafi and tumbled headfirst on to the floor with abandon and Rafi copied the exact same move, climbing over his sibling and somersaulting to the floor with a thud. They took turns repeating the manoeuvre like skilled circus performers and thumped their tails on the floor with delight, yipping and yapping like pups do. Their playtime was a synchronous dance with the mutual benefit of happiness and exercise. Ralph Waldo Emerson crisply put it thus: 'It is a happy talent to know how to play'.

Despite their frenzy of exploration, the pups' energy seemed infinite and their little tanks produced a staggering amount of puppy pee requiring hourly toilet training trips outdoors. Eventually though, they tired and collapsed with exhaustion, curling in as one, a mass of rising and falling fur, out of which came a chorus of soft, puffy snorts. 'They were little black balls of love,' says Wendy.

It was decided that the pups would sleep in the boys' bedroom, in the cardboard box where the children had created a cosy nest for Rafi two nights previously. Gemma continued to sleep in the same room, not wanting to miss the action, giggling with joy at the pups' antics, encouraging their cheekiness. The plan was short-term and would last only while the pups were tiny and getting accustomed to the family. After that they could sleep outside. Their thick, long double-coats were as good as waterproof and would protect them from the vicissitudes of the weather in that part of the country. The Southern Highlands could be covered in snow in winter and as warm as the tropics in summer. But, before the lights had even been turned out that first night, the plan and the box were both abandoned. Gleefully, it should be said. Sarbi and Rafi had burrowed under the blankets and snuggled in with the compliant boys. If happiness could be empirically measured, it was off the scale that night in Bowral.

The puzzlement of pups is not that they are so adorable—that's a prewired by-product of biology—but how they choose us as companions.

Rafi bonded instantly, irrevocably, with the oldest and youngest siblings, Gemma and Marcelo; the livelier, more energetic and rambunctious Sarbi had enigmatically gravitated to Nic, the middle child. There was no reason to it. Nothing had happened that would set one pup on one course and the other on another. Both had been equally indulged with love and affection, over-indulged even, and yet, somehow, canny canine choices had been made, apparently not at random.

Sarbi had not been home more than a handful of hours but the connection with Nic was as if chiselled in stone. As soon as the older brother sat cross-legged on the floor, Sarbi clambered into his lap and squirmed like quicksilver, circling twice or thrice until she found the right spot of warmth, and plopping down to make herself at home. By lights out, the bond was firmly established. Perhaps, as if guided by some divine doggie deduction, Sarbi understood that Rafi had already made his bond and so cleverly opted for the equally attractive alternative. Another shrewd piece of puppy logic also quickly became clear. Sarbi and Rafi eyed Wendy and Carlos as the joint alphas of the pack— something all dogs look for as soon as they find themselves in a new family—and diplomatically bounced from one to the other for tickles and hugs.

The good news was that with Sarbi beside him, Rafi's whimpers and plaintive cries from the previous two nights had all but ceased. The separation from his large pack must have seemed an eternity to him those first 48 hours but he was now reassuringly reunited with a part it, no matter how small. Sarbi was Rafi's comfort; that much was evident from the moment Wendy put the little guy back in the pen at the pet shop and now it was blindingly obvious. The female pup had a dominant and more independent personality, which turned out to be a good thing.

Finally, the entire family—two parents, three children and yes, even the two balls of fur—got a good night's sleep. Wendy's plan had been a success, an ultimately joyous one at that.

The Austrian zoologist and Nobel Prize winner Konrad Lorenz was a fascinating and occasionally controversial man who dedicated his life to the study of animal behaviour, particularly how various species such as birds and dogs interacted with us humans. Lorenz spent decades knee-deep in research—'observation' he liked to call it— and wrote with affection and humour about the animals he so dearly loved. He was so dedicated to the cause of ethology, the study of animal behaviour, that he taught himself to walk and talk and splash like a duck and when needed for science, did all three. He could honk like a goose and had no compunction about spending hours on hands and knees in hides to see what the animals did in their natural habitat.

An animal lover *par excellence*, Lorenz had bonded as a child with a wild goose, or more to the point, the gosling had bonded with him as it would its mother and followed him everywhere, trailing as geese offspring do. This magical experience, known as imprinting, set the inquisitive boy on a lifelong path of discovery about animal behaviour and comparative psychology. Later, when he had completed a medical and zoology degree, Lorenz put the groundbreaking theory of imprinting on the scientific map. Imprinting, or 'stamping in' as Lorenz called it in his native German, is a survival instinct for infant birds. They bond with the first thing they see for protection from predators and mishaps. Usually, the hatchlings imprint with the mother goose but Lorenz's scientific experiments showed how goslings and ducklings would attach themselves to humans in the absence of their ornithological mothers just as that first gosling had imprinted on him in childhood.

In the mid 1960s Lorenz, by then a household name in scientific circles and accepted as the godfather of ethology, broadened the scientific corpus about the animal-human connection. He called the inter-species relationship 'the bond' and defined it as behaviour patterns of an objectively demonstrable mutual attachment. Previously, it was understood that the primary goal of a species was procreation in order to guarantee survival, but the breakthrough on imprinting made by Lorenz and fellow scientists changed that one-dimensional assumption.

Dogs were different again. Dogs took the bond to a higher level. Was it a better bond? Well, if you love dogs you know the answer to that and comparing dogs to geese is rather like comparing chalk to cheese. Doesn't really make sense.

The relationship between our more primitive human ancestors and wild dogs, or wolves in the very first instance, was initially built on the mutual needs of feeding, hunting, protection and cohabitation and is often said to be one of the reasons why Homo sapiens survived so well when the ice age Neanderthals, who showed no primitive affection for dogs whatsoever, didn't. Thousands and thousands of years later, though, modern man and his domesticated dog are bonded in something else as well, something more emotionally compelling—companionship. And companionship has primacy above nearly all other benefits, particularly in Western society where man is dog's best friend and vice versa. As Lorenz puts it in *Man Meets Dog*, his seminal book first published in 1949, 'there is no domestic animal which has so radically altered its whole way of living, indeed its whole sphere of interests, that has become domestic in so true a sense as the dog.'

Cats? Well, yes and no. In fact, forget the feline. When it comes to companionship, the cat doesn't hold a candle to the dog. Sure, it has made its way into our hearts and homes but cats—no, not *your* cat—don't need us like dogs need us. Have you ever seen a cat dance, pant, paw and twirl with unbridled excitement upon your arrival home? No? Didn't think so.

The flamboyant Lorenz was right when he wrote: 'The whole charm of a dog lies in the depth of the friendship and the strength of the spiritual ties with which he has bound himself to man.'

Much more recently cognitive scientist Alexandra Horowitz expounded on Lorenz's work in her wonderful book, *Inside of a Dog*. Horowitz creates a mystical world— the *umwelt* (OOM-velt)—for the canid clan and writes about what life must be like from the dog's point of view at ground level, absent the anthropomorphisms we humans tend to project on to them. She respectfully treats the dog as a dog.

Like Lorenz, Horowitz describes the various ways through which humans and dogs bond. One is contact or touch; another is the greeting ritual—a physical burst of feverish exhilaration that highlights recognition between dog and owner and acts as acknowledgement of their bond. But what really separates dogs from other species, according to Horowitz, is the actual 'timing and pacing' of the dog–human interactions.

Dogs know when they will be walked, the time during that walk when they will be let off the leash, the times they will be fed, or allowed to play. Dogs also know the time for bed. Dogs anticipate all of these activities with the precision of a Swiss watch and let their owners know with a nudge to the thigh or a paws-down play-slap and a *come on, get a move on* rumble of a growl that turns into a single, high-pitched *roooph*. Owners usually comply. Why not? We are bonded and the timing is a tonic.

According to Horowitz, 'human companionship has become dogs' motivational meat'. It works the other way round, too. Yet the curious, or rather, marvellous thing about this inter-species, human–dog bond is the speed with which it occurs. Strangely fast.

Dogs know how to effortlessly inveigle their way into our hearts. Like card sharps and con men, they know an easy mark when they see one. Witness Rafi and Sarbi.

Chapter 5

IT'S A DOG'S LIFE

All dogs have a capacity to understand words and sounds. Moreover, they can detect and isolate the nuances in human language even though they can't actually speak it the way we two-leggeds do. Scientists and ethologists call it the receptive language ability and it applies equally to canines as children. It is easiest to think of it in terms of how toddlers learn language: by hearing and understanding a word but without having developed the ability to speak it. A thirteen-month-old can point to a dog and know what it is, but will not be able to say 'dog', only some cute version thereof. As Stanley Coren points out in *How To Speak Dog*, humans would do well not to underestimate that same knack in dogs.

The average hound can understand between 110 and 200 spoken human words or signals, or a combination of both, but the really clever ones can be quite loquacious, in a silent sort of way. One German dog trainer boasted of teaching his dog 350 words and added that the dog was able to correctly pick out the individual instructional words from a longer sentence and do what he was required to do. Say 'walkies' and your dog knows what it's been invited to do. Say 'do you want to go for a walk in the park?' and it will pick out the word 'walk' and greet you with a physical response that says, *do I ever?* if it hasn't already beaten you to the front door.

Say the word 'treat' and your dog will react differently to an utterance of 'no', which, almost universally, will be met with a look of abject dejection if not an overt sigh of displeasure. (Dogs, Coren points out, actually do sigh and their sighs can have a range of meanings.) Compare 'bath' and 'bone', both short, sharp, strong B-words, and you'll notice how 'bone' is understood as a good thing. Not so, 'bath'. 'Bone' will probably result in your dog licking its chops and his ears standing at attention with greedy expectation. 'Bath' might turn a happy-go-lucky hound into a sullen, immovable block of a dog with the paw-brakes on, one who wants to remain smelling as doggie as possible. Or try saying 'bad dog' in as neutral a tone as possible, minus emotion and volume, and London to a brick your dog will still slink into its *I've just been berated* submissive pose, with its tail under its rear legs and ears flattened, just as it would if you really had said 'bad dog' and meant it.

A dog's receptive language abilities, then, are limited by the time spent listening to its owner and what that human decides to teach his or her four-legged friend over and above the usual commands of sit, stay, down, come.

Sarbi and Rafi were blessed. They had five eager and devoted teachers and the pair proved to be very quick learners. Gemma knew the pups were beginning to understand English when she noticed how they chased and retrieved tennis balls with, well, the zeal of retrievers. The kids would say 'tennis' with a particular intonation and Sarbi and Rafi instantly stopped whatever they were doing and froze, stone-like.

Tennis.

Their ears pricked up, their eyes widened and they cocked their heads, quaking with anticipation.

'They looked like little cartoons,' Gemma says.

The children said the word again. 'T-T-T-tennis', emphasising the T.

The dogs quivered, practically levitating, as they fell over each other, crashing through the back door and tumbling down the steps to the backyard. Sarbi and Rafi had not only learnt the word 'tennis', but every variant of the consonant T.

'We'd tease them by saying things like, "Anyone feel like a cup of Tea? Sounds very TempTing doesn'T iT?" emphasising all the Ts and watching the dogs salivate over the sound. If you played that game, though, you had to then go and throw the ball a few times. It was just too cruel not to.'

Sarbi was more obsessed with chasing the ball and retrieving it than Rafi. Her enthusiasm was boundless. She chased with a blind insistence that bordered on the obsessive. If she couldn't find a ball, she picked up pebbles and dropped them at the children's feet, her front paws splayed and ready to pounce, staring at the rocks with catatonic intensity as if the pile of pebbles was her sole purpose in life. Sarbi was impossible to distract or pat while a pile of pebbles or a tennis ball lay before her. She sidestepped any attempt at physical contact and peered more closely at the stones, more urgently and insistently, hoping someone would get the hint and throw.

Sarbi and Rafi were competitive and frequently fought in their pursuit, occasionally drawing blood while wrangling for the ball but Rafi usually tired of the effort after about 45 minutes. He signalled *game over* by collecting all the balls in front of him and guarding them proprietorially, deliberately denying Sarbi access.

When the dogs were left at home alone, Sarbi gathered rocks and stocked them in neat little piles on the steps leading to the house, where they couldn't be missed if anyone wanted to cross the threshold. 'When I arrived home from school she would have her head poking out from between the steps, staring ferociously at the day's rock collection and dribbling all over it until I let her out and threw them for her,' says Gemma.

Rafi, on the other paw, was obsessed with swimming, a legacy of the sweet-natured Newfoundland in him, and the dogs were introduced to the ocean at the start of summer, within months of arriving at Bowral. The neighbour's property was also ideal. It had a duck pond and, better yet, live ducks that catered to the dogs' instinct to chase. Sarbi and Rafi worked as a team. Rafi herded the ducks towards Sarbi, who chased with sheer determination, gathering speed with each thunderous gallop. Imagine an eighteen-wheeler perched at the top of a hill with the handbrake off and you'll have an idea of her force and momentum. Neither dog was deterred by the electric fence around the pond. Sarbi and Rafi jumped over it or pushed through it, letting out a little *yip* of pain when they made contact. An electric shock could not stop two dogs hell bent on doing what dogs do naturally. Fortunately, Sarbi and Rafi were not fast enough to catch the ducks.

Rafi was a natural swimmer. With massive webbed paws as powerful as oars, he easily outswam the children. Once he leapt into the ocean and kept swimming until he was a dot on the horizon. Wendy quickly improvised and tied a long length of rope to his collar, fearing where he would end up if left to his own devices. Sarbi preferred to chase the whitewash of waves in the shallows, barking and snapping at the foam and delighting in the wake she threw up as she roared along the shore, her ears flopping up and down, her pink tongue hanging from the side of her mouth, drool flying everywhere.

Rafi and Sarbi had landed with their bums in the butter. They grew like Topsy, fast and strong, and within months resembled miniature Shetland ponies, forcing Gemma to give up carrying them down to the local shops in a basket. By now, the dogs were taking the kids on walks, dragging them along at breakneck speed. Even the boys' father, Carlos, was taken for a walk instead of the other way around.

Sarbi and Rafi were afflicted with the Labrador's innate obsession with food, like any member of the proud breed. Wendy bought a second refrigerator to accommodate the growing hounds, that were fed twice daily. Raw chicken necks by the kilogram; leftovers from the dining table.

Family barbeques were a speciality. The cheeky pups sat obediently—for once!—gazes unflinching, begging to be tossed scraps, just as if they'd never been fed.

At six months, it became necessary to feed them separately. Rafi was fierce on the fang—put bluntly, a guts. As soon as he scarfed his food he pushed his snout into Sarbi's bowl and stole her dinner. She responded with a snarl and snap more than once, occasionally drawing blood.

Rafi sneakily found other food sources, including a birthday cake from the family's favourite French patisserie in Bowral, bought for Wendy's birthday by her long-time friend, Anne. The cake was sealed in a box, resting safely on the back seat of Anne's car when she arrived at the house. After being welcomed by the family, Anne reached in to get the cake. Instead, she found Rafi, taking up the entire back seat. He had snuck into the car with the dexterity of a cat burglar and his cake-covered face was as good as a guilty verdict.

'In the time it took us to get through all the hugs and kisses he'd quietly demolished the entire thing,' recalls Gemma.

Fortunately for Rafi, the family could only laugh. After all, our emotional connection to dogs is pure and primal. For the most part, our dogs mirror the connection. As the garden variety dog lover knows, dogs are highly social mammals and experience fear, happiness and love.

In 1872, the evolutionary biologist Charles Darwin published his book, *The Expression of the Emotions in Man and Animals*, in which he included hand-drawn illustrations of dogs (and cats) expressing fear, submission and aggression as well as some of the aforementioned emotions. The dogs' expressions are remarkably similar to our own. Move forward 140 years and scientist Patricia McConnell sees it thus: 'Emotions allow each of us, from an award-winning neurobiologist to a hungry bloodhound, to respond to the world in ways that allow us to keep growing.'

McConnell might have added 'growing together'. Rafi and Sarbi had grown up with the children, marking every significant milestone with the family. Christmas, birthdays, holidays. They were not like the pitiful hounds whose existence is as good as forgotten as they languish alone and lonely in suburban backyards, after the novelty of puppyhood has worn thin and Christmas gone cold. Sarbi and Rafi were family in the truest sense of the word and had free rein of the house. Wendy and Carlos saw how the dogs taught the children empathy and compassion, and helped tease out their natural kindness.

There was more to it, though. Whenever Nic and Marcelo were in trouble or sad, the dogs responded instinctively. Sarbi curled up next to Nic, and Rafi's bulk crawled onto Marcelo's tiny lap, obscuring him. Similarly, if Gemma needed bucking up, Rafi plopped a giant paw ever so softly on her face, leaving it there, almost as if he was patting the teenager. Sarbi, who was not a particularly cuddly canine (nothing unusual there—while we humans love hugging our dogs, dogs are not overly fond of it and see it as a display of social status), intuitively put her head in Gemma's lap and looked up at her with those gorgeous liquid brown eyes. The kids and dogs seemed inseparable. And they were.

Which is why in mid-2005 Wendy and Carlos faced a family dilemma unlike any before.

Nic had won a place at the prestigious Sydney Conservatorium of Music, a twice-daily, two-hour commute to and from Bowral. It was too much for the youngster and the family decided to move to Sydney. Unfortunately, the regional real estate market was in a slump and Wendy and Carlos were unable to find a buyer for their beautiful house. Without a sale, they couldn't purchase a new home with a backyard big enough for Sarbi and Rafi. Despite a suburbs-wide search, they were unable to find a landlord who permitted two huge hounds as canine tenants. The only option was to find a new home for their beloved pets. It was a heartbreaking decision and one the family agonised over.

Wendy placed an ad in the classifieds section of the local newspaper. Ideally, she hoped a like-minded family in Bowral would take Sarbi and Rafi, so they could stay on familiar territory and continue their carefree lives. A couple of families visited but left without the dogs, confessing they were simply too big. Bottom line, they feared they could not handle them.

Wendy and Carlos were getting desperate. The kids, too, fretted over finding a suitable and loving new home for Sarbi and Rafi, one that would resemble their own. The prospect of losing their beloved mutts was bad enough but the added uncertainty was close to unbearable.

Chapter 6

RECRUITMENT DAY

Corporal Murray Young was flicking through the local newspaper in the Southern Highlands in June of 2005 when he stopped at the 'For Adoption' notice in the classified advertisement section. 'Two beautiful, intelligent Labrador Newfoundland crosses—brother and sister need a new home.' The words struck a chord with the experienced soldier, a member of the Explosive Detection Dog (EDD) Section in the Australian Army, a tight-knit team of men always on the lookout for good, strong dogs to join the niche unit with a reputation as one of the best of its kind.

The army has a long history of using dogs in the line of duty but, save for a brief time in the 1970s, did not breed its own hounds. The official policy was and is to adopt dogs that have failed to make the grade in customs or police work, or rescue dogs from animal shelters and council pounds. The latter also serves an altruistic purpose and saves unwanted and unloved dogs from being 'put down', the deceptively anodyne phrase meaning 'euthanised'. Besides, the army has a high regard for dogs found at the Royal Society for the Prevention of Cruelty To Animals (RSPCA).

'The RSPCA dog is like the Aussie soldier, he's resourceful,' former chief handler Corporal Fred Cox once said.

Then there are the dogs adopted from families in the unenviable position of having to find a new home for them. They tend to be a better proposition still as they come with a known history and a pen sketch of their personality, skills and talents. And, importantly, a well-loved dog usually means a good disposition and you can never overstate the value of that.

Murray scanned the ad and liked what he read. Experience had shown the best EDDs, as the dogs are known, were mixed-breed mutts like Sarbi and Rafi, and those with a working pedigree such as kelpies, Labrador-crosses and border collies. He picked up the phone and called the number.

Murray explained the army was recruiting dogs for the EDD Section at the School of Military Engineering (SME) based in the Sydney suburb of Moorebank. The unit trained dogs to sniff out a vast range of lethal explosives found in weapons, bombs and ammunition used by enemy forces. Dangerous work. The dog was paired with a handpicked soldier and together they went through a rigorous training program to build a symbiotic working relationship. Known as an EDD team, the dog and handler were then deployed to various regiments in the army including the three Combat

Engineer Regiments (known as 1CER, 2CER and 3CER) located in New South Wales, Queensland and the Northern Territory, or the elite Incident Response Regiment (IRR) based at the Holsworthy barracks in New South Wales. The IRR was raised in response to the September 11 terrorist attacks and unveiled by the then Australian defence minister Robert Hill in 2001. When fully manned, the regiment's 300-plus troops are trained to respond to terrorist attacks involving chemical, biological, radiological, nuclear and explosive hazards in Australia and abroad.

The first version of the dog section was established in Sydney in 1953 and was devised to train a variety of hounds to detect hidden mines and act as guard dogs.

This was not what Wendy expected. Like many, she had no idea that the Australian Army used dogs. Police dogs she knew about. Those gorgeous, hard-working beagles, Labs and spaniels that trot around the legs of exhausted travellers, sniffing their luggage for contraband and drugs illegally imported into the country or between states, yes. But army dogs, no.

Wendy was curious. She and Carlos had what seemed like an unsolvable problem. No one wanted to take their beloved Rafi and Sarbi. So when Corporal Young, then the chief instructor at the SME, stepped in to the equation with a potential solution to their agonising predicament Wendy heard him out.

The Australian Defence Force has long employed a veritable military menagerie that has fed, fought, clothed, defended and supported its two-legged brothers- and sisters-in-arms on foreign fields. Among the feathered, furred and woolly troop have been pigeons, rabbits, cockatoos, camels, chooks, cats, horses, sheep, monkeys, donkeys and, of course, dogs. The first animal army deployment was a contingent of about 40,000 horses sent to assist Commonwealth soldiers in the Boer War in South Africa in the 1890s.

Dogs were officially introduced to army life in the First World War, as messengers and ratters in the forlorn and fetid trenches, ribbons of graves that tunnelled cancerously through the earth for mile upon miserable mile on the Western Front. One messenger dog, working with the Fourth Division Signal Company in France in 1918, gained notoriety for its, ahem, unreliability. Named Bullet, the mutt worked to its own schedule. One day it took a mere eight minutes to deliver an important message but a few days later the canine courier took a very elastic nineteen hours.

Infantry patrol dogs and tracker dogs were used in the Korean War. A patrol dog scouted ahead of the troop to find enemy positions and weapons and, once detected, a tracker dog, working on a leash in tandem with its handler, searched through the enemy positions, to help neutralise the threat. The teams were so successful that it made sense at war's end to formalise the program in Australia, and in subsequent years dog teams were deployed as offensive and tactical tools to new battlefields in Borneo and again during the Malayan emergency.

The Tracking Wing was officially established in 1966 at the School of Infantry in Ingleburn in Sydney, with a solitary mongrel liberated from death row for the princely sum of three dollars. The first dogs to be enlisted into what were then known as Combat Tracking Teams were named after Roman emperors and given lofty titles including Cassius, Marcus, Caesar and Tiber. The last three had the distinction of being the longest serving of the eleven Australian dogs sent to the Vietnam War in 1967.

Once trained, these freshmen trackers were deployed to infantry battalions, to track fleeing enemy soldiers through impenetrable jungle woven thick with foliage. Like most of their canine predecessors in the First and Second World wars, none ever made it home.

Australia's strict quarantine regulations prevented the return of the hero dogs, which was utterly soul-destroying for the men with whom they had bonded and whose lives they helped save. The Diggers took solace knowing their mates had found new homes in embassies or with civilians but they never forgot their best mates.

The early success of the tracker and mine dogs led to an ambitious attempt by the army in the 1970s to breed its own military working dog in conjunction with the CSIRO. Called the Psycho-Genetic Breeding Program (PGBP), the goal was to breed a miniaturised version of the German shepherd crossed with kelpie and border collie working dogs that would be small enough to be carried under one arm by a soldier in combat conditions. George Hulse, then a captain at the SME, was in charge of the program. He enlisted in the infantry at the age of seventeen and served in Malaya, Papua New Guinea and South Vietnam. By the end of the 1960s, he was an officer in the corps of engineers and one of the famous tunnel rats in the Vietnam War who took part in the battle of Coral and Balmoral.

In 1970 the brass dispatched Hulse to the United States to see how the allies went about producing mine and tunnel detection dogs. At the Aberdeen Proving Ground in the state of Maryland, Hulse noted that the US Army was also breeding its own dogs. On observing the pups, he realised that the little balls of fluff would learn various behaviours with minimal human-designed training processes. The observation convinced the Australian captain that there were development opportunities for canines in the military far beyond their current employment capabilities.

The goal of the PGBP was to breed lightweight, quiet, robust dogs with a strong retrieval drive that would not be gun shy or frightened by loud explosions. Hulse had one other criterion for the dream detection dogs.

'It needs to be jungle green,' he says now, with a laugh.

Scientifically speaking, he wasn't joking. He believed it could eventually be done under the right circumstances.

The official response?

'Forget your green dog.'

The first iteration of specially bred German shepherds was born at SME in 1972. Each breeding pair delivered about six dogs, 50/50 male and female. Over the next eight years, four generations of pups were born, and the best of these were to be crossed with kelpies and border collies for another four generations (a canine generation is two years) to produce a new 'bloodline'. The plan then was that the best of the new bloodline would be in-bred for two more generations to produce a 'phenotype', or a specific dog breed that met the criteria for passive detection purposes.

'The aim was to minimise the size of the "chassis" before

out-crossing to the other working-dog breeds,' Hulse says now.

He wanted to breed the dogs down to about 16 kilograms without losing their working-dog attributes. German shepherd dogs usually weigh between 30 and 40 kilograms and bitches between 22 and 32 kilograms.

The dogs showed promise and the pups were exposed to a whole inventory of combat conditions and battle noise simulation at the age of three weeks—when they opened their eyes. They were tested for courage and timidity, and tried on various transport media, with every pup's performance noted daily on a score sheet for later analysis.

The program got off to a fine start but politics and fiscal restraints within the defence department meant it would be short-lived. The out-crossing to kelpies and border collies, under supervision from the CSIRO, did not happen. As a result, the program didn't have the necessary time required to identify emerging trends or to see significant genetic changes in the breed. As Hulse says now, at least ten generations were needed.

'This was the shortest time possible that the CSIRO could indicate a dog possessing the attributes we wanted,' he says. 'The next breeding program would have been to consolidate the breed standard and continue to develop the dogs to undertake very specific roles—for example, conduct reconnaissance at night controlled by radio and other remote-control devices. The dogs could be equipped with state-of-the-art mounted devices such as cameras and infrared detection scanners. The dogs could be trained to patrol routes and housing areas to detect caches, IEDs, personnel and ambushes. At least, that was the promise. I firmly believe that dogs are capable of all these things, and more. It's just that we need to develop the dog and its training program for it to know what it is that we want it to do.'

The end of the program, however, didn't mean the end of dogs in the Australian Army and, as it turned out, military working dogs went on to do exactly what Hulse had hoped in the 1970s.

In more recent years, Australian Explosive Detection Dog teams have served in war zones in Somalia, Bougainville, East Timor, the Solomon Islands and Iraq. Currently, several are on duty in southern Afghanistan. Fortunately, most have returned to Australia. After a month in quarantine they either continue working or retire to live out their days as pampered pets with their soldier-handlers or other adoptive families.

Not every canine is cut out for service, and fewer still are cut out for nerve-racking work in dangerous conditions. Some don't have the patience or the smarts required. Others are incapable of being quiet and calm in stressful situations, when nerves of steel are required. (A wide yawn is a canine self-relaxation technique and usually does the trick; humans yawn for oxygen, dogs for calm.) Some hounds refuse to acknowledge commands or choose to respond in their own time (bad dog); others are unable to master the discipline required to hunt for the olfactory information that says 'explosive' when more delightfully pungent smells—well, at least to dogs—are calling.

Finding a pliable and workable dog was therefore

essential, which is why Corporal Young had one, and only one, question for Wendy.

Do the dogs like chasing balls?

She laughed.

'No dogs like chasing balls and retrieving balls more than these two,' Wendy replied.

That was exactly what Murray wanted to hear. He wasn't interested in how well trained Sarbi and Rafi were—though Wendy cheerily confessed, not very. They were innocently playful, mischievous and insistent, even demanding. Sarbi and Rafi were cherished and indulged family pets, she said, and pretty much got away with anything and everything. Gemma later reminded her mother how upset she had been when Sarbi chewed a pair of brand new boots, but her anger faded at the hound's apparent contrition and Wendy consoled herself by buying another pair of the same boots. Even Marcelo laughed when pointing out the missing nose from his favourite Teddy, a huggable toy he had had since the age of one. Then again, as Gemma says, her younger brother was in no position to complain about a chewing pup, for it was Marcelo who had bitten off Teddy's ear.

None of this worried Murray. On the contrary, he said, it was easier to train new canine recruits with negligible or no training than to undo previous training, in order to mould them into explosive detection dogs. He assured Wendy that the army dogs were happy and thrived in their challenging jobs. A team of dedicated, dog-friendly soldiers would care for them. Many had waited years to get into the elite EDD Section and considered it the dream job in the ADF.

The army preferred to take dogs between eighteen

months and three years old, an age at which they normally should be out of the excitable, uncontainable puppy phase. Sarbi and Rafi were not quite three. They sounded perfect on paper yet the skilled dog handler needed to cast his eyes over them to be sure. Should Rafi and Sarbi pass muster their first deployment would be at the forthcoming Commonwealth Games in Melbourne. It all sounded positive.

That night Wendy told the children about the surprise phone call. After much discussion the family decided the army might just be the perfect fit for the energetic and rambunctious dogs; they would have an exciting and adventurous life while patriotically protecting our national interests at home and abroad. Even if the work was extremely dangerous. And Sarbi and Rafi would have company almost 24/7. That was a bonus.

There was one more key issue for the family and it was the lay-down misère.

'We knew Sarbi and Rafi would also be able to save some lives,' says Wendy.

No higher calling could there be for man's best friend.

Corporal Young arranged to visit on Sunday, 19 June in 2005. It was the start of winter but Sydney was in the middle of its fifth mildest June on record and the day, which began as cloudy as it would end, was almost summery. The sun was shining in a clear blue sky and the mercury crept close to a comfortable twenty degrees Celsius. Murray, handsome with a kind face and of medium height and build, arrived dressed in casual gear rather than his uniform. The only indication he was army was his hair, cut to regulation length. The dogs introduced themselves to the friendly stranger with signature enthusiasm; they circled and sniffed, and generally ran amok.

Sarbi and Rafi were in terrific condition, not overweight as Labs have a tendency to be. Murray asked to see the dogs in action. The children said the magic word. *Tennis*. Rafi and Sarbi sprang to attention and ran around in front of the children, then sat back on their haunches, muscled bodies taut and ready to launch. The dogs stared at the children, brows crinkled, jaws ajar, tongues out, heads cocked to one side, the same side. They looked like they were smiling because they were. Labs smile.

Sarbi and Rafi correctly read every false move the children teasingly made, reacting with tiny jerking movements in the same direction, indicating where they expected the ball to be thrown. Sufficiently encouraged by the familiar play, they took a few steps backwards, rumps in the air, tails wagging, front legs positioned wider than their shoulders. Sarbi had her left paw raised up and tucked back under her chest like a true pointer, a habit she had had since her puppy days. Eyes pleading.

As one, the children belted the tennis balls with racquets, sending them sailing 100 metres down the tree-lined backyard. Rafi and Sarbi thundered off, barking competitively as they raced to the prize. Each found a ball and charged back to the waiting pack, dropping the balls with an accommodating bob of their heads as if to say, *let's go again, again*. A few reward pats and *Good Rafi, Good girl, Sarbi*, and whoomph! Off they went, following the arc of the balls through the air.

The dogs were the apotheosis of natural-born retrievers,

with a fanatical drive. That was the one thing the army's dog handlers looked for and it trumped all other character traits. Dogs could be taught to do any number of complex tasks and tricks—sniff, detect, drop, high-five—but they could not be taught the retrieval instinct. Without it, they were cute and lovable but practically useless.

'That's what we need,' Murray said.

He turned to Wendy and offered to take Rafi and Sarbi on the spot. Right then and there. Today. Now.

Wendy and Carlos were proud their dogs had performed so well but they were stunned by the immediacy. It was so sudden. And they were torn. They thought they would have days to say final farewells and shower the dogs with love and treat them with favourite food from the barbeque. Give them a few more days of romping through the backyard in wild pursuit of the tennis ball, or chasing the neighbour's ducks in vain, the pretend hunters. And watch with delight as Sarbi's ears pricked up at the sound of an unseen bus before romping down the driveway shadowed by Rafi, to wait excitedly at the front gate for the kids to come home from school. To consider the possibilities, maybe even to work out a compromise, a way to keep their cherished pets.

Wendy was nervous about the decision. Murray struck her as one of them, which is to say, dog people, and she and Carlos believed in their heart of hearts that Sarbi and Rafi would be looked after. She extracted a firm promise that the kids could visit the dogs at the army barracks in coming weeks and that they would receive regular updates of their training and work, but that held little currency right there and then.

If you've ever been stared at longingly by a devoted dog nestled at your feet, or felt its wet nose chiselling under your hand for a tickle under its chin, you'll know why she hesitated. You'll know the true meaning of mateship and how easily a dog can fill your heart. Imagine that multiplied by two and you'll appreciate how difficult it was for Wendy and Carlos.

Reluctantly, Wendy agreed it was probably best to have the miserable task done as quickly as possible rather than draw it out, prolonging the painful goodbyes, delaying the inevitable and torturing everyone with the knowledge that a sad departure was imminent. She braced herself and broke the news to the children. Nic and Gemma burst into tears; Wendy too. Marcelo says bravely that only his father and he were able to keep their emotions in check.

The family smiled for a group photograph with Murray but deep down, the children's stomachs were churning. Their idyllic world was about to implode. Nic, desolate, had his arms wrapped protectively around Sarbi, who was wearing a pink collar for the occasion. Gemma tenderly patted the big girl on the head. Carlos crouched next to Rafi for a hug and Wendy smiled but it was a smile born of politeness, not happiness. She and Carlos were equally forlorn. No amount of reassuring talk had convinced their children they should give up their dogs for adoption. Even to the Australian Army for seriously important life saving work, even though they knew it was absolutely the right thing to do, the best thing to do. Hard. But right.

And then they were gone. The lovably lumbering, clever dogs that had brought so much joy and given themselves so selflessly to the family were loaded in to Corporal Young's vehicle and driven to their new lives.

The Bowral house echoed with emptiness and the family felt the dull ache of loss. As Wendy says, 'There was a lot of sobbing in our house that night.'

PART TWO

Sarbi the Soldier

Chapter 7

BOMB SCHOOL

Steele Barracks at the School of Military Engineering is where it all happens for the explosive detection dogs in the Australian Army and it would be home to its new recruits, Sarbi and Rafi, for a slightly shortened version of the standard nineteen-week training program. The EDD Section is part of the Royal Australian Engineers Corps (RAE), located on a vast tract of land in the suburb of Moorebank, just 30 kilometres southwest of Sydney, adjacent to the Holsworthy Army Barracks. Backing on to the banks of the winding and muddy Georges River, lined with dense shrubbery and towering gums and native trees, the grounds boast one of the best golfing secrets in Australia, the eighteen-hole RAE Golf Club. Sadly, though, the dogs don't get to play on it, possibly the only restriction imposed on the military working dogs. Signs hanging by the Major

General Sir Clive Steele Memorial Gates warn visitors that the hounds and their handlers have right of way within the barracks area, indicative of their value and the high esteem in which the dogs are held.

Inside the heritage precinct stands a proud memorial, chiselled from rock, to commemorate the dogs killed while on active duty in the Middle East Area of Operations (MEAO) since 2005, when the first two EDDs were deployed to Afghanistan. A poignant monument for the fallen soldiers from the engineering corps stands nearby. Erected in 2007, the memorial for the dogs bears a brass plaque that captures with profound clarity the perilous nature of the job. *Dedicated to the explosive detection dogs who have paid the ultimate sacrifice so that others may live.* An additional, perfectly simple poem honours the unbreakable bond between the humans and hounds and serves as a rueful reminder of the sacrifices made so that soldiers survive and return home, and the ominous knowledge of sacrifices yet to come.

> *My eyes are your eyes,*
> *To watch and protect.*
> *My ears are your ears,*
> *To hear and detect evil minds in the dark.*
> *My nose is your nose,*
> *To scent the danger of your domain.*
> *And so may you live, my life is also yours.*

The Explosive Detection Dog Section is an elite unit in the army, more like an exclusive club, a vital but (regrettably to the army's hierarchy) there just aren't enough dogs or handlers. Only a handful of soldiers go through the one EDD handlers' course held each year, not nearly enough to cater to the growing need for the dogs' specialist life-saving skills, to counter an increasingly active enemy and its deadly improvised explosive devices, the booby trap of choice for the Taliban.

It is difficult to overestimate the impact of the dogs on the survivability rates of their soldier masters. The EDD teams have one of the most dangerous frontline jobs in the army. Often, all that stands between a Digger and death, or serious injury, is an explosive detection dog. They are highly manoeuvrable four-legged explosive radars.

The dogs and their trusted handlers are called in to investigate disturbed ground or objects suspected of being improvised explosive devices, or compounds and sites suspected of containing dangerous caches of weapons and bombs. The unpredictable nature of the terrain and potential for fatalities makes for a permanent sense of threat on every patrol.

The handlers and dogs crawl around, often prostrate on their stomachs, prodding, poking and scratching for the explosives to ensure threat avoidance and survivability. They provide an initial clearance for following soldiers to traverse safely from A to B. If an IED or any other kind of bomb or ammunition cache is detected, the explosive ordnance disposal (EOD) technician is deployed to defuse or destroy it. The dogs and their handlers march towards danger, confronting it full on. Theirs is precarious work, often dubbed 'follow the sapper'. He, in turn, follows his dog and it follows its instincts and training.

A veritable chorus has championed the uniqueness and unrivalled abilities of the dogs. '[Their capabilities] cannot be replicated by man or machine,' said Lieutenant Colonel John Carey, the commanding officer of the Australian Army's 2nd Combat Engineer Regiment (2CER) in Afghanistan in 2010.

'The best technology for sniffing explosives is still the dog,' reckoned Ralph Whitten, an executive at an American company in pursuit of the Holy Grail in the high-tech world of chemical sensing—a computerised, nano-technological nose.

'We trust these dogs more than metal detectors and mine sweepers. They are 98 per cent accurate,' said Andrew Guzman, a dog handler in the US Marine Corp, a corporal with a recent tour of duty in Afghanistan under his belt. Marines are tough men, they go in first and go in hard, and don't waste words or emotions—except for their dogs.

A Vietnam War veteran once said: 'They are the only weapon system we ever devised to save lives.'

Hardened warriors won't say it for fear of being seen as soft, but the relationship between soldier and dog is more than professional and reflects a mutual faith in the other's abilities to serve and protect. 'We have a saying—In dogs we trust,' says D, the Australian soldier who would train Sarbi.

The SME began the explosive detection dogs program in 1981. An earlier version focused on training dogs to detect mines, and to scout and patrol in the jungles of Vietnam but, as had always been the case with the protean nature of modern warfare, a new approach was needed to counter new weapons and tactics. Different wars make for different circumstances. Techniques, tactics and procedures—TTPs—change. Contemporary commanders would no more dress canine soldiers in body armour and speared collars today than, say, a tutu. Same for detection work.

The current crop of explosive detection dogs are taught to sniff out raw explosives used in ammunition, weapons and associated deadly devices—detonation cords, igniters, time fuses and blasting caps—in a complicated and gradual process known as scent imprinting. The dogs are trained on approximately eight base compositions. All ammunition and explosives are made from different percentages of those compositions. Once trained, the sniffing detectives can detect thousands of different types of military and civilian explosives and, according to one highly optimistic Doggie, up to 25,000.

Among the military-grade explosives are Composition B (also known as CompB, used in land mines, rockets and projectiles) and PE4 (a conventional plastic explosive). The dogs also learn to detect base chemical compositions including black powder, gunpowder, the well-known TNT (trinitrotoluene), the lesser known RDX (nitroamine), PETN (pentaerythritol tetranitrate) and NC/NG (nitrocellulose and nitroglycerin) based propellants.

RDX is considered the most powerful of all high military explosives and was used in some of the first plastic explosives in the 1930s. PETN is often used as a base charge in detonators or detonation cords. When mixed with other compounds it can be turned into semtex and other plastic explosives. Self-confessed al-Qaeda member Richard

67

Reid used PETN in his unsuccessful shoe bomb attempt to blow up American Airlines Flight 63 en route from Paris to Miami in 2001.

The dogs learn to sniff out fertilisers such as ammonium nitrate, a key ingredient in the Taliban's homemade explosives (HMEs) and roadside IEDs. This skill is particularly important. A recent report by the North Atlantic Treaty Organisation (NATO) found that between 80 and 90 per cent of the lethal roadside IEDs in Afghanistan contain ammonium nitrate. And almost half of the Australian soldiers killed in action in Afghanistan have been killed by IEDs.

With the rapidly rising number of IEDs and other homemade explosives in Iraq and Afghanistan, the explosive detection dog is the most in-demand of all hounds in the global war on terror. The Australian Army routinely deploys several dogs to the Australian base at Tarin Kot. The well-armed Americans have 300 WMDs (working military dogs) sniffing for explosives in Iraq and Afghanistan and frequently employ civilian contractors for the role of handlers.

The dogs and handlers are trained separately. You can't train a soldier while teaching old dogs new tricks. The handlers' course at the SME takes thirteen weeks, during which time soldiers are aided by dogs that already know the ropes. The first two weeks of the EDD handlers' course are arguably among the most difficult. The incoming two-legged recruits have to bond with the dogs assigned to them, which is, as one soldier said, 'like sticking two total strangers together and forcing them to spend a lot of time with each other to form a friendship'.

Dogs study us with Talmudic care; they anticipate us, watch for our signals, interpret our intent, monitor our moods, adapt to our response. They feed off our energy, our anxieties, our confidence and our timidity. In fact, the more time you spend with a dog the more it comes to know you, in precisely the same way you come to know it. The relationship develops organically.

Our pet dogs may watch us, but the EDDs watch even more closely. Their lives depend on it. Their soldiers' lives depend on it. Key to building a successful explosive detection dog team is ensuring the canine and human personalities complement each other. Partnering hound and handler requires the deft touch of an alchemist or, in the army's case, an experienced handler who can read each dog's personality and gauge the person with whom it will do its best work. Some dogs need more confident and secure handlers, of strong voice and demeanour, or they won't work—or, to be more generous, won't work to the five-star standard set for them. Similarly, matching a shy dog with a handler who has an overly strong personality could hinder the dog's performance. And a dominant dog with an inexperienced handler is a recipe for disaster—there can only be one top dog in any relationship and it can't be the dog.

Working with dogs requires a unique set of skills, athleticism, determination, ingenuity, tenacity and toughness. It also helps to have a can-do spirit and an ability to work with a tight team of warriors in highly variable conditions. The Doggies pride themselves on being among the most proactive members of the defence force. They initiate training searches on a daily basis and devise new ways of challenging, testing and advancing their dogs. Some sappers, as the handlers are technically called before they have been promoted to a rank, have been known to make their own leashes with which to work more efficiently.

Most importantly, though, the handlers must have a general love of the scrappy hound with all its quirks, foibles and strengths. A soldier lacking a genuine affinity for man's best friend won't last long. The course supervisors know it and so do the animals. In fact, the intuitive dogs use it to their advantage, picking up the nervousness of a handler only to manipulate it to its own advantage. One dominant golden retriever at the SME recognised a distinct lack of experience in her new handler and ran roughshod over the sapper, disobeying commands and ignoring well-intentioned entreaties. Named Mandy, she bolted off into the bushes to play hide-and-seek every time she was given an instruction, hoping to be chased instead of working.

Sarbi was perfectly placed with EDD instructor D, an athletic, tall man with thigh-thick biceps and broad shoulders. Confident and intelligent, he has a mellow, handsome face uncreased by age. His Central Casting good looks once won him a male modelling contest in 2003, a fact he acknowledges he will probably never live down and for which he is constantly ribbed by his fellow Doggies, who occasionally attach a beefcake picture of him to the monthly duty roster. He smiles at the piss-take.

D joined the army in 1995 as a nineteen-year-old, with every intention of being a dog handler. He had a border collie as a child and after that bred a mixed-breed bitch. He named her Chelsea Brown because Chelsea was cute and brown she was. 'Not very imaginative, I know,' he says now with signature soldier-like economy. Chelsea Brown, a boxer-mastiff cross, threw a litter of beautiful pups and, being a motivated teenager with an entrepreneurial flair, he sold all six for a tidy profit.

Originally from Mackay in northern Queensland, he moved with his sister and mother 1600 kilometres south to Griffith in western New South Wales after his parents divorced. He attended the local schools, and played rugby and excelled at darts and hockey. But, like so many restless teenagers eager to get on with life, he left school at the end of year eleven. Raised in a family that appreciated the value of hard work, D got a daytime job as a trainee manager in a fast food outlet and a part-time job delivering pizzas by night, both of which proved less than satisfying for someone keen on adventure, the second even more so because his clapped-out car wasn't up to the task. Not so incidentally, neither accounted for his passion for dogs. He cast around for a better-fitting career and remembered a school visit from an army recruiter, who had informed the student body about the various jobs available in the Australian Army, including the explosive detection teams. The only familial link to the military was through his grandfather, who had been in the army decades before, but D researched the EDD Section, figured it would be ideal for a young man like himself, and signed up to serve his country.

He began the thirteen-week basic recruit training at the First Recruit Training Battalion at Kapooka in southwest New South Wales, where he and a couple of dozen other new recruits were taught basic military skills—shooting, navigation, first aid. After the passing out parade, his platoon was offered a range of positions across the army but the idea of working as a cook or clerk or in the quartermaster's store held no appeal. D was driven. He wanted to join the RAE to be a dog handler. As it happened, eleven places were available in engineer corps and he listed the RAE as his first, second and third preference. He was determined but D's dream of working with dogs would have to wait. The army had other ideas for him. Despite his first three choices—in fact, his only choice—the brass allocated him elsewhere.

'You are going to be an air defender,' the commanding officer said.

'I don't want to do that,' the disappointed recruit replied, forgetting he really had no choice in the matter, this being army, not a project meeting.

'We need a couple of the smarter guys to do it,' came the final pronouncement.

'I think they were trying to build me up, to make me think it was a good thing,' he says now with a measure of self-deprecation.

The young soldier was assigned to the Sixteenth Air Defence Regiment in Woodside, South Australia, as part of the artillery corps, and in August reported for duty as a 'missile number' for the Rapier surface-to-air towed missile launcher. It wasn't his dream job but it was, at least, action driven. 'You're basically shooting missiles at enemy planes.'

He moved west, bought a flash car and fancy motorbike, and made himself at home. For now. In his head, the gunner had the future mapped out. He expected to make a good impression and, after completing the first mandatory year, apply for a corps transfer to the RAE. Things were working according to plan until a sharp bend in the Adelaide Hills got in the way of things. The motorbike aficionado came out of one bend in the twisting and picturesque hills at the legal limit but was too fast for the next hairpin turn and crashed his powerful CBR 600 Honda motorbike. The end result was a leg snapped in four places that required a 45-centimetre pin inserted into the bone, held in place by three screws. The injuries gave him an early education in the scale of pain from one to ten, which he would draw on years later in Afghanistan, when a Taliban ambush left his body riddled with shrapnel. A painful and slow recovery delayed the corps transfer until 1997, when D was posted to the 1st Combat Engineer Regiment (1CER), a mechanised unit of the RAE at Holsworthy.

From gunner to sapper, he was one step closer to the Explosive Detection Dog Section but still had to mark time for a couple more years as a combat engineer. He easily mastered the fundamentals of engineering in the initial employment training (IET) and was a dab hand at demolition, bridge building, watermanship and mines. His official duties also included ferrying troops in an Armoured Personnel Carrier (APC) and chauffeuring the regimental commanding officer, the latter of which came with certain privileges.

The regiment moved to Darwin in late 1999 and soon after was deployed to East Timor as part of the International Force for East Timor (INTERFET), a peacekeeping mission under the command of Major General Peter Cosgrove, raised in response to the civil strife that erupted after the East Timorese voted for independence from Indonesia. After four months driving a thirteen-tonne APC through the dangerously narrow and steep streets of Dili, D finally scored a coveted spot on the EDD handlers' course with four other soldiers. He received orders to report to the SME for the course beginning in March 2000.

'I finally got there,' he says.

The sapper was teamed with Vegas, a stock standard, good-looking yellow Labrador retriever true to the breed; eager, biddable, food and ball obsessed, and as loyal as could be. At two years of age, Vegas was at the tail end of puppyhood and had only just finished her own nineteen-week training course. She had had little, if any, follow-up training during the Christmas holidays and was a little bit rusty and a little bit disobedient when D began working with her. It meant he had to work harder to pull the dog into line while learning the ropes himself.

Their days started with an early morning run with the dogs, for fitness and to burn off the dogs' excess energy before training, followed by mucking out the kennels, a sure-fire way to get to know how healthy your dog really is. The first two weeks were devoted to basic obedience training, the theory of dog behaviours and the role of the EDD Section. The handlers were taught how to transport their dogs, and safety and first aid for themselves and the hounds. This included carrying the heavy mutts if they were incapacitated on patrol by slinging the dog up and around its handler's neck and across the shoulders with the front and rear paws held together at the chest. This variation of the fireman's lift was usually no problem with the smaller dogs but a tough task with the bigger hounds that could weigh as much as 35 kilograms, especially when the soldier is loaded with his regular weapons, webbing and pack. They trained on agility and obstacle courses, over barrels, up and down ladders two metres high, across logs, through tunnels, windows and doorways, in preparation for deployment.

Four weeks were devoted to learning intricate search patterns for four distinct and separate locations: buildings, open areas, vehicles and routes, with a week to master each. It was exhausting work. The cut-off point was the end of week six, by which point if the handler lacked aptitude he would be booted out of boot camp, no correspondence entered into. This is life saving work—you don't get second chances in a war zone.

'It's quite stressful for the guys on the course, thinking, "here comes week seven, the cut off. If I am no good, I'm out",' says D. 'And you can still fail even at the end of week thirteen after the two-week final assessment, which is called "Mad Bomber". You can fail on the very last day, and that's it, you're out.'

Failing was not an option. He'd waited five years for this gig and he had no intention of throwing it away. Mad Bomber tests the sappers' dog-handling skills and overall search abilities in public venues around Sydney and in the bush, or any environment to simulate every type of threat. The handler is also assessed for leadership qualities when working in a team. Human and hound are evaluated together but the burden of responsibility remains with the handler. The sapper has to recognise when his dog has failed to follow procedure and correct its behaviour, and keep the animal motivated and on track for the 40-minute searches over several kilometres. The pressure is enormous, particularly with an instructor standing a metre behind you every step of the way, with a notebook in hand, writing critical notes that could determine the end of a career with the dogs before it has even begun.

'The biggest failing point is on safety for the Doggies—either walking into an unsearched area or missing areas,' says D. 'You have to maintain situational awareness at all times, to know where you've been, where the dog's been, what has been searched, what hasn't been searched. The other failing point is not being able to read the dog's indications. You need to recognise when the dog has a change in posture to indicate to you that something may be in the area.'

All dogs have a tell, much like a poker player when on to a winning or losing hand—a slight twitch of the eye, a faint smile, or two fingernails clicking against each other. The tell is an honest and consistent response, an instinctive reaction, and the well-trained handler can recognise his dog's tell instantly. Some dogs freeze; others put their tails straight up or out, or raise a paw, or prick up their ears. Some might even signal verbally, though this is uncommon.

Sapper D and Vegas passed and went straight to work at the Sydney Olympic Games in 2000 with the entire EDD Section. The Olympics occurred in the pre-9/11 days when the clearest and most present danger wasn't hidden explosives or weapons of mass destruction, but over-eager tourists and athletes wanting to pat the lovable dogs. The golden Labrador retriever sniffed her way through countless athletes' villages, venues, vehicle checkpoints and public spaces. Vegas, with her smiling Lab face, always drew attention despite being a professional military working dog on a mission.

Even Queen Elizabeth II fell for Vegas's canine charms. D and Vegas were part of the security detachment for the Golden Jubilee Royal Tour of Cairns in 2002 and had lined the red carpet at the airport waiting for the Queen and Prince Philip, to stroll past as custom dictates. As the animal-loving royal made her way up the receiving line she spied the soldier with Vegas sitting neatly beside his left leg, a fine example of an obedient and well-trained dog. Her Majesty is a die-hard dog person. She fell in love with the quirky corgi breed as a child when, in 1933, her father King George VI brought home Dookie and Jane, the first of a long line of famous royal corgis. These days the Queen has several Pembroke Welsh corgis and dachshund-corgi crosses that tootle behind Her Majesty through the hallowed halls of royal residences across her vast kingdom. Many of her current pack are descendants of a corgi she received as a gift for her eighteenth birthday, that the young princess gave the un-doglike name of Susan.

Queen Elizabeth stopped in front of Vegas. Her handler was surprised, not exactly expecting a one-on-one royal audience but like every soldier, he came prepared.

'Good afternoon, Your Highness,' he said with a smile, posture ramrod straight, shoulders back. As the small talk progressed above her, Vegas surreptitiously went to work on the new smorgasbord of scents that had materialised in front of her. With as much dexterity as she could muster from her seated position, the cheeky Lab craned her neck as far as she could, her inquisitive nose testing the air, twitching with each inhalation. Seconds later, an emboldened, black, wet schnozzle sniffed the royal handbag, as if searching for treats. Had Her Majesty not been so fond of dogs, Vegas's wayward sniff could have been a diplomatic disaster reminiscent of Paul Keating's infamous 'lizard of Oz' moment in 1992, when he undiplomatically snaked an arm around the royal back.

'The Queen just laughed,' D says now.

Pooch protocol, being slightly more relaxed than political protocol, had not been breached and you couldn't blame Sergeant D for thinking Vegas had just received the royal imprimatur, however unofficial. D, too, got the unofficial royal thumbs up. When it came to the Doggies, he was blessed, as would become clear years later in Afghanistan.

Chapter 8

A NOSE FOR WAR

Canis familiaris, more humbly known as man's best friend, has been going to combat since 400BC—possibly even earlier. Back then dogs were used as forward attack elements in the Peloponnesian War between the Greeks and Corinthians. Attila the Hun relied on dogs as sentinels during his conquest of Europe in the fifth century. Eleven hundred years later the Italian naturalist, Aldrovandus, detailed how the ancient Greeks bred particularly ferocious war dogs, trained to 'be an enemy to everybody but his master'. They were given names indicative of their roles: *Symmachi*, for allies, and *Somatophylakes*, for bodyguards.

The English were fond of the fighting dog too. King Henry VIII and his daughter, the first Queen Elizabeth, used hundreds of hounds in battle. Across the English Channel the French emperor Napoleon, no lover of dogs as previously noted, employed them against the enemy and famously chained them to the walls of Alexandria to warn of looming danger. Napoleon later wrote of being stirred to the point of tears at the sight of a devoted dog sitting beside his slain master at the end of a battle in Europe in 1798. The dog's grief haunted him unlike any other tragedy he had witnessed at war.

Soldiers in the Confederate and Union armies in the American Civil War trained dogs to catch fleeing prisoners and called them, somewhat ominously, 'hounds of hell'. The author of *War Dogs, A History of Loyalty and Heroism*, Michael G. Lemish, writes that the escapees would have been terrified of the massive beasts on their trail, for to be caught 'meant severe mutilation or death'.

In the Second World War, the United States military finally caught up with its Australian counterparts and officially used canines to patrol the coastline. Shortly after, it began the Dogs for Defence program in which Uncle Sam called on the public to donate healthy, obedient dogs to defend the nation. To support the war effort, President Franklin D. Roosevelt enlisted his dog in the army. Fala, a Scottish terrier, achieved the rank of private. The promotional stunt worked and more than 19,000 family pets were contributed, of which more than half passed the recruitment test. Dogs have been deployed ever since.

Over time, war dogs have been used as messengers, mascots, ambulances, combatants, carriers, couriers, trackers, scouts and sentries. They have attacked approaching enemy fighters and horses wearing body armour and sharply spiked collars, and guarded fortress perimeters to prevent entry as much as escape. They pulled carts loaded with machine-guns and small cannons and wagons with wounded soldiers; they delivered messages to distant commanders, located fallen troopers, dragged them from the line of fire and delivered medication, water and, poignantly, comfort to the dying. Fast and agile, they also made for smaller targets and thus were more difficult to shoot than humans.

Fast forward to the present day. High-tech dogs abseil out of helicopters and parachute from planes to land with their masters in otherwise inaccessible places. The dogs love it. They have no concept of height and the rush of wind on the dog's face is their equivalent of nirvana. The highest human-hound air assault was a 30,000 foot leap by a US Navy SEAL and his dog, Cara.

The now famous SEAL Team 6 that tracked down and killed the world's most wanted man, Osama bin Laden, took with them a highly trained dog named Cairo. The fearsome warrior was winched down into bin Laden's for-tified compound in Pakistan from the MH-60 helicopter along with the twenty hardened Marines. Details of Cairo's mission are closely guarded but he was trained to sniff out explosives or find the high-value target if he had been hid-den in the compound. Cairo was also trained as an attack and guard dog. Cairo, a Belgian Malinois, has since had a private audience with President Obama and will be remem-bered for his role in one of the most daring combat raids in contemporary military history.

The modern military dog like Cairo fares much better than its historical counterpart. Today's combat hounds wear sophisticated body armour and custom-built life vests.

Heavily armoured assault jackets have been constructed to be bulletproof, stab proof and shrapnel proof. They even have vests equipped with long-range GPS systems. According to *Foreign Policy* magazine, the elite SEAL dogs like Cairo have infrared night-sight cameras and intruder communications systems able to penetrate concrete walls.

For all their brilliant agility and utility, the dogs also provide something more. Loyal guardianship.

In Afghanistan three stray dogs named Sasha, Rufus and Target prevented a suicide bomber from penetrating a US army barracks where 50 soldiers were relaxing in 2010. The mongrels attacked the intruder who detonated his suicide bomb vest, blowing himself up with 25 pounds of C4 explosives. Sasha was killed but Rufus and Target, who was pregnant and would later give birth to five pups, survived the blast. The soldiers nursed them to health—'they were our babies'. The grateful men whose lives they saved repatriated Rufus and Target to the United States. Unfortunately, Target was later wrongly euthanised by an animal shelter when she wandered away from her home. Her tragic plight and pretty beseeching face made headlines around the world. Dog lovers grieved as if they had lost their own cherished pet.

Dogs grieve too. In 2011 animal experts said it was possible that an explosive detection dog with the British Army had died from a heart seizure just hours after his devoted companion, Lance Corporal Liam Tasker, was killed in a firefight with insurgents in Afghanistan. Theo, a springer spaniel-mix, was not quite two years old. 'I think we underestimate the grieving process in dogs. Some dogs react very severely to their partner's loss,' a senior veterinarian said after Theo died.

With such loyalty, it is no wonder dogs have been hailed as heroes, honoured with military funerals and awarded an array of medals for bravery and service. Monuments have been built and portraits painted to record dogs' unyielding loyalty to man.

And yet. Much of it has not ended well for the devoted dog conscripted to war.

One of the most disturbing uses of man's best friend was by the Soviets in the Second World War, in a savage effort to repel invading German tanks. The Russians trained dogs to find food hidden under tanks. In the days before the expected confrontations, the hounds were starved. As enemy tanks approached, soldiers strapped an explosives-filled coat on the backs of the innocent canines, freed them from their bonds and sent them in search of food. The dogs did as trained and crawled under the tanks, which triggered a raised detonator attached to the top of the coat. The bomb exploded, the dog was killed and casualties and fatalities were inflicted on the enemy. It is remarkably easy to feel sorry for them, these trusting hounds callously written off as expendable military equipment.

Thankfully, the Russian barbarity was abandoned when soldiers discovered that, while obedient and smart, the dogs had some limitations—the most serious being an inability to tell the difference between enemy and Soviet tanks. Dogs might not be colour-blind in the full sense of the word but they were blind to national insignias. That wasn't all; no matter how desperately starved they were, some dogs were gun shy. Instead of barrelling headfirst into battle, they shied away from it, an instinctive fear that reduced their reliability and effectiveness but saved them from blowing themselves up.

Other nations and combatants also have been callous in their disregard for the kindliness and willingness of dogs to please and serve us humans, and it makes one wonder. If dogs can read human gestures and human behaviour better than any other species, including the marvellously intelligent chimpanzee, as American scientist Brian Hare recently argued, it seems an especially cruel oversight that they can't read or foretell man's duplicity. The tragedy of the anti-tank dogs shows the purity of canine loyalty.

The easiest and perhaps surest way to understand a dog is to accept that it sees the world through its nose and that it is, quite literally, a nose-aholic. The canine nose is the dog's lifeline and it uses it in every interaction it undertakes. Dog noses are different to our human ones, physically and functionally. As well as having pride of place on a dog's face, the nose has front nostrils that extend into flexible side slits to assist the sniffing process, and its shape is specifically designed to breathe in and out at the same time. Impressive, yes?

The nose has an internal membranous and bone structure built for smelling, armed with millions of receptor sites to process whatever smell, foul or otherwise, they have inhaled deeply and repeatedly. Compare. We humans have just six million receptor sites. The average dog has 220 million. A bloodhound, considered the *crème de la canine* of nose work, has about 30 million more. No wonder it has been dubbed 'a nose with a dog attached'. As Alexandra Horowitz writes in her best-selling book, *Inside of A Dog*, 'Dogs have more genes committed to coding olfactory cells, more cells, and more *kinds* (her emphasis) of cells, able to detect more kinds of smells.'

And what smells!

The non-profit Pine Street Foundation in California has taught five dogs to detect ovarian cancer in humans by smelling samples of their breath. The dogs are all pets of families who live near the research facility in San Anselmo, located 32 kilometres north of San Francisco. None of the volunteer hounds had any scent training before their proud owners signed them up to be scientific researchers. The canines were trained using operant conditioning, with a clicker and using food as rewards, and are now ready to go to work. By the end of 2011 the foundation will have completed recruiting ovarian cancer patients to then 'closely examine the chemistry of exhaled breath,' says the foundation's research director Michael McCulloch.

McCulloch hopes the study will lead to the discovery of a new non-invasive test for this insidious disease, known as the 'silent killer' because it is usually detected in its later, more aggressive stages when treatment is less effective.

Pine Street has a strong track record. In 2006, researchers led by McCulloch taught another five dogs to sniff out the chemical changes in people who had recently been diagnosed with breast and lung cancer. The scientists worked out that canines can differentiate between cancerous and healthy cells because cancerous ones emit different metabolic waste products. The dogs accurately detected cancer cells at all four stages of the disease and across all age groups within 12,000 samples from 55 lung cancer patients, 31 breast cancer patients and 83 healthy controls.

In 2010, McCulloch and Emily Moser from the New College of Florida went on a search mission to examine all peer-reviewed studies on cancer-detecting canines. They narrowed in on six studies in which dogs had been used to detect breast, ovarian, lung and prostate cancers and melanoma. Their conclusion after reviewing the work was optimistic. 'Early successes with canine scent detection suggest chemical analysis of exhaled breath may be a valid method for cancer detection.'

That man's best friend really is the top dog in scientific research when it comes to scent and sniff should come as no great surprise. Pups are born blind and begin life relying on smell and touch. Ground scenting and air scenting—in fact, any scenting—comes naturally. In 1989 the respected British medical journal, *The Lancet*, reported the first known case in the United Kingdom of a dog owner whose hound alerted her to a melanoma by repeatedly licking the cancerous spot on her leg. That tongue-lashing saved her life. A few years before that, on the other side of the Atlantic Ocean, a Shetland sheepdog in New York detected a virulent form of melanoma on its owner's back. The discovery ultimately led scientists to test the diagnostic abilities of dogs in a project partly supported by the National Institutes of Health. 'It may well be that, someday in the future, inspection by a dog may become a routine part of cancer screening,' said Richard Simmons, a research associate who worked on the project.

McCulloch believes the dog nose is 'one of the most sophisticated odour detection devices on the planet', so sophisticated that it can sniff out a few tiny molecules in an Olympic-sized swimming pool. McCulloch's colleague and the medical director at Pine Street, Michael Broffman, puts it rather more charmingly, 'We often refer to our dogs as the best and original PET-scan.'

Knowing and accepting our limitations and as we learn more about the fine intelligence of man's best friend, humans are increasingly calling on dogs to do a range of complicated and dexterous tasks. We faithfully put our lives directly in their paws. They guide the blind, hear for the deaf, help the physically disabled, find the lost, in body and soul, and even nurture stressed victims in criminal trials. They aid search and rescue missions when Mother Nature has unleashed her worst, or when the unthinkable happens, such as the 9/11 terrorist attacks in the United States.

A retired Canadian search and rescue police dog named Trakr located the twentieth and last survivor of the World Trade Center attacks buried beneath ten metres of concrete and twisted metal. Genelle Guzman-McMillan had been trapped for more than twenty-three hours when Trakr indicated to his handler, James Symington, that he'd detected a human being close by.

'Trakr came to a sudden stop . . . [his] body became still and erect . . . Trakr's ears perked up and his tail stiffened. There was no doubt about it at that point: Trakr sensed somebody close by was buried alive. That somebody was me,' she writes in her autobiography, *Angel in the Rubble*.

Four hours later, Guzman-McMillan was cut free from her concrete tomb in the mountain of burning debris.

Dogs also have been taught to detect pending seizures in epileptics and hypoglycaemic attacks in diabetics. They can smell fear, because fear smells. They can smell confidence and anger, too, for as Horowitz points out, pheromones are released when we are alarmed and charmed and our bodies go through physiological and metabolic changes. They magically teach prisoners and juvenile delinquents the meaning of compassion, care and responsibility. Therapy canines calm and comfort the sick. Doggie soothsayers foretell imminent earthquakes and thunderstorms.

Right now in Australia scientists at Monash University in the southern state of Victoria are investigating whether dogs can detect the range of raw human emotions, with a focus on determining whether dogs prefer happy or sad people. 'There is some anecdotal evidence that if you have had a bad day at the office when you get home your dog knows it and comes up and gives you a nuzzle,' says Melbourne-based animal behaviourist, Kate Mornement.

We have no qualms about giving canines the dirty and stinky work and it helps that they love it. Sniff for cadavers? No problem. Bed bugs, termites, dead game and fowl? Easy. If it really reeks, great. You might be turning your nose up but remember that dogs eat faeces, a habit known as coprophagia—disgusting to us but delightful to them. They also sniff other dogs' urine and excrement and then, more often than not, sign the same spot with a splash of their own. Call it doggie graffiti. Think of how a dog introduces itself to another member of the species—straight to the rear end where its genitalia are located.

Dogs are not prejudiced: they don't limit themselves to their own species. Remember the last time a dog decided to invade your personal space with an inappropriate sniff of your groin that had you shifting from foot to foot with embarrassment? Dogs have no time for embarrassment, especially when it comes to smells. To the dog, that invasive sniff was the most straightforward way to gather information about you, though, thankfully, we'll never know what it discovered because it won't tell.

Take your dog for walk and you will lose count of the times it sniffs repeatedly at something imperceptible to you. Dogs collect a veritable library of information about what's gone on from invisible and visible stink spots—who's been there, when they were there, what they did, what they ate for breakfast, if it was healthy, who they were with, on heat or not, dominant, submissive, aggressive, large, small.

Horowitz calls these cumulative piles of aging yet invisible scents from a parade of passing pooches a 'community centre bulletin board', and this seems about right. Humans need obvious cues, and many of them, to determine such things; dogs just need their schnoz, one big sniff and some form of physical, even disgusting, nose contact.

Hound expert Stanley Coren likened a dog on a sniffing mission to a human reading a newspaper. Pulling the dog away before it has finished sniffing means it has only 'read the headlines', not the whole story. As Coren says, it seems rather mean to deprive the dog of its daily gossip.

The father of modern philosophy, René Descartes, coined the phrase, *I think, therefore I am*. The canine *Cogito* would be: *I sniff, therefore I am*.

Chapter 9

TEACHING OLD DOGS NEW TRICKS

As is often the case in life, chance played its hand as much as circumstance. A fortuitous combination of both, mixed with the felicity of fate, had Sarbi assigned to explosive detection dog handler D. His facility with dogs had seen him promoted from handler to instructor and, more recently, rise up a rank. He was, in short, something of a dog whisperer, and was without an explosive detection dog for the first time in five years when Sarbi and Rafi arrived at the SME in June 2005. Vegas, his beloved golden Labrador retriever, had been retired to live out her life as her handler's pet after a distinguished career serving her country alongside D at home and abroad, including a six-month stint in the Solomon Islands on Operation Anode.

Rank has its privileges and the EDD Section's chief

trainer, Corporal Murray Young, chose to train Rafi. By default the dogless D took Sarbi.

He immediately noted Sarbi's retrieval drive was excellent. She didn't game, that is, chase birds or prey, a habit that can mean the end of an EDD career before it has even begun. And she had the hallmarks of a good working dog: eager to please, a disposition to work closely with a master and a love of playtime, the latter of which turned out to be a strong point because, in reality, all work for the explosive detection dog is a form of playtime.

The explosive detection dogs' role is straightforward, though training them is not. The nineteen-week course revolves around a few fundamentals, starting with the dog's innate retrieval drive, the tennis ball—the reward—and a custom-built harness, all of which leads to teaching the dogs how to detect the chemical compounds of explosives through the process of scent imprinting. The dogs are not trained with food as a reward because it is impractical for their handlers to carry extra food on patrol when their packs already weigh in excess of 40 kilograms, not including webbing, weapons and equipment.

Sarbi and Rafi took to the basic training and obedience lessons with alacrity and sailed through the initial two-week assessment period designed to see how they coped in various situations and conditions: indoors and out, with various physical and audible distractions. They trained over a specially made obstacle course consisting of ramps, platforms, ladders, tunnels, A-shaped walls and simulated windows and doorways, to prepare them for the harsh terrain and exacting mission demands of real patrols. EDDs search tight and unfamiliar spaces, compounds, caves and bunkers, under and in trucks, tanks, in cargo containers, aircraft holds, on board airplanes and in helicopters. In fact, wherever it is suspected that dangerous materials and weapons are hidden, even under water. There are no off limits.

Dogs have acute hearing and are sensitive to the noise and percussive impact of exploding rocket propelled grenades, roadside bombs, mortars, and machine-gun and small arms fire. Sudden, nerve-jangling explosions will spook them. The high pitch of chopper blades, the roar of aircraft engines and the racket of tanks and trucks can be their undoing. Therefore, they had to be conditioned to cope with the thunderous noise of war.

A meticulous program to desensitise the EDDs to battlefield noise has been developed over the decades and is used around the world. D began by firing a starter pistol from about 100 metres away, to familiarise Sarbi with the sound while she was calm and settled. He moved in small increments closer until she could withstand the gunfire and percussive shock waves at close range, including when tethered by leash to his body armour. Most dogs are initially affected by weapons fire—in other words, gun shy—and their reaction can make or break their careers. 'The initial testing is to determine that the dogs won't run away or react badly or savagely,' says D. 'Dogs are generally fight or flight and if they can't get away they might bite.' He had never seen a dog bite anyone when exposed to gunfire or explosions, but he never discounted that dogs were dogs.

But all this is mere entrée. The real work of scent

imprinting came next, the moment the dogs had been waiting for. The aforementioned harness is the trigger for the dog to know it is about to go to work. 'It's a game for the dog, he thinks he is looking for a tennis ball. As soon as the search harness is put on the dog he knows he's in for a game,' said Corporal Fred Cox, a former chief trainer at the SME.

D unpacked the explosive training kit and stashed the first explosive odour that Sarbi would be trained on in a metal cage. He held Sarbi while Corporal Young ran down to the explosive, where he placed a tennis ball next to the cage. Sarbi didn't take her eyes off the tennis ball and watched in anticipation. When Young ran back past Sarbi's handler without the ball, the dog instinctively knew what to do. She waited patiently for her cue, the magic words from her handler.

Sarbi, seek on.

The trainee hound sprinted down to the cage and picked up her ball not knowing that her handler was actually training her to associate the smell of explosives with the tennis ball. Sarbi was smart, but for her this was a simple game of retrieving the ball. As the training progressed Young repeated the exercise, but over time, instead of putting the ball beside the cage, he hid it in his pocket and ran back empty handed. D released Sarbi with the routine command.

Seek on.

Sarbi ran down to the cage and couldn't find the missing ball. But she recognised the explosive odour that she had been trained to associate with her ball. She stared at the cage that was emitting the newly familiar smell. Young threw the missing tennis ball in over Sarbi's head. Fortunately, he had a well-trained arm and the ball landed precisely on the cage. The dog was ecstatic—her ball had appeared out of nowhere. The training was done in small steps, working towards the required response, and after a week Sarbi was able to follow a dummy run and sit within one metre of the cage containing the explosives and stare at it without moving. Sergeant D quickly identified her signature tell; it was obvious. She froze, raised her tail and went into a slow motion sit, staring intently at the object, just as Gemma said she had done as a puppy in Bowral.

Good girl.

D repeated the process until Sarbi automatically identified a range of explosives. In no short time she proved that her explosive detection skills were not to be sniffed at.

'Some dogs learn slower than others, some never pick it up,' he says. 'Sarbi was pretty much excellent right from the get-go after her initial training. Once she learnt it, she was very good. She is an awesome searcher, very responsive. I don't have to try to control her too much because she searches everything that needs to be searched. Quite obedient and very steady under all conditions. And she loved the tennis ball.'

Her schnoz finesse and TTPs were tested daily on simulated patrols and in mock situations. Every morning D loaded Sarbi in the EDD Section's purpose-built vehicle, dubbed the 'ice-cream van' because it looked like a refrigerated van and could carry up to eight dog teams, and headed out to search. He and Corporal Young spent hours with

Sarbi and Rafi, hiding weapons and explosives until both dogs effortlessly identified any number of hazardous threats in any situation. D hid explosives from the explosive training kit for Rafi and Murray to discover, and vice versa. Both handlers and dogs were tested. They rarely failed. Sarbi had become a canine Sherlock Holmes. Ditto Rafi.

Nose-work is only one part of the game. Sarbi was taught the same four basic search patterns D had learnt years earlier—building, area, route and vehicle. EDDs searching for improvised explosive devices on routes work in a box pattern, up one side of the road, across and returning down the other side to the starting point. For vehicle searches, Sarbi circled a vehicle and checked under it before going through one door and out the other, front seat first then rear, followed by trays and truck sections. Large open areas are zigzagged, left to right with the dog off leash and metres out in front of its handler. The teams search vulnerable points and choke points including bridges, river crossings, riverbanks, and defiles, army speak for places where the road or route narrows due to a man-made or natural obstruction, increasing its risk as a site for ambush or attack.

Circumstances dictate the distance at which the animal works. Each handler has his own preference for how far the dog should be ahead of him. D liked Sarbi to roam at least 40 metres in front of him but she could be as far as 70 to 80 metres from her handler, depending on the segment of the search pattern. Monitoring distance is absolutely vital. As he says, the dog is in the most vulnerable position and the crucial element in each search is to ensure the safety of the following troops. Visual hand signals and audible commands for the dog remain the same in every instance. Consistency is king.

To the untrained observer, the intricate teamwork between man and mutt must seem magically telepathic and, in a way, it is. It is as if the dog has insinuated its way into the handler's head, and vice versa. They have become attuned to each other's needs. 'Streamlined and instinctive,' he says.

When trained, the military mutts can detect lethal explosives from 100 metres, with a nose that is ten to 100,000 times superior to the exceedingly limited human olfactory tool. In monetary terms, they are worth an estimated $90,000 and cost thousands of dollars a year to run. The American military working dogs cost $40,000 a year to maintain and care for and are designated rather coldly as a 'highly specialized piece of equipment'. It's worth remembering that the eleven Australian dogs that served in Vietnam were also robbed of their actual dogness and described as 'engineer stores'. Decades later the faithful hounds were finally afforded the respect they had earned and deserved when granted a proper title, explosive detection dog. But the dollar figure and designation devalues the true worth of the smart animals. To their handlers and the soldiers whose lives they save, ensuring they will go home safely, they are priceless.

For these dogs had skills other than those for which they had been meticulously trained. How could you put a price on the ability to boost troop morale or comfort the grief-stricken or provide faithful companionship or act as an emotional crutch for young soldiers who put their lives on the line daily for their countries? What price their unconditional love, as pure and as old as the ages, or the happiness they bring by just being a dog? All the mutts want in return is to be loved, fed and taken care of. Occasional playtime is a bonus. As warriors go, there are none more uncomplicated than the four-legged variety. They are creatures of unbidden affection as well as marvels of military training.

Sarbi and Rafi were trained to a gold standard and knew every hard edge and right angle of operational deployment. They proved to be star performers and graduated in November 2005. Yet, for the first time in their lives, the dogs that had done so much together were to be separated. Corporal Young chose to take Rafi, now with the official rank of EDD 435, to Townsville and he reported for duty in January of 2006. EDD 436 Sarbi remained with D, who was assigned to the specialist Incident Response Regiment at the Holsworthy Army Barracks under the aegis of the Special Operations Command.

It was time to seek on, for real.

Chapter 10

SARBI, GO SEEK

Explosive Detection Dog 436 Sarbi made her professional debut in 2006, in one of the greatest national security challenges on Australian soil—ensuring terrorists did not unleash a reign of terror on the Commonwealth Games in Melbourne. The so-called friendly games were the second international sporting event held in Australia in the post September 11 environment and the Federal and State governments and law enforcement authorities were on high alert. For good reason. The threat of a terrorist strike was a daily reality.

Echoes of the bloodbaths in Bali and London the previous year were resonating still. On 1 October 2005 twenty tourists were slaughtered while dining on a beachfront restaurant at the popular Indonesian resort of Jimbaran Bay, the second terrorist bombing to target Western holidaymakers in the Islamic archipelago in the space of three years. Three months previously, on 7 July, four suicide bombers with ties to al-Qaeda hit London. They detonated crudely made bombs during the morning peak hour on three trains in the Tube and on a red double-decker bus on a crowded city street. Fifty-two innocent men, women and children were murdered. Another 700 people were seriously injured.

The attacks shattered Britain's fragile sense of security, now permanently altered.

The eighteenth Commonwealth Games presented another potential opportunity for religious and political extremists. Terrorists abhor a vacuum. They need an audience, crave it. An audience fuels and sustains the brutal objectives of terrorisers, who use violence against civilians and non-combatants to exact revenge for perceived wrongs. Equally dark and insidious is the desire to instil fear in and intimidate or influence a targeted population, often with irrevocable and devastating effect. As terrorists had shown on so many occasions in so many locations around the world, they had no compunction about targeting civilians.

Terrorists weren't the only concern. Individuals fixated on public figures, serial pests with a history of disrupting public events, minority groups with single-issue grievances and even those suffering mental illness posed real and significant threats.

It was for these reasons that the contours and consequences of an attack in Melbourne were addressed from every imaginable perspective, by a coalition of agencies experienced in counter terrorism, rapid responses and cataclysmic consequence management. 'It was not as if the threat of terrorism was new, but the concern was around issue-motivated groups. There was a possibility they would use your event to push their own cause,' recalls a senior member of the contract security team for the games.

Security for the Commonwealth Games was logistically complicated. More than 4500 athletes from 71 countries converged on Melbourne to compete in 247 events in sixteen sports, fourteen of which were held within three kilometres of the southern state's central business district. Hundreds of thousands of spectators were expected to attend more than 60 sporting venues and public domains, all of which had to be searched and secured. Chief among them were the sprawling 'precincts' for the road events, the only venues where unscreened, non-ticketed spectators could actually reach out and physically touch an athlete competing in the walk and mountain bike events, and the popular road cycle races, marathon and triathlon.

The opening and closing ceremonies at the Melbourne Cricket Ground, on 15 March and 26 March respectively, presented even bigger propaganda opportunities for potential terrorists. Queen Elizabeth II was opening the games before a retinue of royalty, heads of state, VIPs and dignitaries. For terrorists, they were high-value targets. Tens of thousands of jubilant locals and tourists, all with their guard down to celebrate the glory of the games, were also at risk. Hundreds of thousands more were invited to free events at public venues. Public transport would be stretched to capacity. There was no overstating the fact: the city would be a target-rich environment. Nothing could or would be left to chance.

Federal and State law enforcement agencies joined with intelligence, military and government bodies plus a civilian army of 6000 private security contractors to make the games safe, or as safe as could be.

Two thousand six hundred personnel from the Australian Defence Force—navy, army and air force—were selected for the event. In typical style, the ADF named its mission, calling this one Operation Acolyte, the Greek word for 'helper' or 'assistant'. Highly trained soldiers from the Special Air Service Regiment, the 1st and 2nd Commando Regiments, the Incident Response Regiment and the entire Explosive Dog Detection Section were among the 1200 defence members specifically conscripted to provide security for the Games, patrolling the skies, land and waterways. Their collective specialty was counter-terrorism and rapid responses to terrorist strikes.

Blackhawk helicopters supported a Tactical Assault Group (there are two, known as east and west and located in Sydney and Perth). Maritime and airborne assets, including amphibious landing vessels and FA/18 Hornets, were ready to intercept vessels or divert aircraft to counter specific threats should they arise. Soldiers from the IRR would respond to any chemical, biological or radiological (CBR) threats, as well as perform air crash rescues.

The devil was in the detail. The success or otherwise of an operation as vast and complicated as the Games was in the planning, training, rehearsing and readiness. Operation Acolyte presented new training opportunities for D and another handler, Sapper Craig Turnbull, and EDD Razz because they were attached to the Commandos and SAS, with their superior firepower, machinery and equipment.

D and EDD Sarbi hadn't been working together long but he didn't reckon that as a disadvantage. He had every confidence in her and believed she was up to the task. As dogs go, he had seen none better. Still hasn't. She had proven her mettle as an all-terrain, all-conditions dog during doggie boot camp. Sarbi knew her TNT from her RDX, her detonator cords from her time fuses; she was able to sniff up wind, down wind and across wind. In short, she knew the ropes and the smells.

The EDD teams developed extra searches to assist the elite Special Forces soldiers and devised new ways of winching two dogs side-by-side out of Blackhawk helicopters for rapid response insertions. One handler fast-roped out of the chopper to the ground first, followed by the dogs that were winched out the other side in harnesses, then the second handler fast-roped to the ground.

D strapped Sarbi in and hoisted her up a tree to determine her reaction—remarkably calm, considering the situation. She didn't, however, appreciate the noise and downwash of the rotor blades when winched from the chopper, not uncommon for the hounds. The dogs were compliant, if not overly happy about their aerial activities, unlike the rush of wind they love when abseiling. 'I wouldn't say they like it, they tolerate it,' he says.

The dogs were also taught to detect explosives concealed on humans, to counter the threat of suicide bombers. That required a new skill set. Dogs recognise humans as people—not inanimate objects with an explosive scent—and respond accordingly. The innovative handlers tweaked the proven methods of detecting explosives and the dogs dutifully adapted.

The hounds and handlers had honed their skills and drills to their highest standard yet, constantly sharpening their ever-evolving TTPs. They were fully prepared for any situation, however unpredictable. D, calm and process driven by nature, didn't let things faze him. He had worked the Sydney Olympics and Sydney Special Olympics with EDD Vegas in 2000 and his experience would complement his hound's natural-born sniffing skills. Sarbi was good to go.

The EDDs searched, cleared and secured the athletes' villages and prepped them for lockdown. Once done, nothing could penetrate the established security zone. They helped other agencies at vehicle checkpoints, with the dogs sniffing for explosives and associated contraband.

The dogs' mere presence among the public was psychologically reassuring from a security perspective. The feel-good effect was rated a bonus. Animal lovers all stopped and offered a pat and kind word. The flow-on effect and goodwill was infinite.

The intense preparation paid off. The event was a masterpiece of top-level domestic security and lived up to its nickname of the 'friendly games'. The VIPs went home happy; Melbourne's proud boast that it is the sporting capital of Australia remained unchallenged.

It was a prelude for what would come next.

D and Sarbi returned to the Incident Response Regiment

in Sydney and the other Doggies flew back to their bases around the country. Before long the handlers were hearing whispers about their next deployment.

There was then a 200-member Australian Army Special Operations Task Group (SOTG) partway through a year-long deployment known as Operation Slipper. They were based at the multinational Camp Holland in the remote and dangerous province of Uruzgan in Afghanistan.

To outsiders, Afghanistan is a place that time forgot. A nation for which past is prologue. Afghans boast a proud warrior culture some 2000 years old. They have ruthlessly repelled Persians, Greeks, Arabs, Mongols, Tartars, the British and, finally, the Soviet Union (the Cold War superpower was humiliated in defeat after a nine-year war that ended in 1989). No nation has been able to conquer with any sense of permanence Afghanistan's ethnically diverse tribes, sub-tribes and clans. The infamously fractious populace has a reputation for independence, blood feuds, ferocity and a near mystical ability to disappear into the mountains and villages, the latter trait for which the Russians dubbed them *dukhi* and *dushman*—ghosts and bandits. Not for nothing is the landlocked country known as a graveyard of empires for, historically speaking, it has been.

Uruzgan, the southern province where the Australians were deployed, is hauntingly beautiful but treacherous. The terrain is tailor-made for guerrilla warfare, dominated as it is by the Hindu Kush mountain range. Uruzgan bleeds slowly in to the southern edge of the Hindu Kush that splits the country from north to south and rises into jagged, steep and impenetrable hills pockmarked by elaborate cave systems and rutted with deep crevices. In the sweeping valley below, mud hut compounds known as *qualas* nestle along tree-lined rivers that feed creeks and streams used to irrigate the surrounding fertile fields farmed for opium poppy and a handful of other crops. Subsistence farming. Beyond the green belt, the land turns harsh, hard and barren. The arid desert plateaus are littered with rock as hard as flint and pebbles sharp enough to shear through combat fatigues. Seasonal temperatures swing from extreme highs to dangerous lows, notable for sandpaper-like dust storms and biting blizzards.

The high-tech machinery of a modern army is, strangely, at some disadvantage against the dramatic natural features of the landscape. Movement is limited, communications obstructed and observation restricted.

As the commanding officer of the task group, Major General Mike Hindmarsh said later, the soaring desert mountains are so remote and difficult to access that local villagers believed the Australian soldiers who arrived in August 2005 were Soviet soldiers returning to fight the war that ended in 1989.

It had been almost four years since the first Special Operations Task Group withdrew from the country, after an initial twelve-month deployment in response to the 9/11 attacks in the United States. Their mission then was to support the American-led operation to catch or kill the elusive al-Qaeda leader Osama bin Laden, who used Afghanistan as a training ground for his terrorist network.

They missed bin Laden but the Taliban was quickly

ousted in 2001. A fledgling democracy was desperately trying to take hold under President Hamid Karzai, who had been democratically elected in 2004. The economy remained fragile amid widespread corruption. The nation was susceptible to the growing number of insurgents flowing across the badlands along the porous 2430-kilometre border Afghanistan shares with Pakistan on its eastern and southern sides.

In 2005 the governments of the United States, United Kingdom and Afghanistan asked Prime Minister John Howard to redeploy Australian troops to join the International Security Assistance Force (ISAF) as they expanded south in the next stage of the war on terror. The country was on the cusp of another round of national elections.

'In recent months there has been a resurgence [of enemy activity] and it's very important in the war against terror, because of the obvious connection between al-Qaeda, the Taliban and Afghanistan, that those attempts of recent times, renewed attempts to undermine the government of Afghanistan, are not successful,' Mr Howard said in a packed press conference in Canberra.

By 23 September 2005 two large SAS and Commando units from the task group were patrolling the hostile terrain, pushing 70 kilometres north of their base at Camp Holland in Tarin Kot, the capital of Uruzgan. They were to provide overwatch on remote polling stations and gather intelligence, or intel.

The prime minister revealed that a 200-member Provincial Reconstruction Team (PRT) would deploy in August 2006, to help stabilise the Afghan government and aid locals with rebuilding the war-torn country. The troops would build schools, hospitals, bridges, roads and even a dam to provide irrigation and electricity, while also providing humanitarian, medical and veterinary support to locals. 'What you might call the hearts and minds side of the operation,' Howard said.

The Special Operations Task Group had a dangerous mission—to target terrorist groups and their supporters and disrupt the hardcore Taliban leadership and al-Qaeda elements in their traditional sanctuary of Uruzgan. In other words, to capture or kill the enemy in its own backyard. 'It was akin to poking an ant bed with a stick,' said Major General Mike Hindmarsh.

To succeed they would penetrate hostile terrain on joint combat patrols with American, Dutch and British Special Forces and the Afghan National Army. They would perform long-range reconnaissance and surveillance to gather intelligence on the enemy's routine, intent and movements, particularly across the so-called 'rat lines', treacherous donkey trails and goat paths that fed the Taliban and al-Qaeda fighters over the Durand Line dividing Pakistan and Afghanistan.

The anti-coalition militia (ACM) was an implacable enemy. Hindmarsh had a list of adjectives to describe them. Tough. Resolute. Agile. Determined. 'And more dangerous than anything Australian Special Forces have encountered at least since the Vietnam War.'

The ACM was the sum of many parts—splinter groups, tribal warlords, religious fundamentalists, criminals and foreign fighters, with diverse commands and motivations.

The Taliban drew primarily from the Pashtun tribe but, as Bing West writes in his authoritative book *The Wrong War*, 'it is a distortion to use the word Taliban as synonymous with the insurgency . . . [though] the true Taliban advocates comprise the centre of the rebellion.'

Moreover, they were close, danger close, just fifteen kilometres north of Camp Holland. The Taliban 'wanted to make life difficult' for the ISAF troops. 'The threat is ever-present; it could be missiles or rockets and there are tonnes of unclaimed ammunition lying around this country. We are fighting a counterinsurgency and for the people we are up against, almost nothing is taboo and they will keep coming up with new ways to achieve their objectives,' an Australian officer said.

Decades of fighting had armed the enemy with every conceivable weapon, including the ubiquitous rocket-propelled grenade (RPG), mortars, heavy machine-guns, recoilless rifles and Stinger surface-to-air missiles, although those were used much less in 2005 than against the SFTG in 2001–2002. Local bazaars did a brisk trade in small arms and a variety of Russian-made weapons. The insurgents had Dragunov sniper rifles, DShK machine-guns (Dishka), RPK light machine-guns, RKM Kalashnikov machine-guns and the common AK47. They were also increasingly using new and deadly tactics picked up from their counterparts in Iraq: improvised explosive devices. 'A cheap and effective way of fighting an insurgency campaign,' Hindmarsh said.

There were about 80 IED incidents per month throughout the country, which accounted for a large proportion of coalition and civilian casualties. They were unpredictable and 'becoming more technical and constantly updated to defeat known coalition protection and detection systems', Hindmarsh said.

All soldiers deploying to the Middle East area of operations were trained to mitigate the threat of IEDs. Every EOD (explosive ordnance disposal) operator underwent rigorous pre-deployment mission rehearsal exercises, specific to the theatre in which they would operate. In March 2006, the Australian Defence Force established the Counter IED Task Force in Canberra to reduce the dangers of IEDs. 'The work of the Counter IED Task Force includes the acquisition of equipment, scientific research, intelligence, discussion with allies, development of doctrine and the delivery of training,' the defence force said in a statement.

The army had humans trained to defuse and disassemble the IEDs where possible, to study their provenance and identify the bomb-maker through his signature methods. And it had heavy and light remote positioning vehicles (RPVs), or robots, to detonate or defuse the IEDs. It also had another asset in reserve.

The Doggies.

Explosive detection dogs and handlers had not been deployed to Afghanistan but their successes in other areas of operation gave them an edge. The army command decided to exploit the four-legged advantage and called for a two-man, two-hound contingent to test the section's capabilities in Uruzgan.

D and Sarbi were at work at the Incident Response

Regiment at Holsworthy when word came that EDDs Jasmine and Sam were to be deployed with handlers Corporal John Cannon and Corporal Phil Grazier. Between them, the soldiers had at least 25 years of service in the regular army and Cannon had racked up time as a paratrooper, mortars man and physical training instructor. The mutts were getting on in age, about eight years old, but they were extraordinarily competent and viable operators.

'The SAS and Commandos recognised the need to have engineers there to provide engineer support to search the routes and compounds,' D says now. 'The EDDs have always worked with the engineers so it was a given they would be deployed. They were the forerunners and set us all up. They were the pioneers.'

Cannon and Grazier got their gear together in seven days and flew to Camp Holland with their respective dogs, Sam and Jasmine. Once in the country, they went straight outside the wire with the Special Forces soldiers, searching routes and compounds for IEDs, caches and ammunition. A lot rested on those eight paws—not only the lives of their handlers and fellow two-legged soldiers but the future role of the section in Afghanistan.

Sam and Jasmine worked at the front of the patrol as nose-driven sniffer scouts. Their handlers walked several metres behind, followed by members of the patrol, who fanned out on the flanks to provide cover. The EDD teams had their skills and drills but Afghanistan was a new environment presenting new challenges. They adapted, using each new patrol as a learning curve. It helped that they spent all their spare time together, strengthening the bond between hound and handler. In theatre, the dogs and handlers are inseparable, which benefits the patrols. The handlers are alive to their dog's every nuance. The ability to read the dog pays off when the harness goes on.

'He's your best friend, he's your best mate and you treat him as such. When you've got down time you know you hang out with your dog, you know, you sit around reading a book—he just hangs out with you,' Cannon said. 'You need to be able to tell when your dog has found something that is potentially dangerous and to be able to call him away from it before he gets injured or you get injured.'

Sam and Jasmine detected seven caches, proving the value of the Doggies in the war zone. They were indispensable. Their superior noses and detection skills led to the permanent presence of the Doggies in Uruzgan, as an essential asset in the search for IEDs and deadly explosives.

'They had some decent finds and found caches and weapons and explosives. They made a good impression with the SAS and Commandos and they were happy to keep working with the Doggies and engineers,' D says now.

Sam and Jasmine remained in Afghanistan when Cannon and Grazier returned to Australia after an extended deployment. The dogs were too successful to withdraw from service. It was a strategic decision for the commanders, and one that was heartbreaking for Cannon and Grazier. The men had the wrenching task of passing their beloved mates to the sappers who arrived with the next rotation of troops and with whom they would continue patrolling.

'I found this part of the deployment really hard. I knew that Sam had to be re-teamed with his new handler, which meant that I had to ignore him and show him no affection,' Cannon said. 'He had been one of my closest mates and had worked so very well in the rough stuff, and now here I was treating him with indifference. Poor Sam didn't understand this and I felt so bad about it. I found myself weeping with grief for the little bloke. I boarded the C130 for my outward journey without a decent word of goodbye for him.'

The sad separations were unavoidably commonplace for many of the handlers who followed.

Sam and Jasmine were honourably retired upon their return to Australia. They were nearing ten, or 70 in dog years—well past the age of human retirement in the Australian Army.

Operation Slipper, however, was gaining pace. Another rotation of troops was going in. In December the brass handed D an early Christmas present. He and explosive detection dog Sarbi would be released from the Incident Response Regiment and attached to the Second Reconstruction Task Force (RTF) for a seven-month deployment starting in April 2007.

Next stop, Afghanistan.

Chapter 11

WELCOME TO AFGHANISTAN

Sergeant D and Sarbi spent the first three months of 2007 training for deployment, rehearsing every move the EDD and engineers in the EOD teams would make on route searches and compound clearances in Uruzgan. It was mission-specific training, geared towards real operational threats, with staged scenarios as close as possible to those that had previously occurred in the lawless province. The exercises focused on lessons learned and real-time reports from the areas of operation. Weekly reviews of the latest information and intelligence ensured technical accuracy and relevance for those about to deploy. No two firefights or battles are ever the same and if enemy tactics changed, so did the training.

Soldiers prepare. Battles hinge on split second decisions. So does staying alive. Luck is only partially involved, so the Aussies believed in making their own through practice and preparation: finessing TTPs as if lives depended on it because, truth be told, they did. Train hard; fight easy.

The mission rehearsal exercises were conducted in Queensland with the platoons they would deploy with, in terrain and environment similar to that of Uruzgan. D quickly got acquainted with the Magnificent Bastards of the Second Combat Engineer Regiment, as the blokes are proudly known, and sharpened up some more on the tactics, techniques and procedures. To create a realistic and stressful threat environment they used functioning replica IEDs, landmines, explosive charges, explosive hazards and simulators. They practised search patterns and close-quarter combat drills. Every mission was evaluated and every response by the troops monitored and adjusted where necessary.

They drilled on their area of operation, the enemy threat and the enemy's known TTPs. As Sun Tzu wrote in the seminal *Art of War*, 'If you know the enemy and know yourself, you need not fear the result of a hundred battles'.

It was practical, hard-going, hot and sweaty work, carried out in the middle of an Australian summer, useful because they were going into the Afghanistan fighting season when temperatures reached 50 degrees Celsius. Sarbi didn't complain. She was having a blast being with D every paw of the way and her devotion to him was getting deeper by the day, if possible. More protective. A loyal guardian.

D was scheduled to stand piquet—guard duty—midway through a sweltering night. Sarbi slept snuggled beside him, standard operating procedure when on patrol. One of the guys coming off piquet tried to wake the handler but Sarbi jumped up and went into a defensive stance—four legs locked at the elbow, neck craned, ears back as she let out a low-level growl that rumbled down her sturdy chest. D's mate, too frightened to move closer to the menacing hound, pelted the soldier with rocks to wake him. 'Yeah, Sarbs was pretty protective. The guys would have to throw rocks at me because she'd jump up and bail them up,' he says. The handler was proud of her protectiveness but could have done without the rocks. 'A few hit me in the lower extremities. Deliberately, I think.'

The Diggers were disciplined, thorough, determined. They weren't mucking around; they couldn't afford to. Their unofficial credo was 'don't let your mates down'. One soldier had his chest tattooed with the words 'I will not fail my brothers'.

Australia had been blessed to date. Only one soldier had been killed in Afghanistan and that was in 2002, but nearly twenty had been injured, some seriously. Seventy per cent of injuries were caused by IEDs. The US Army had lost 103 soldiers to IEDs. The Aussies heading in wanted to maintain the status quo. Nobody wanted a mate's name added to the statistics.

The Australian Army has what it calls a layered approach to protecting its troops. The year-old Counter IED Task Force worked closely with the Pentagon's Joint IED Defeat Organization and other allies to gather the latest intelligence on the enemy's IED techniques and tactics, to reduce or neutralise the threat. Incidents in Iraq and Afghanistan were reviewed and analysed CSI-style. Where possible engineers recovered disarmed IEDs and roadside mines and sent them to the Combined Explosives Exploitation Centre in Kandahar, where every feature of the weapon was examined for common traits to identify and track down the bomb-maker, and develop effective countermeasures. In-field intelligence pinpointed bomb-making facilities and unmanned aerial vehicles (UAVs) buzzed over villages on surveillance flights picking up signatures the human eye had missed.

The army's commanders and IED specialists considered the IED fight 'a mini arms race against a fairly agile and fairly smart enemy'. Lieutenant Colonel Russell Maddalena, the operations officer—OpsO in army slang—of the task force admitted 'there is no one silver bullet' to defeat the scourge of homemade explosives, but the ADF and its coalition partners had harnessed what he described as some of the best military and scientific brains in the business to protect the troops. Stay ahead of the threat.

D was a professional. He listened up, trained hard, and put in the hours. He got the inside running on the lay of the land in and around Camp Holland. He studied the Australians' rules of engagement (ROE) for the RTF2, a strict document that outlines when and under what circumstances the soldiers can return fire and engage the enemy. 'That's set out in stone,' he says now. 'When you get there if there are any changes to the ROE they let you know.' The key focus was minimising the loss of civilian lives, protecting coalition forces and completing the mission. He treated with similar respect the first Standard Operating Procedure of the task force—the rules of soldiers' conduct that prescribed how soldiers should deal with Afghan villagers and their cultural and tribal practices. All deploying troops are given a quick immersion course on local customs—*Pashtunwali* 101. It was essential.

Uruzgan is a complicated place and 'in the conservative south, it was the most isolated and backward province' of Afghanistan. Ethnically, the population is 91 per cent Pashtun, 8 per cent Hazara and 1 per cent 'other'. The Pashtun is a tapestry of tribes of whom the Durrani in the south and Ghilzai from the east are the two largest, not to mention historical arch rivals. 'A Pashtun is never at peace, except when he is at war,' goes a national proverb.

The Pashtun live by a code of conduct known as *pashtunwali*—translated literally 'the way of the Pashtuns'. It is based on honour, hospitality and a primitive eye-for-an-eye revenge otherwise known as *badal*. 'The need to secure revenge for any slight, any insult, has been part of the Afghan's life through his history. Blood feuds between individuals, between families, and between clans or tribes, are endemic,' writes Mohammad Yousaf in *Afghanistan, The Bear Trap*. 'The Afghan will never turn the other cheek, a killing must be avenged by a killing, and so it goes on from generation to generation. A family will never forget a debt of honour.'

Another element of the code is *hamsaya*—'one who shares the same shadow'. As the *Military Review* noted, *hamsaya* is a form of servitude in return for protection from stronger tribes or the provision of goods, which explains, in part, the rise of the Taliban. Afghans historically follow the strongest tribes, or those who have prevailed in battle. 'Pashtun history is filled with heroes who played both sides for the benefit of tribe, family and honour,' notes *The Christian Science Monitor*.

The anonymous author of the 2005 book *Hunting al-Qaeda* was more blunt. Pashtun warlords have spent decades 'betraying each other on a daily basis'.

Sergeant D also received the standard Operational Deployment Guide issued to all troops, outlining the potential stressors he might encounter in Uruzgan. The soldiers are encouraged to share it with family members, who also feel the stress of their absence, possibly more. Worry is a crippling curse.

After pre-deployment training, D flew home to Sydney to spend a week with his girlfriend. Seven days for seven months.

A week out from deployment for the RTF2, the dog mafia moved to the Gallipoli Barracks at Enoggera in Brisbane, from where they would deploy.

D, of course, wasn't travelling alone. He had responsibility for an expensive piece of military hardware that ran on four paws and a lot of love, EDD Sarbi. His workload was effectively doubled. There was a lot to do and a lot of paperwork to fill in.

Sarbi had a complete medical check-up at the veterinary clinic and requisite inoculations to prevent her contracting local diseases. D took the warning about the dangers of rabid Afghan dogs in his stride. Sarbi didn't seem too worried either. Unlike a lot of dogs she wasn't vet-shy. To her it was just another social outing and another two-legged to charm for pats. Sarbi was a canine prima donna; she knew how to work a room. The handler filled in the official forms and permits and filed them with the Australian quarantine and customs services, to guarantee Sarbi's exit and re-entry with minimal fuss. He prepped the EDD gear, ensured the transport kennel was sound and made an inventory of equipment needed to keep his hound safe. Sarbi might be a dog but she didn't travel light and she had a combat wardrobe that would make the most pampered poodle green with envy.

The terrain and climate was as ruthless an enemy as the Taliban. The cold in Afghanistan could freeze the diesel in the Australian Light Armoured Vehicles (ASLAVs) and Long Range Patrol Vehicles (LRPVs) and the summer sun turned the ground into a bed of hot rocks.

Sarbi wore custom-made dust and fragmentation protection glasses, aptly named Doggles—think Jackie O-sized sunglasses for dogs. She also had four canvas booties to protect her paws from sharp rocks and prickles that could crack and wear down the dogs' pads. The course bulldust would get between her claws and wear away skin. The booties were a fetching red with circulation holes punched in the fabric. They had canvas soles reinforced by tough rubber grips for added protection. Sarbi had custom-designed earphones to block the sonic boom and over-blast shock waves of explosives and the *pop pop pop* of rifle fire. The earphones were similar to the reactive hearing protection Peltors that the soldiers wore. Constant exposure to weapons fire could have a deleterious effect on the dogs' ears and in some cases, their psychological state. For the colder months at the start of spring and winter—when D and Sarbi would be ripping in and ripping out of Uruzgan—Sarbi wore a fitted oilskin jacket known as a Doggie Drizabone. Very *Dogue*. D also carried a heating pad for her outdoor kennel on base and a thin canvas-covered mattress for sleep-outs on patrol. 'The dogs appreciate it,' D says.

D and Sarbi were part of a three man and three explosive detection dog team joining RTF2. The unit was tight, a brotherhood within the brotherhood. He and his fellow Doggies, Sappers Zeke Smith and Pete Lawlis, looked out for each other. Zeke had a black kelpie named FloJo and Pete took a three-year-old blue heeler called Merlin. The dogs, like their handlers, got on well.

Sarbi was a dominant bitch and didn't put up with any dog's nonsense. She'd tolerate it for so long before putting an annoying mutt in its place. Sarbi, D says with a chuckle, had sent a few of the other dogs to the veterinary clinic for emergency stitches back at the SME, but she got on fine with Merlin and FloJo. Who knows, they had probably worked out who was going to be top dog already. D suspected it would be Sarbi.

The Second Reconstruction Task Force staged out of Brisbane on 12 March 2007.

D was keyed up. This is what he had been training for but, at that moment, Sarbi was his priority. Dogs know when their masters are about to leave them and turn on a serious case of the sulks, complete with downcast looks and droopy tails. *How could you leave me?* Sarbi was a canine frequent flyer and had a Zen-like temperament when not chasing the ball, but D didn't want the big mass of fur stressed about their impending separation, even if she didn't know she'd be locked in her first class custom-built crate for the long-haul flight. He gave the hefty hound a well-earned rub behind the ears and offered a few reassuring words, just in case. *Attagirl, Sarbs.* Focusing on Sarbi had another benefit, too. 'That took your mind off any nerves or thinking about what's to come,' he says now.

Sarbi was loaded into the chartered 747 aircraft for the flight to the Forward Logistics Area (FLA) in Kuwait. Given the length of the flight and her requisite confinement, D didn't feed her. There was no point. The dogs didn't have the luxury of using a bathroom in the cargo hold. Besides, Sarbi would curl into a tight ball and sleep most of the way, her only movements in response to doggie dreams that made her snout quiver and paws twitch as if in chase.

The plane touched down on 13 March and the handler collected his hound, who was happy to be free of her crate. They had ten days to cool their heels in Kuwait and went through a series of mission briefings and more drills. The dogs were trained daily to maintain situational awareness.

D was issued with essential war-going equipment and collected new front and back Kevlar ballistic plates for his body armour vest and soft-moulded shrapnel fragment protection inserts that hug the curves of the body and the small of his back—and a cache of weaponry. 'Things to keep me alive,' he says with signature cool.

Sarbi was already sorted. Everything she needed was stowed in her handler's bag.

The troop left Kuwait for Afghanistan on 23 March. Hitching a ride on the C-130J Hercules were two official war artists from Melbourne, Lyndell Brown and her husband, Charles Green. The history of war art began in the First World War and the fine tradition is now enshrined for perpetuity in our national culture by an act of Parliament.

Brown and Green had spent the latter part of February in Baghdad photographing the action they saw, capturing the pathos of Australian soldiers at war and riding in armoured personnel carriers down Route Irish, said to be the one of most dangerous roads in the world. Back home in the southern state of Victoria they would use the photographs as the basis for a striking collection of artwork that eventually toured the country, before being added to the official collection at the Australian War Memorial. Now, though, the artistic collaborators were en route to visit an Australian contingent in Kandahar, via Tarin Kot.

The flight line was a mass of restless waiting. 'The army maxim—hurry up and wait,' Green recalls wryly. He spied a huddle of SAS troopers, identifiable by their Ned Kelly-esque beards and strong, lean physiques. They kept to themselves, shooting the breeze like they were knocking back a beer or two at the pub on a Friday night, not about to go into one of the most dangerous places in Afghanistan.

Nearby, Green watched the Doggies—three men and three hounds. The handlers actively engaged with the dogs, issuing commands and tossing them tennis balls as treats. The dogs never strayed more than a few metres from their handlers and seemed happiest when leaning on their two-legged mates. 'Strong, quiet Aussie blokes,' Green says now. With an artist's searching eye, he looks beyond the physical and finds emotion in the action. To him, a soldier's calloused hand draped casually around his dog's neck conveyed nuance and mood, quiet authority and easy command. The dogs were content, calm and controlled. The partnerships were almost poetic.

'The handlers were all very close to their dogs, it was quite cute, really,' Green says. 'They were continually playing and petting the dogs, and the dogs were continually huddling up to their handler, lying across them. These men are highly trained and yet there is this intense bond. At the same time they are very proud to be in Afghanistan, to be deployed with these dogs.'

The sight of fully armed, muscle-bound soldiers looking after their hounds with profound tenderness seemed incongruous—yet so perfectly natural. It gave the artists an idea. 'In the back of our minds, always, was the idea of a dog portrait. How cute can you go, but not in a mocking way,' he says. 'The ADF is made up of men and women who are like firemen. They are putting their lives on the line and they are highly trained and taught to reflect on what they are doing. The effect of being in the presence of those people was like being sent to the moon and watching history unfold. It strips out any desire or ability to editorialise—you are in documentary mode.'

Once at Camp Holland, Green and Brown photographed Sarbi and D, FloJo and Zeke and a yellow Labrador retriever, Aussie, who was on his way home after completing the First Reconstruction Task Force (RTF1).

Looking at the photographs now, one is reminded of the Stoics. The handlers stare directly ahead as the dogs stare directly at them, heads tilted up in expectation of a command and reward to come. The bond is as natural as breathing. In one image, Sarbi sits obediently at D's left leg, her brown leather leash doubled over and held in his right hand. D, ramrod straight, squared-off shoulders atop a broad chest, looks like a man who means business, with his Browning 9mm handgun strapped to the outside of his right thigh. He never left home without it, at least when in theatre.

Sarbi, her white blaze not yet smudged by the dust and grime of Uruzgan, looks positively serene. She has followed D's gaze and looks exactly where he does. Like her master, she is poised, ready for action.

'When the story broke of what happened to Sarbi and what she'd been through we thought, "we know that dog",' says Green now. 'And so we decided to paint the portrait we always wanted to paint of the army dogs.'

The dogs were all heroes but there really was no better canine candidate to sit for an official war portrait than Sarbi. The artists used lush oils on linen and painted Sarbi sitting next to Sergeant D, who is crouching down on the rocky gravel. The striking portrait measures a mere 31 by 31 centimetres but Sarbi's strength and beauty are rendered to perfection.

Said Brown: 'It's an incredible story of hope from the field of tragedy that is modern warfare and it is something that ordinary people can relate to.'

Chapter 12

CAMP HOLLAND

An early spring had eased into southern Afghanistan when D and Sarbi joined Task Force Uruzgan at Camp Holland at the end of March 2007. An Australian officer once described the base as 'a dusty shit-hole' and it was. The sprawling rectangular compound sat on the valley floor, ringed by towering snow-capped peaks. The rock-strewn ground changed from red to brown to grey depending on the season, the arc of the sun and whether there were clouds or rain. Gravel and dust got into everything, including the woolly beards that soon sprouted on the Diggers' faces. The base was surrounded by tumbleweeds of barbed wire and rock-filled HESCO bastion containers, in place to keep the enemy out and protect against rocket attacks.

The town of Tarin Kot was visible in the near distance,

encircled by a rich, deep-green belt. It was home to 10,000 people and located about 120 kilometres north of the dangerous city of Kandahar, long known as the spiritual home of the Taliban. Kandahar was the birthplace of one-eyed (literally) Taliban leader Mullah Muhammad Omar, the self-proclaimed 'commander of the faithful' who led the repressive regime for much of the Dark Ages decade it controlled Afghanistan.

Camp Holland was established by a United States Marine Expeditionary Unit as Forward Operating Base Ripley in May 2004. A Dutch-led contingent from NATO's ISAF took over Ripley in 2006 and renamed it Camp Holland for obvious reasons. The Australian Special Operations Task Group named its section Camp Russell in honour of Sergeant Andrew Russell, the first Australian SAS trooper to be killed in action in Afghanistan, when his long-range patrol vehicle hit a landmine in 2002.

A row of flagpoles at the base entrance paid homage to the various nationalities that formed the International Security Assistance Force in Uruzgan. Dutch soldiers followed the wartime tradition and erected bright yellow signposts pointing to towns back home—5248 kilometres to Brabant, 5235 to Ede and 5291 to Slootdorp.

They obligingly tipped the hat to the Aussies and the small contingent from Greece, adding a sign pointing to Darwin, 6914 kilometres in one direction, and another to Chania, 3819 kilometres the opposite way. No one knew if the distances were correct, but no one cared either. The arrow at the top of the post pointed to the only place that did matter—the badlands beyond the barbed wire. On it was stamped the word 'Taliban'. The enemy was within RPG range. Force protection was a priority. 'Stay with your weapon, always,' the soldiers were told.

Camp Holland featured a state of the art combat emergency hospital, a 1.8-kilometre runway, more than a dozen helicopter landing pads, arming and refueling points, and accommodations and recreation areas for several thousand soldiers.

The Australian Reconstruction Task Force headquarters announced its presence with a massive sign hung on a HESCO wall. The sign was unmistakably Australian, with a leaping red kangaroo over a V-shaped black boomerang. The commanding officer (CO) of RTF2 was Lieutenant Colonel Harry Jarvie, a stocky man with salt-and-pepper hair and an open, optimistic face that maintained its boyishness despite his age. Jarvie removed the number 1 from the RTF HQ sign and replaced it with 2 to signify the handover from the first task force to the second.

RTF2 had strengthened troop numbers and comprised a full company of infantry from the Royal Australian Regiment for greater force protection, and cavalry support via the ASLAVs and Bushmaster Protected Mobility Vehicles.

As was the custom, Jarvie welcomed the task force in a ceremony during which he reiterated the troops' task in rebuilding the province and assisting the local Afghan people. He also outlined the dangers. 'We must outsmart those who want to disrupt Afghanistan's development and our mission,' he told the assembled troops. 'We must make them irrelevant.'

Sergeant D bunked down in the Feldlager living quarters,

a series of interconnected shipping containers, equipped with the luxury of air conditioning, that were undergoing an upgrade by the resourceful engineers. He shared the sleeping quarters with two other Doggies, Pete Lawlis and Zeke Smith. He dropped his gear in his designated accommodations and claimed a bunk.

Sarbi was housed in kennels built by the RTF1 carpenters on the south-west edge of the base, not far from the red dirt runway. *Not too bad*, Sergeant D thought to himself, even though there was no strip of grass on which the hounds could exercise.

At the mandatory RSOI (reception, staging, onward movement and integration) briefing the task force was familiarised with the base, personnel, equipment and materials required for tactical operations during their deployment. The integration was a highly synchronised handover of incoming units into an operational commander's force prior to executing missions. Knowing the minutiae meant a better chance of survival. Heard. Understood. Acknowledged. The soldiers also received an update on the reconnaissance, surveillance, operations and intelligence. 'They take us around and show us the area and emergency bunker in case there's a rocket attack,' D says nonchalantly.

The overarching goal of RTF2 was the reconstruction and stabilisation of Uruzgan, to rebuild the basic infrastructure so its impoverished people might have a viable future. The mission was focused on community-based projects, and Dutch and Australian soldiers met with local elders in weekly *shuras*—council meetings—where they drank gallons of sweetened tea before deciding what the Afghans wanted and how the coalition could provide it.

D was no innocent abroad, he'd travelled well and far, but Tarin Kot looked like an alien landscape trapped in a time warp, hundreds of years old. Uruzgan was recognised as the least developed of Afghanistan's 34 provinces. To the trained and even untrained eye, it lacked the basics: villages had no electricity or running water and in 2006 there was no mobile telephone coverage—which, to the digital natives who made up the Western military machinery, seemed positively anathema. Only 10 per cent of males in the province were literate. For women, the rate was zero.

The thrust of the mission was an extreme backyard blitz, Afghan style. The Taliban had done its best to destroy whatever flimsy infrastructure there was and RFT1 was midway through building local schools and redeveloping the Tarin Kot hospital. RTF2 would continue the good works by adding roads, bridges and dams to the To Do list. They also helped train the Afghan National Army.

The insurgents were resolute. They wanted to reimpose the repressive rule of the Taliban in the rural regions and prevent the rebuilding program by the 'Christian invaders'.

That's where Sarbi and D and their fellow Doggies came in. The EDD section provided force protection for the men and women moving beyond the wire for the rebuilding work. The two biggest risks were IEDs and roadside bombs.

'I was a little bit nervous. There had only been one reconstruction task force before us and they spent most of their time developing the base at TK,' D says. 'Once we were there we were straight into work outside the wire. It was quite intimidating because the IEDs were starting to be a problem.'

IEDs are made of five main components: a container to hold the lethal bomb together, a power source such as a battery, a switch or circuit to initiate the device, a detonator, and the explosive charge. Most IEDs until then had been victim-operated pressure plate devices but the enemy tactics were changing. It used whatever it could get its hands on. Old-fashioned mousetraps, washing machine timers, cell phones, batteries, and wireless remote controls from modified doorbell equipment and model cars had all been used to detonate IEDs.

The Chief of Defence Angus Houston confirmed the rising use of radio-controlled devices and command-initiated devices. Insurgents even used infrared sensors to detect passing vehicles and detonate bombs. IEDs had been found buried in roadside rubbish piles, moulded into concrete blocks, even stuffed in animal carcasses and the fetid entrails of dead dogs.

By 2007, the insurgents turned to a version of IEDs known as an EFP, or explosively formed penetrator (or projectile). The explosive shockwaves of the blast splinters the metal liner and turns it into hundreds of individual metal pellets of death. The intensity of the blast shoots the projectiles with enough speed and force to penetrate trucks and reinforced personnel carriers. They also used DFCs—directional fragmentation charges—that operated a similar way.

Whatever the enemy employed, D and his fellow Doggies and engineers were prepared.

'We changed the TTPs mainly for safety; we wanted to keep everyone safe. We had to develop new techniques for how and where we stood and where and how we sent the dogs in and how we worked with the engineers behind us,' says D. 'It was still just as dangerous for the dogs because they are the first ones out there.'

After EDDs Jasmine and Sam were deployed to Afghanistan in 2005, section supervisor John Cannon adjusted the course at the SME to better deal with the changed environment and tactics of the anti-coalition militia. Taliban insurgents and al-Qaeda terrorists buried the roadside bombs in the cooler winter months, before the height of the so-called fighting season in the spring and summer. The explosives became more difficult to detect because they had been covered for so long. In response, Corporal Cannon developed 'buried hide training'.

As D says, all Doggies are highly motivated, self-starting, innovative soldiers. The handler buried weapons and explosives in rural showgrounds at the end of regional annual shows, when the earth was ripe with animal odours, excrement and urine. The additional odours proved infinitely alluring for the dogs but they were trained to work through the new distractions and challenges to detect the appropriate explosives.

Another of those involved in the new training was Sapper Darren Smith from the 2CER in Brisbane, who was killed alongside his explosive detection dog Herbie in the Mirabad Valley in Uruzgan in 2010. Twenty-six-year-old Smith, dubbed Smitty, helped rehabilitate Herbie from an injury that would have ended his EDD career without his handler's attentiveness and care. Smitty had drawn sketches and diagrams for the buried hide program when posted to the 1CER in Darwin. The revised training improved force protection and made route clearances safer for both hounds and handlers.

As a result, one week in every three is now dedicated to the buried hide training at Tarin Kot, often around the waste treatment area, colloquially known by the soldiers as the shit pits.

'There were a lot of areas, routes and roads that we could train around. Unfortunately, if the wind was blowing in the wrong direction you'd get a good whiff of it,' says D. Pity the handler whose dog decided to roll in the seepage and ooze. 'Yeah, that happened.' Shrug.

The Doggies ripping in got a comprehensive handover briefing from the handlers ripping out: what to expect at villages, vulnerable points (VPs) and compounds. The departing handlers' message was 'expect the unexpected and don't get complacent'. The transfer was seamless. Training was continuous.

'You never stop learning,' says D. 'You learn from your mistakes; you never repeat them. You don't want to be responsible for letting your mates down. Or worse.'

What was worse remained unspoken. No point jinxing yourself.

Sarbi's orientation was top-notch. The unfamiliar terrain and swirl of invisible new scents that danced across the airwaves kicked her olfactory senses into overdrive. And she was becoming a hit around Camp Holland.

Sarbi didn't recognise rank or nationality but returned

whatever affection was sent her way with a waggle of her rear end and a front-pawed dance. D didn't mind her popularity with the troops. He knew how important Sarbi and her fellow dogs were for morale. A couple of soldiers told him they appreciated seeing her on her morning runs in the exercise area; it took their mind off the quotidian routine of army life, the distance from loved ones thousands of kilometres away, and the threat beyond the wire.

'It was a huge boost for them because it made them think of their dogs back home,' he says.

The experienced EDD handler was relaxed about allowing soldiers to pat and interact with Sarbi. He understood the psychological benefit his dog brought and had studied the scientific literature that explained the positive physiological changes that canines cause in humans. Patting a dog, he knew, can be its own opiate. Some of Sergeant D's peers preferred to quarantine their dogs to maintain their focus and drive. D's strategy was to 'turn off the pats' to instil discipline if Sarbi misbehaved or went rogue on patrol, but she hadn't so he didn't. She was working well, never missing a beat or a scent.

Sarbi's only moment of canine uncertainty occurred when she first set eyes on a man wearing the traditional Afghan *shalwar kameez* and turban. Sarbi went stiff, raised a paw, stared, cocked her ears at a comical angle, and tilted her head. She was a picture of concentration, focused on the strange new sight. Her highly trained nose went to work, inhaling the novel hybrid odours of the Afghan's exotic diet and, perhaps, his less than rigorous approach to hygiene. In weeks to come D would suffer the same, courtesy of the unloved Dutch stodge served in the mess tent at Camp Holland and days-long patrols under a crucifying summer sun, with only a splash of water to keep clean.

Sarbi decided the foreign figure was no threat and moved on. But her handler concedes she never developed a great affection for the locals. She didn't bark at them but Sergeant D could feel the tremor of a low-pitched growl vibrate up from her collar through her leash when she was close to a local. And she never romped over for a pat as she did with the Aussies behind the wire, or arch her back and flex into the downward dog position—a pose well known to yoga aficionados—with her front toes splayed as wide as they can go, waiting for a tickle. Sarbi kept the locals at a distance, even when she became more familiar with the friendly men who set up their weekly bazaars outside the base.

Sarbi's inbuilt radar was alert to the rhythms of hazard and danger. Perhaps she intuitively knew that Afghans do not share Westerners' inexplicable love for dogs. Or maybe, as Sergeant D says, she was just more familiar with combat fatigues!

Chapter 13

OUTSIDE THE WIRE

Sergeant D and Sarbi had deployed into a hornet's nest. More than 4000 people had been killed in 2006, making it the deadliest year in Afghanistan since the Taliban was ousted in December 2001. As the insurgency escalated into full-blown slaughter one Taliban leader, Mullah Hayat Khan, swore to make 2007 the 'bloodiest year' yet, using a martyrdom army of 2000 suicide bombers against the coalition forces.

Suicide bombers had been on the rise. In 2002, there was just one recorded case of a suicide bomber in Afghanistan. The following year that number had doubled to two. In 2004 it tripled to six. In 2006, the number had multiplied to 139. The rise was significant. The increase marked a radical change in tactics as Afghans traditionally had not included suicide bombings in their deadly arsenal.

Remotely detonated bombings more than doubled from

783 in 2005 to 1677 in 2006; armed attacks tripled, soaring from 1558 in 2005 to 4542 by the end of December 2006. IEDs killed 492 civilians and injured at least 700 more. NATO troops held the major towns throughout the country, but it also suffered 90 fatalities in 2006.

The local population was helpless. The ruthlessness of the Taliban's 'retribution against "collaborators" neutralised much of the Afghan population'. They terrorised villagers into supporting them by delivering pamphlets known as 'night letters'—*shabnamah*—warning the impoverished people of horrendous retaliation if they aided the coalition forces or Afghan government. According to Thomas H. Johnson from the United States Naval Postgraduate School in California, the 'Taliban relies on the educated populace to transmit the *shabnamah* to illiterate villagers. Often these "letters" are pasted to the walls of mosques and government buildings and promise death to anyone who defies their threats or instruction.'

'A bullet to the head is all it takes,' a soldier said.

The Australian Special Operations commander Major General Tim McOwan described the night letters as 'death threats to intimidate and terrorise' and said the Taliban contrived 'situations where innocent men, women and children are likely to become caught up in their fight'.

Afghan observers noted the insurgency 'has become ever more daring and deadly in the southern and eastern parts of the country, while extending its presence all the way to the outskirts of Kabul'.

That was exactly where Sarbi and Sergeant D were operating, 'striking . . . at the heart of the Taliban strength' and doing 'the heavy lifting' with the US, the Netherlands, the United Kingdom and Canada.

The bleak news and statistics didn't bother Sarbi. She was happy to be with her handler and he was more focused on ways to avoid adding to the statistics. Tactics, techniques and procedures.

Sarbi quickly attuned to the thrum of life on an army base, the rockets and weapons fire and constant noise from hundreds of aircraft movements daily. She recognised the start-up groan of the LRPVs and the rumble of the Australian workhorse, the fifteen-tonne Bushmaster with its distinctive V-shaped hull, designed to save lives.

The LRPV was a specially adapted Land Rover that the enemy years earlier had dubbed the 'devil vehicle' because of its sheer versatility. The vehicles were like six-wheeled motorised mountain goats. No enemy sanctuary was beyond their reach. They were heavily armed and mounted with a 50-calibre heavy machine-gun and two 7.62-millimetre MAG 58 general-purpose machine-guns. They were also loaded with extra weapons systems in the back, including a Javelin anti-armour missile system, a Swedish-made Carl Gustaf 84-millimetre anti-tank rocket launcher and 66-millimetre rockets—for use whenever and wherever needed.

Sarbi had learned that the Bushmaster engine revs were a call to work. She eagerly leapt into the back, and tucked herself in between D's legs next to his automatic rifle— barrel pointed down. He kept a tight grip on her leash as they bumped along the potted roads and dirt tracks, until they reached a search destination or a forward infantry scout radioed for the EDD team to search a defile or vulnerable point. Their job was to provide manoeuvrability and survivability for RTF2 troops to and from construction destinations.

But they weren't going in blind. The soldiers relied on field intelligence and had a good handle on whether the situation was benign or hostile. 'Generally, if a compound is occupied, you know the locals aren't going to booby-trap their own house or have an IED set up in there,' Sergeant D says.

As soon as the request came over his communications (comms) system, D removed Sarbi's collar and snapped the search harness around her chest, attaching the leash. He sensed the instant shift in her concentration and interpreted it as a comment, as if she was trying to tell him, *now this is going to be fun.*

Sergeant D's rifle was locked and loaded and ready to engage. Awareness levels were elevated but he was conscious of not feeding his nerves to Sarbi. He surveyed the ground to determine the search type and unhooked Sarbi's leather leash, giving her distance to ensure the safety of the platoon. He didn't like sending her out on her own, but safety protocols were non-negotiable. The dog waited, obediently.

'Sarbi, seek on.'

The 27-kilogram black mass moved off, following the route patterns drilled into her at the SME. D's heart rate went up; he was relying on Sarbi more than any other soldier. So were his mates out on the flanks. He watched her backside swing with each step as she padded along silently, alert to every noise and movement in the immediate area, ready to 'take a knee' (kneel down) to reduce his profile if he detected her tell. The hyper-vigilance was a learned skill.

Soldiers work as a team and each also has his own responsibilities. D was responsible for reading and understanding his dog's body language, and recognising indicators of unexploded ordnance and IEDs. He kept his eye out for irregular signs on trees or stakes that had been posted by the insurgents to signal to their fellow fighters where they had planted bombs. He checked for piles of stones and random objects and debris that looked deliberately placed on the road. Similarly, recent road repairs and new or covered tracks were considered suspect until proven otherwise.

D kept a watchful eye on any Afghan locals and observed their movements around the compounds. The human terrain was loaded with information. An absence of women or children in a village usually indicated potential ambush or attack. A lone man sitting on a hill could be watching, spectator-like, knowing action was about to unfold. Someone hurrying away could be departing the scene after planting an IED or a knowing civilian not wanting to get caught in the crossfire. A teenaged boy on approach could be about to blow himself into martyrdom.

The first searches were the hardest. Sergeant D's heart pumped faster as he worked out the most likely place for an IED and positions from where the enemy or unfriendly locals could be watching. TTPs. 'After a couple of searches it started to become more streamlined and instinctive,' he says.

The Australians had been lucky and, as every soldier going into battle knows too well, luck eventually runs out.

On 24 July Sergeant D and Sarbi were on patrol, performing routine clearances in and around the fortified compound housing the governor of Uruzgan, on the main road to Tarin Kot. An infantry section was on a dismounted patrol through TK, on a road leading away from the compound. Intelligence intercepts picked up local radio chatter, a warning that the insurgents were using certain types of trucks as vehicle-borne IEDs. In particular, the ubiquitous Toyota Hilux.

Around 1pm, with the sun directly overhead, a truck fitting the description came in from a side street and made its way up the road towards the patrol, gaining speed as it approached the soldiers at the top of the hill. Men yelled at the young male driver to stop but he stepped on the accelerator. They signalled visually, their hands held aloft in the internationally recognised halt signal. The vehicle continued speeding. D and Sarbi were in the governor's compound, at the bottom of the hill about 150 metres away, watching.

The Australians immediately took up fire positions. Just in case. They had experienced too many near misses to give the driver the benefit of the doubt.

Weeks earlier a young male had approached Australian and Afghan soldiers at a vehicle checkpoint. A teenager. He refused to stop when ordered and walked purposefully towards the unit. The task force took up fire positions and aimed their weapons but before the soldiers could fire a thunderous *boom* shook the checkpoint. The Taliban extremist had blown himself up using a crude homemade device. His torso was ripped in half, limbs dismembered.

One Australian and two ANA soldiers were wounded. It was the first suicide bomb attack against the RTF. The Australians were lucky. Or as defence boss Angus Houston preferred to say—equipped and prepared. 'The situational awareness of the RTF patrol, their reaction to the bomber and their personal-protective equipment ultimately prevented a more serious incident.'

It was a salient lesson.

The Australians on patrol outside the governor's compound in Tarin Kot were equally prepared.

Insurgents had warned they would attack Afghans who worked with coalition forces. The Uruzgan governor's compound was a high value target. Dozens of soldiers and civilians near the building were at risk. So, too, those working inside.

Sergeant D watched as the truck drove faster up the road. Under their rules of engagement, the Aussies could use lethal force when they faced a 'real and present danger' and this was as real and present as it gets.

The Australians fixed their target. The driver was not slowing down and went about 50 metres after being ordered to stop. They opened fire.

D, prone in the dirt with his weapon ready, watched as bullets cracked overhead. Sarbi, clipped to his hip, instinctively dropped on her belly on the dirt, lying next to her handler.

'Sarbi, stay.'

'Everyone was running around and taking fire positions until we realised what was going on. Sarbi was calm. She just dropped down next to me and didn't move,' he recalls.

The bullet-riddled vehicle limped to a stop but the

danger wasn't over. The truck could be packed with high explosives and armed by a remote control detonator.

Troops cordoned off the area and moved locals to safety, out of a possible blast zone. A platoon commander radioed D and Sarbi with instructions to conduct the initial search, to make sure the dead driver wasn't behind the wheel of a booby-trapped truck.

'If it had been a vehicle borne IED it could have taken all of us out,' he says.

Sergeant D brushed himself off. He called Sarbi to heel.

He was about to go on what seemed like the longest walk of his life.

With an engineer team behind him, Sergeant D stepped off, in tandem with his dog. Weapon locked and loaded. Scanning for enemy snipers or spotters.

He approached from the rear, straight up the hill from the Governor's compound. Out in the middle of the road he may as well have had a target on his chest. Forty metres away from the disabled vehicle, D released EDD 436 from her leash. *Okay girl, don't let me down*, he thought. The engineers stopped a few metres behind him.

'Sarbi, seek on.'

Sarbi trotted up the driver's side of the vehicle, her nose testing the wind for explosives, quivering and twitching with each inhalation and exhalation. She moved at a steady pace around the front of the truck. The seconds she was out of sight dragged on and felt like minutes. D was relieved to see her black nose round the corner, followed by her solid torso.

Sarbi manoeuvred down the passenger side of the vehicle, clinging to it like a limpet, her head bobbing up in short, sharp bursts with each sniff as she air-scented. Her methodical drive reaffirmed D's faith in his hound and their training. He watched for her tells—freeze, front paw up, stare, slow-motion sit. Nothing. He searched for any slight change in her behaviour that might indicate uncertainty, something not quite right. Nothing.

Sarbi turned again and walked across the back of the truck. Search complete.

She did not indicate the presence of explosives. *Right*, D thought, *that meant one of two things. No explosive or Sarbi had missed it.*

Highly unlikely, but not impossible. Every dog can have its off day.

D was composed and in control, but still apprehensive. His adrenalin pumped and his pulse thumped. Better that than being complacent, he figured. Complacency kills.

'Sarbi, come.'

She trotted back, happy at her master's positive tone of voice, her bright pink tongue hanging out of her mouth. She had her usual look of expectation that she'd be rewarded with a tennis ball, which, of course, did not materialise for safety reasons.

Sergeant D grabbed his push-to-talk radio mike off his shoulder and spoke to the platoon commander.

'EDD did not indicate explosives. Will conduct systemic search, over.'

Could Sarbi have gotten it wrong?

The handler reassured himself. 'During all of our training previously in TK and back at home she very rarely missed any explosive.'

D checked his weapon. He reattached Sarbi's leash to his hip and slowly walked to the truck, in sync with his hound. He scanned around the area for potential threats, hoping no insurgent lay in wait with a remote control detonator. The Hilux truck could still be a death trap. All eyes were on Sarbi and Sergeant D.

As they drew closer, D saw the driver, dead, slumped forward in the seat. The blood-splattered windscreen was shattered; bullet holes pierced the metal door panels. A thought raced through his head. *He just should have stopped.*

D guided Sarbi as close to the truck as possible and they began the painstaking process of searching around and under the car. He gently directed Sarbi's nose to the door cracks, the wheels and wheel hubs. She sniffed as trained, paying particular attention to Sergeant D's splayed hand indicating each location. With the external search complete, he began the internal search. Slowly, with as much care as possible, D opened the driver's door.

'Go on, Sarbi.'

With balletic grace, the big girl gently reared up on her hind legs to rest her front paws on the doorstep, hindquarters planted on the road. She ignored her primitive canine instinct with its preference for blood. She sniffed as if the corpse was another inanimate article to search, not a human being that seconds earlier drew breath. Sergeant D was quietly proud. 'She was nice and focused on the job,' he says now.

No signs of explosives. He exhaled with quiet relief.

Sarbi hopped down.

Ten minutes and they were done. D radioed the commander.

'All clear.'

He patted his dog.

'Good girl, Sarbs, good girl.'

The engineer team moved to search the stalled Hilux and driver for a final clearance before it was towed away.

For whatever reason, the civilian driver simply had not stopped and it got him killed. The needlessness of the man's death was evident but there was no good to come from dwelling on it. No point weighing the 'what ifs'. It was a war zone. There were rules and regulations. Number one: you stop at vehicle checkpoints. Obey orders.

Back at Camp Holland Sergeant D took Sarbi to the kennels. He groomed her and inspected her paws for injuries. Standard operating procedure.

Sarbi wolfed down a bowl of Eukanuba dry food. If the cooks were feeling generous, and they usually were when it came to the explosive detection dogs, particularly after they had discovered an IED or weapons cache, they gave the hounds fresh mince topped with an egg. Occasionally, Sarbi had steak. 'Better fed than most of the task force,' D jokes.

Once Sarbi was settled and bedded down for the night, Sergeant D decommissioned his equipment, cleaned his weapons and gear, recharged the batteries of his radio, refilled fuel, water and rations for him and Sarbi, and restocked the vehicles. Team gear first, then personal gear. Recocked and refigured.

The patrol gathered for a forensic debrief and intel

update. The Aussies were vigilant about their post-operation routine in case they needed to push out at short notice. If the word came in, he and Sarbi were ready to go in less than five minutes.

It was just as well.

Chapter 14

RIP MERLIN AND RAZZ

On 31 August 2007, four months after Sarbi and her handler arrived in Afghanistan, the Australian contingent was rocked by its first fatality since the 2002 death of SAS Sergeant Andrew Russell in the neighbouring province of Helmand. There was a sense that luck had shone on the task force for the two years that the Australians had been back in Uruzgan and that it was bound to end, sooner or later, though it would be a foolish soldier who said it out loud. Why tempt fate in a war zone, especially in the height of the fighting season when the enemy was ratcheting up its use of IEDs, suicide bombers and roadside explosives? Prime Minister John Howard had recently warned 'there is a distinct possibility of casualties, and that should be understood and prepared for by the Australian public'. For their part, the Aussie soldiers knew they were on borrowed time. Truth is, every soldier always is, but no one had seen this coming.

Sergeant D was inside the wire, working with Sarbi on continuation training, when he was summoned to the RTF headquarters mid afternoon.

The message was blunt.

Explosive detection dog Merlin had been killed on the outskirts of Tarin Kot, while on a routine mission providing force protection for a reconstruction team.

D felt his heart drop. He knew Merlin and his handler, 27-year-old Sapper Peter Lawlis, who hailed from Bredbo, a small country town in the Snowy Mountains south of Canberra, known for its history and beauty. 'Mate, you've got no idea how many people used to stop at Bredbo and put their snow chains on thinking they were at Thredbo,' he says with a laugh. He preferred to be called Pete but he didn't mind that his army mates called him Lucy. 'As in my last name is Lawlis and Lucy Lawless played Xena Warrior Princess.'

Lucy and Sergeant D were old mates. Lawlis, who enlisted in the army as a combat engineer on 11 November 1999, had done his handlers' course at the SME in early 2004. He was appointed the school's operational handler later that year when D and Murray Young were conducting an instructors' course.

He had been chosen to take part in the Doggies' coveted exchange program, *Long Look* in Aldershot, England, in 2005. Lawlis was despatched to the British Army's 101 Military Working Dog Support Unit as its only dedicated 'arms explosive search dog handler' for several months in the middle of the year. The commanding officer of the unit,

Major R.C. Pope, noted that the young Aussie was a likeable chap who 'has a natural affinity with dogs and people' and 'fitted in very well with all ranks'.

Major Pope sent the CO of the SME a report filled with nothing but praise for Lawlis and the work he carried out in exercises and operations during his time in England. 'Sapper Lawlis's performance has been excellent,' the major wrote that September, at the end of the exchange. 'His drive and enthusiasm quickly gained him the respect from those he worked with and for, and his willingness and desire to learn was infectious. He has been an excellent ambassador for his country and his Service'.

Lawlis, like Sergeant D, was a professional. They shared the same accommodations on RTF2, and Merlin and Sarbi were kennel mates at Camp Holland. The black and white blue heeler cross graduated as a fully-fledged detection dog immediately after Sarbi and was designated EDD 437. Like Sarbi, his first operational role was at the Commonwealth Games in Melbourne. Merlin had also done a tour of duty in East Timor.

When D heard the sad news about Merlin, his thoughts turned to his mate.

'Is Lucy all right?' he asked, concerned that Merlin's handler had also been killed.

Lawlis was not hurt but, understandably, he was distraught. The sapper was Merlin's first and only handler. He was assigned the mutt in 2006 when he was a 'green dog and a bit of a ratbag', Lawlis says now.

Merlin, who had been adopted from an RSPCA shelter in Queensland and was originally called Buster, could be a touch aggressive. Some of the boys in 3CER called him 'Tipdog', but he was a pussycat with his handler, who loved the scrappy hound with whom he had seen so much.

Shortly after Anzac Day the pair were on a vital asset-protection patrol, searching vehicles at the Wanow Bridge, the main passage in and out of Tarin Kot across the Tiri Rud, when a young Pakistani suicide bomber blew himself up.

'I was on the north side of the check point walking south. He was about 40 or 50 metres away and I just thought he'd been let through,' Lawlis recalls. 'The suicide bomber walked up and popped himself. I saw him—then he was gone. It was an eye-opener for me.'

Lawlis had been lucky. He felt the blast but wasn't hurt. A private from D Company, 1RAR wasn't so fortunate. He was pulling piquet and manning a MAG 58 on a Bushmaster when he sighted the approaching man from about ten metres away. He swung his machine-gun on the bomber, a sixteen-year-old boy, who detonated himself before reaching the bridge, his intended target. The private sustained shrapnel wounds to his left arm and shoulder. His quick response in identifying the suicide bomber was later credited with saving lives. Two Afghan nationals were also wounded in the attack.

The next few days would be nerve-wracking for Lawlis.

He conducted vehicle searches at the Wanow bridge with Merlin. The electronic warfare experts were intercepting Taliban chatter over the radio, suggesting that insurgents would target a dog team with a vehicle-borne IED packed with high explosives.

'I honestly thought every culvert, every rock that was

out of place was going to kill me,' Lawlis says now. 'I was doing my best not to get blown up. I was super-duper hyper-vigilant. Don't get me wrong, I trusted Merlin, I trusted the dogs but dogs can have an off day. You have got to rely on yourself. It was quite stressful.'

Lucy and Merlin had been through a lot since then.

Lawlis now had the heartbreaking task of getting Merlin's lifeless body back to the Australian base. His dog was a fully-fledged, highly qualified and respected soldier; he would be afforded the same dignity in death as his human counterparts. Their departure caused a logistical problem. The patrol was effectively stranded without an EDD team to get it back to Camp Holland safely.

Sergeant D and Sarbi had a mission to complete. He donned his webbing, grabbed his pack and weapons and collected his dog from the kennels. Shortly after that he was on the ambulance convoy, blasting across the desert to fill the vacancy.

Sergeant D and Sarbi arrived in a burst of dust at the patrol near the Spinkechah defile, effectively a small bridge over the Tiri Rud. D took one look at Lawlis and could see the anguish etched on his face. He was racked with guilt.

'The handler was apologetic, as if his dog's death was his fault. Because of the bond, the handler was devastated and he was blaming himself,' says Sergeant D.

The accident occurred around 1405 hours local time at the defile, which was a magnet for IEDs and enemy attention. Lawlis says it was always a point of 'vigorous searching'. The defile was en route to a remote Dutch patrol base and not far from the Talani Boys' School, where members of the RTF2 had done some incredible restoration work in a ten-hour backyard blitz that pleased the school principal no end.

The day had been a scorcher, around 50 degrees Celsius. Men were soaked through with sweat. Merlin and Lawlis worked solidly all morning.

'Merlin was searching really well. He was on fire, super keen, and you could just tell he was having a good time. He was loving it,' Pete says now.

Lawlis and Merlin searched 1500 metres on one side of the Spinkechah defile and fellow EDD handler Zeke Smith and FloJo searched 1500 metres on the other side. The two EDD teams were with a section of engineers, working with the forward reconnaissance boys from the Second/Fourteenth Light Horse Regiment, the cavalry who provided overwatch protection for the other RTF2 vehicles as they moved through the defile.

Merlin and Lawlis had just finished a long, vulnerable point search, which took 50 minutes. Despite working well, Merlin suffered heat exhaustion and had started to throw up. Lawlis decided to give his dog a break in the shade of one of the 2/14's ASLAVs, an eight-wheeled, high-tech monster of a vehicle that resembled a tank and provided the only shelter from the sun in the area. He dropped down beside the vehicle and Merlin sat down next to him, crawling under the ASLAV, out of the sun.

They'd been resting a while when Pete heard the gears engage and the vehicle unexpectedly roared to life. The sapper was almost run over but managed to jump out of the way. Merlin was trapped under two of the wheels.

'Then he went under the another two,' Lawlis recalls.

The handler was shocked but he could do nothing. The driver couldn't see him due to the inherent blind spots and he couldn't hear Lawlis's shouting through the heavy metal doors and reinforced glass windows.

The truck crushed Merlin. Lawlis dropped to the ground screaming and scooped his dog up, cradling him in his arms.

'It was a prick of a day,' he says. 'Merlin was alive for about five minutes. I was going to shoot him with my pistol but I didn't have the guts.'

The ASLAVs moved off to provide security further up the route but Lawlis refused to go.

'I wasn't moving. They took up the overwatch on another ridge. We were covered because those guns could reach where we were,' he says.

Lawlis cradled Merlin until he died. He was in shock.

Twenty minutes later a lance corporal took a body bag to Lawlis and he gently placed Merlin's warm but lifeless body in it.

'None of the boys were talking because they were all upset as well. It was a bit of a blur after that for me. One of the blokes put an Australian flag over Merlin's body bag and then we were back in Tarin Kot.'

Merlin had successfully uncovered weapons caches and defied the Taliban's best attempts to kill him with IEDs and landmines, which made his accidental death seem especially cruel. No one expected the four-legged warrior who looked like he had a permanent smile on his face to be run over while taking a rest break.

The driver of the ASLAV was gutted. Like Lawlis, he blamed himself.

'He was a bit ashamed to come up to me for about a week after that but I didn't blame him. It was my fuck up; it was my fault. I didn't hold anything against him,' Lawlis says now.

He took full responsibility but manning up didn't make losing his mate easier to bear. Merlin had worked with the soldiers for months and been on patrols that lasted several days. He woke up in the harsh landscape next to his two-legged brothers in arms, sleeping beside them and keeping his ears and snout sharp to alert them to looming disaster. He waited patiently, politely and bravely for scraps from the pre-packed Meals Ready to Eat (MREs) and loped around expecting free rubs behind the ears for being so damned cute. The mixed-breed mutt, whose coat was flecked with grey, somehow made things seem less warlike, if that was possible. Tipdog had become everyone's best friend, irrevocably wriggling his way into their warrior hearts. It was hard not to fall in love with the hero hound ready to sacrifice his own life for theirs. Possibly because he was a rankist—a dog who had a habit of having a go at the officers whenever they appeared, much to the amusement of the sappers and privates.

It was even more gut wrenching knowing that EDD 437 Merlin was the first explosive detection dog to be killed on operations. That was a milestone no one wanted to claim.

Back at Camp Holland, Lawlis put Merlin's body in refrigeration and smoked three packets of cigarettes with an EOD technician at the back of the medical facility, next to the watch-house. The brass wanted him to see the padre for counselling but Lawlis wanted to be left alone; he was trying to figure out a way to get his dog repatriated to Australia. It was the least he could do for his four-legged mate.

Back in Australia, Brigadier Andrew Nikolic announced the terrible news of Merlin's death. 'Merlin is the first army explosive detection dog to die on operations. His death will be keenly felt by the RTF and the wider Royal Australian Engineers, particularly their specialist dog handlers,' he said.

Nikolic's comments were poignantly borne out five days later when dozens of soldiers from the RTF and Special Operations Task Group gathered at the kennels complex for a memorial for Merlin. Army Chaplain Craig Potter presided over the service. Merlin's fellow explosive detection dogs were also present, sitting at attention at their handlers' sides, paying their last respects with doggie dignity.

Task force tradies from the RAE built a special coffin for their little mate, and fashioned a metal plaque and nameplate they attached to the outside. They also built a headstone with a commemorative inscription. The talented craftsmen wanted the casket and final resting place to reflect the esteem in which Merlin was held.

Before the ceremony got under way, Lawlis and Zeke Smith dropped a couple of tennis balls in the coffin, with some snacks and a picture of Smith's dog, FloJo. 'FloJo and Merlin had a bit of a love affair in Afghanistan,' Lawlis says fondly. 'They hung out together. We put a photo of FloJo in the coffin so he wouldn't be lonely.'

Sergeant D, a Browning 9-mm strapped to his thigh, and another Doggie with his AuSteyr assault rifle slung over his back, carried Merlin's coffin to a burial plot overlooking the kennels where he'd lived for the past four months. The casket was draped in an Australian flag, as is customary to honour the fallen. A photograph of the little fellow, sitting in a green field dotted by blossoming red poppies and wearing his search harness, was fixed to the wire-meshed fence. It bore the words, *Merlin Oct 03–Aug 07*. He was two months shy of his fourth birthday.

Soldiers stood at attention as the padre said a prayer and paid tribute to Merlin. Then, with a solemnity to match the occasion, Sergeant D and two others gently lowered Merlin's remains into the ground.

There you go, boy. Good fella, Merlin. Rest in peace, Digger.

There were no tears, but there were many among the toughened and battle-scarred soldiers happy to have their eyes shielded by impenetrable wrap-around sunglasses.

Afterwards, the soldiers named the dog complex Merlin Kennels, upholding an Australian Army tradition to honour those killed in action.

Three weeks had passed since the EDD Section interred Merlin in the red earth of Afghanistan. Sergeant D received a call from the Special Operations headquarters at Camp Russell on the other side of Camp Holland—then home to a mix of commandos from the Fourth Battalion Royal Australian Regiment (4RAR) and troopers from the SAS. Together, the highly trained soldiers formed the elite of the Australian Army and had been taking the battle to the insurgents and Taliban fighters beyond the wire as part of the Special Operations Task Group 4 (SOTG4) component of Operation Slipper.

SOTG4 also had its own Doggie contingent and explosives ordnance disposal team, made up of Lance Corporal Craig Turnbull and EDD 409 Razz from the Incident Response Regiment, and a handful of specialist explosive ordnance engineers.

Razz was a textbook perfect black Labrador retriever with softly rounded features and eyes the colour of melted cocoa. He had a sweet habit of lolling his big, rose-pink tongue out the front of his mouth—a welcoming gesture that never failed to get a smile in return. Razz began his working career with Australian Customs before transferring to the army in 2002. Like the other dogs in Afghanistan, he was experienced and proficient. 'A top EDD and very intelligent,' Turnbull said. Razz had worked on the Commonwealth Heads of Government Meeting in Coolum on the Queensland coast in 2002, and the Commonwealth Games in Melbourne alongside Sarbi.

Turnbull and Razz were tight. In fact, the soldier regarded Razz as a member of the family. 'We spend every minute with the dog, even while asleep,' Turnbull said later. 'You are with the dog 24/7. It's brilliant. It is great teamwork.'

Sergeant D was told that the headquarters had taken a call from the area of operations, requesting an explosives detection dog be sent out urgently to link up with the SAS units.

He and Sarbi were good to go.

The SAS boys had been tasked with providing intel to members of 4RAR, who were conducting a series of village clearances in a vast sweep of the valley floor, a 36-hour operation. A six-man SAS patrol with an Afghan interpreter staged out of a remote American forward-operating base (FOB) known as Anaconda. Anaconda was named for a massive US-led operation in 2002 during which SAS Signalman Martin 'Jock' Wallace became the first Australian soldier since the Vietnam War to receive the prestigious Medal for Gallantry for courage under fire and bravery in perilous circumstances in the Shahikot Valley, otherwise known as bandit country, in Paktia Province.

Anaconda was in hostile country. In August insurgents had failed to capture the base during four separate large-scale attacks. They roamed the countryside in small, fluid units, launching hit and run attacks on the coalition troops. The SAS patrols established observation posts several kilometres out of FOB Anaconda. Before long, SAS snipers identified and killed several insurgents and 120-plus 4RAR commandos, travelling in a convoy of about 40 vehicles, successfully pushed the enemy out of the valley.

On 21 September, a day after the SAS celebrated its fiftieth anniversary with a bells and whistles ceremony at its home base in Swanbourne, Perth, the Australian contingent began the long trek by road back to Tarin Kot. They kept an eye out for enemy fighters and Taliban spotters.

The vehicle-mounted patrol was travelling along a route when the interpreter picked up radio chatter that insurgents had been monitoring their movements. The road was a choke point and there was no way around it, with the mountain rising on one side and a slope running down to a creek on the other, and the open *dasht* (desert) off in the distance. It was a perfect site for ambush or IED.

Boom!

The lead LRPV struck an IED, detonating two Russian anti-tank mines stacked on top of each other, packed with enough high explosives to leave a crater several metres wide and half as deep. Troopers were thrown from the trucks and two sustained serious bruising. One also smashed an elbow in the blast. Miraculously, no one was killed.

Bloody lucky bastards.

Soldiers rushed to help their fallen mates and the injured were treated at the site. Their wounds were assessed as slight by combat standards but one trooper eventually would be returned to Australia for further treatment. The six-wheeled LRPV was out of action.

An SAS sergeant coordinated an American air medical evacuation and before long the two injured men were on a Blackhawk medevac chopper back to the ISAF hospital at Tarin Kot, escorted by the ferocious AH-64 Apache attack helicopters that fire 625 rounds per minute and are renowned for being 'as close to "one shot, one kill" as you can get'.

Hours later, the Afghan interpreter intercepted more enemy traffic over the radio. A second IED was in the area.

The Doggies were called forward and Turnbull unleashed Razz.

'Seek on,' Turnbull instructed.

The black Labrador padded forward, following his nose, with his handler and an EOD engineer armed with a mine detector a few metres behind.

The rest of the patrol stayed back a couple of hundred metres for safety and to provide covering fire if needed.

Razz indicated an explosive and sat down but the indication was vague and he returned to his handler. Turnbull needed a stronger tell to positively identify an IED; he needed Razz to sit and stare at the spot as trained, perfectly delivering the required passive response.

The slow, methodical process was deliberate.

'Razz, seek on,' he said.

He trotted back to investigate, tail wagging, happy to be working. He hadn't got far when—*bang!*

A massive explosion roared through the defile and sent shockwaves echoing up the mountain, blasting rocks and debris hundreds of metres in every direction. Turnbull was knocked off his feet. Unconscious.

'It was a huge bomb and poor Razz wasn't only killed in action, he was vaporised,' said George Hulse, the president of the Australian Defence Force Trackers and War Dogs Association.

There was nothing left of Razz, no remains to bury. The only evidence of his existence was some black fur that fell over the front cars and a few bits of harness.

There was nothing left of the massive IED, either, and no way to determine if the bomb was detonated by remote control or pressure plate. Fortunately, Turnbull regained consciousness and was well enough to resume work to help secure the patrol. But they were down a dog.

Back at Camp Holland, Sergeant D listened to the news, absorbing the information.

Not again, he thought to himself, anguished by the loss of another fine four-legged soldier.

Time was of the essence. He and Sarbi had to replace

Razz and Turnbull as soon as possible, to maintain protection for the force out among the bad guys.

Sergeant D returned to the Feldlager on the other side of Camp Holland and gathered his pack and weapons. Sarbi was in the kennels. She began to dance with excitement when she saw her master, as if to say, *let's get going then!*

An Australian Chinook dropped the EDD team in later that day and extracted the damaged LRPV along with Turnbull. The two handlers tag-teamed on and off the chopper and Sergeant D was relieved to see Turnbull standing on two legs unassisted. He didn't appear too badly wounded.

Turnbull was gutted and blamed himself for the death of his beloved Razz, feeling he'd cheated the covenant of loyalty between dog and handler by sending him directly into harm's way. Yet he had had no choice.

'He was devastated,' says Sergeant D.

Razz was the first member of SOTG4 killed in action.

'It was pretty harsh, but he saved my life,' Turnbull said later. 'A bad experience, but better than one of our soldiers.'

A fellow soldier who survived the blast acknowledged Razz's ultimate sacrifice with a tattoo that read *In dogs we trust.*

The SAS patrols and commandos were still a couple of days out from Tarin Kot and Sergeant D and Sarbi had to fit in with a new bunch of blokes, with whom they'd never worked. They were Special Forces and did things their own way.

'All our drills are standard across the board and you can jump in and out as required, but it is better to work with them pre-deployment so that you know their idiosyncrasies, the little quirks that they may have,' D says now.

The SAS boys were kitted out with different body armour, and were more agile and faster over the ground. Sergeant D noticed the difference instantly, but he was super-fit from daily hour-long sessions in the gym and hauling Sarbi's extra load on his back. He kept up. Sarbi had no problems.

The next morning Sergeant D and Sarbi moved out with the SAS patrols in LRPVs, through a village suspected of housing a known IED facilitator. The troop cleared the village and searched the young men who had gathered around the central bazaar. Sarbi went to work with her handler but there was nothing to find.

That night they slept in the open and the temperature bottomed out close to zero. Sarbi was fine. She had already begun growing her winter coat. It bulked her up, particularly around her chest and neck. The miracle of breeding and genetics kept her as warm as toast. She snuggled up next to Sergeant D and they fell asleep.

The following day the patrols came to another village, with the 4RAR convoy trailing them. Sergeant D and Sarbi were in the second LRPV. Just luck.

The Afghan interpreter with the unit intercepted more Taliban chatter over the radio. This time, the Taliban had set up an ambush for the infidels but they weren't in place fast enough.

'The SAS boys were leading and we had gone through the area before the Taliban managed to set up,' recalls Sergeant D. 'When the commandos came through, that's when the Taliban initiated the ambush.'

As the convoy moved through the valley between the mountain and green belt the Taliban opened up with small arms fire. The SAS circled around to take the high ground, to provide cover and put flanking fire on the enemy. The commandos got through the ambush zone without taking any casualties. But they were angry and ready for a fight.

'All of a sudden half the countryside was being shot at from the 4RAR boys who were itching to get among it,' Rob Maylor wrote in his book, *SAS Sniper: The World of an Elite Australian Marksman.*

Maylor and his mates spotted two bad guys running for cover behind a mud building and used two 84-millimetre anti-tank rocket launchers to fire high explosives simultaneously over the compound. Sergeant D and Sarbi were sitting on the LRPV next to them.

'I covered Sarbi's ears with my hands to protect her from the 84s firing, which is enough to knock your teeth out,' D says now.

Maylor gave the fire command to his fellow troopers.

'Ready, ready.' He paused. Standard operating procedure.

'Ready, ready, ready. Stand by. Fire!'

Shwwooosh. The soldiers saw a bright flash and a split second later the sonic boom of the explosions hurtled through the valley and up the hills.

'We were covered in rocks and dust by the rockets,' D recalls.

The powerful 84s made a mess but they did the job.

'If the blast didn't kill them the shrapnel would have. There was no movement after that,' Maylor wrote.

The commandos and SAS patrols moved off, heading back to Tarin Kot.

'It was one contact. It was quite small,' says Sergeant D with typical understatement. 'We just went on. We didn't bother following up, mainly because of the area.'

Back at Camp Holland, Sarbi and her handler returned to the Reconstruction Task Force. The rotation was drawing to a close and Sergeant D began preparing a hand-over brief for the incoming Doggies. He considered himself lucky. He and Sarbi got through the deployment without any injuries and had performed solidly. Sarbi got a bath and a bone for her efforts.

The command in Australia recognised the operational efficacy and great sacrifices of the explosive detection dogs and announced a memorial would be built at the SME to specifically honour the hard work of the EDDs and remember those who lost their lives while serving their country. Merlin. Razz. Two months later on 23 November, a black and tan kelpie named Andy was also killed, hit by a car at Camp Holland.

'In this case, the dogs have paid the ultimate sacrifice to ensure the safety of the Australian soldiers on operations,' said Major General Ash Power.

The dog mafia in Afghanistan were quietly pleased. No longer were the military working dogs relegated to the lowly, inhumane status of 'engineers stores'.

On 11 October Sergeant D and Sarbi arrived in Sydney, where the four-legged hero spent a month at the Australian Quarantine and Inspection Service, to ensure she hadn't picked up any exotic diseases during her seven months in Afghanistan. She had passed the requisite veterinary checks before leaving Afghanistan but was still kept in isolation as a precaution.

It was a lonely time for the sociable hound used to company 24/7, and hardly seemed a fitting reward for her good work, but those were the rules. At least times had changed since the Vietnam War when the dogs were left behind, as soldiers were forced to walk away from their best mates, tearful and heartbroken.

Sergeant D took a well-earned break. He needed it.

He and Sarbi were heading back to Afghanistan in 2008 six months later as part of Special Operations Task Group 7, working with the Commandos and SAS to kill or capture the Taliban and insurgent leadership and give the Afghan people a real chance at a peaceful future, free from the tyranny of oppressive rule.

Sergeant D didn't know it then, but he and Sarbi were about to become a part of Australian military history.

Chapter 15

ONCE MORE UNTO THE BREACH

Sergeant D and Sarbi rotated out of Sydney with Special Operations Task Group 7 (SOTG7) on 24 June 2008. He was 32 years old, unattached, as fit as he'd ever been, physically and mentally, and at his peak in command of the Explosive Detection Dog Section in Uruzgan. He had spent the previous six months in a series of exacting pre-deployment exercises in Sydney, practising ways to minimise battlefield risks and improve operational effectiveness. He was ready for the hardcore work with the Commandos and SAS.

The new rotation was heading back to Afghanistan at the height of the the fighting season. Their task, and the message to the enemy, was clear. As the head of Special Operations in Afghanistan Major General Tim McOwan said: 'We will find you. We will hunt you down. Your time is limited. Leave now and go back to a normal life without violence.'

Australian newspaper headlines in recent days had painted a picture of an Afghanistan riddled by endemic government corruption amid a failing NATO campaign to win the hearts and minds of the locals. In a story headlined 'Afghanistan's deadly double whammy', Fairfax journalist Tom Hyland wrote that Afghans were caught between a vicious insurgency and a deeply corrupt state. In another, headlined 'Hearts and minds not won', Hyland quoted a report by European aid agencies that claimed Afghans believed reconstruction efforts were 'misplaced and even counterproductive' until the government was free of corruption and security had been established.

'It was measurably more dangerous than the first time I was there,' Sergeant D says now. 'Our role was totally different to the previous ones. We were doing a lot more compound searches and clearances getting to and from places. We were basically trying to get the local populace to follow the government rather than the Taliban and to do this we were trying to capture Taliban commanders, and have *shuras* with the local elders to see what they needed from us.'

By then, Australia had suffered four more fatalities in Uruzgan Province and the wounded numbered almost 40. On 27 April 2008, Lance Corporal Jason Marks, a commando with 4RAR and a father of two, died from a single shot to the back of his head. Twenty to 30 insurgent fighters attacked his vehicle-borne force element with small arms and RPGs as the Australians prepared for a targeted assault. Marks, a respected and commended soldier, was leading his platoon when he went down. Four other commandos were wounded in the three-hour pitched battle, one seriously as he heroically tried to help his leader.

On 23 November 2007, Private Luke James Worsley died in a buzz-saw of fire from a PKM heavy machine-gun as he stormed a known Taliban bomb-making compound 30 kilometres away from Camp Russell. His warning to his mates behind him saved their lives. They repaid him by fighting for hours to reclaim his body and carry him back over rugged terrain to their forward operating base. Not a single enemy survived the firefight.

A month earlier, SAS Sergeant Matthew Locke was shot in the heart by a single round from a 7.62-millimetre heavy machine-gun, fired by a Taliban gunman in a cornfield in the Baluchi Valley along the Tiri Rud. Locke had recently been awarded the prestigious Medal for Gallantry for courage under fire in the Chora Valley with fellow SAS trooper Ben Roberts-Smith, a specialist sniper and assaulter who would later win the Victoria Cross for single-handedly wiping out three enemy machine-gun posts, saving his mates' lives. Locke's small unit was on a mission to disrupt insurgent forces within a key Taliban line of communication when it was ambushed. It was a clear morning at 0749 hours local time. 'He was one of these guys who would stand up in the middle of a firefight, in front of a wave of fire and just hook in,' said Roberts-Smith. Locke's grieving father Norm said his son 'absolutely loved the army. He loved what he was doing'.

In October 2007, David Pearce, a member of the 2/14th Cavalry Regiment, died when the ASLAV he was driving ran over a pressure-plate operated improvised explosive device. The ASLAV, call sign V30E, was struck just six kilometres outside Camp Holland, on a road the Aussies dubbed 'IED Alley'. Pearce, who had only celebrated his forty-first birthday a few days earlier, was killed instantly, the second Australian to die in Afghanistan and the first from a direct contact with the enemy.

The death toll was mounting among civilians, too. On 24 June 2008 the US Commander of the Combined Joint Task Force 101 in Afghanistan, Major General Jeffrey J. Schloesser, turned a televised press briefing into a lament for the loss of civilian lives. He said IED attacks and small arms assaults had increased by 40 per cent on the same time the year before. 'The enemy ... [is] aggressively targeting what I will call both development and governance at a local level,' Schloesser said. 'They're burning schools ... and they are also killing teachers and they are killing students.' Later, he added: 'The people that they're killing, first and foremost, are innocent civilians.'

The Australians with SOTG7 knew what they were heading into. After ripping in, Sergeant D received a series of intelligence briefings and a couple of weeks' worth of practical updates from the departing Doggies.

He was based in Camp Russell, the central nervous system of the Australian Special Operations Task Group. The SOTG area was a significant improvement on Camp Holland, even though it was within it and located just a couple of hundred metres away. For one, the special ops blokes had better food than the stodge provided in the Dutch mess tent and enjoyed a traditional Australian Sunday roast and weekly barbeque and seafood spread. The recreation and eating area was well equipped with books, huge television screens, computers, and pool and ping-pong tables. The sleeping quarters were five-star by comparison, too. D bunked in a reinforced concrete dormitory that slept five or six men. Overcrowding and privacy issues were sorted with the utilitarian resourcefulness typical of the sappers.

'Engineers being engineers, we scrounged around for timber and whatever we could get hold of to partition the large room into individual little rooms,' he recalls. 'Some of the more skilled guys managed to do some excellent work to make their bed spaces as comfortable as possible.' But not all were equal in size.

'There were some real estate discussions,' Sergeant D concedes. 'Eventually it was all sorted out and everyone was happy with the end result.'

Sarbi had settled in effortlessly. Her needs were far simpler than her handler's and she placed no demands on anyone other than a daily run, a spot of grooming and ongoing training when not on patrol.

Sergeant D and Sarbi were initially attached to the commandos, before switching to the SAS patrols when one of the SOTG dogs went on leave to give its injured paws time to recover.

The Australian Special Operations Task Group was formidable. The troopers were the hardest, fittest, and among the most thoroughly trained and tattooed soldiers in the Australian military. They were extraordinarily agile and highly manoeuvrable; adaptable, self-sufficient and trained to survive any conditions. They were as physically tough as they were psychologically strong. In a word, fearsome, and that gave them a distinct psychological advantage over the anti-coalition militia.

The task group used the classic hammer and anvil approach to warfare. The commandos had superior combat power and launched ground assaults to destroy the enemy threat with the aid of coalition air support. They fought hard and up close and were also equipped to act as a rapid reaction force to support the SAS when needed, or help extract patrols and other Coalition elements under fire. The combination of artillery and aerial bombardment, or 'arty and air', was fearsome. The British, Americans and Dutch provided Harrier GR7A jets, Apache gunships and the lethally effective AC-130 Spectre gunships, which the enemy called 'spitting witches' due to its formidable firepower.

The soldiers were self-reliant. Everything needed was stowed in their vehicles and backpacks and attached to their Molle system webbing. They hauled water, single-ration combat food known as MREs, radio and communications gear, sleeping gear, weapons, night observation devices (NODs), emergency medical equipment and more. Their entire loads weighed between 30 kilograms and 80 kilograms, depending on the equipment required for the operation and the personal weapons the soldiers brought along for the show, the 7.62-millimetre SR-25 sniper rifles, 9-millimetre Browning pistols, 9-millimetre USPs, hand grenades and M4 automatic rifles.

Most of their work was done on foot at night, in response to actionable tactical field intelligence and highly advanced surveillance. They relied on a complex web of human sources and intercepted enemy radio 'chatter', rendered intelligible by local interpreters who spoke Pashto or Dari, two of the main languages in Afghanistan. The ACM spoke in code but it was easy to break. In the notorious Korengal Valley in the north-eastern province of Kunar, insurgents called the ISAF soldiers 'potatoes' and their own weaponry 'sugar'. As in, 'I'll wait for your nine potatoes and give them some sugar'. When they added 'but I only have a few lumps left' the interpreters knew they were running out of ammunition.

The SOTG missions lasted days to weeks. Scouts tore through the countryside on quad bikes to gather intelligence. The patrols exited Camp Russell by Bushmaster or LRPV and drove to a lay-up point where operators and engineers infiltrated by foot, walking several kilometres under the cover of darkness to pre-determined mission sites.

They set up hidden observation points (OPs) on harsh and ragged hilltops at nose-bleed heights, feeding information to other force elements. They used magnified spotting scopes and sophisticated ground-to-air radio comms to call in offensive air support to take out identified enemy targets. If the OPs were compromised, they moved.

They searched suspect compounds for material and insurgent fighters, using specialised night fighting equipment and Ninox night vision goggles, named after a powerful and aggressive native Australian owl.

Prudent planning meant the drivers, vehicle crew and support staff remained with the harboured vehicles, monitoring radio networks for enemy chatter, ready to move when needed, which was almost always. As McOwan would later say, 'once outside the wire, our troops are in harm's way' and in 'some form of contact or firefight' on almost every patrol.

On 15 July 2008, Sergeant D and Sarbi and a large commando contingent had completed a compound clearance mission in a village nestled in the green belt several kilometres out of Tarin Kot. The patrol had been working for days, on heightened alert after the death the previous week of SAS signaller Sean McCarthy, who died from wounds sustained when his vehicle struck an IED elsewhere in Uruzgan.

The commandos were divided into two platoons spread out over a couple of hundred metres, moving through the green zone, away from the compounds. Sergeant D and Sarbi were in the middle with the headquarters element. There are no hard and fast rules when fighting the Taliban but the soldiers generally considered the open desert safer than the green belt with its soft cover of vegetation and fields. The enemy couldn't fight the coalition troops with their superior weapons systems as effectively in the exposed terrain of the *dasht* but, as D had previously discovered, it is never safe to assume.

The first platoon had moved ahead, followed by the headquarters element. There was no evidence of roadside bombs and no suspect movement from locals. Sergeant D and Sarbi were next. The Afghan interpreter and a soldier from the Afghan National Army trailed them by 40 metres. They were *shohna ba shohna*—shoulder to shoulder—with the Australians.

Suddenly an unexpected shock wave ripped across the ground. *Boom!*

The interpreter and ANA soldier behind D and Sarbi had just been blown up, killed instantly.

'I was lucky,' D says now.

A motorbike was spotted racing away in the distance but it was too late to intercept it. 'We worked out it was remote detonated. It was just lucky they weren't targeting Doggies that day,' D says.

The platoons immediately dispersed into flanking positions and took cover, combat-ready to counter an enemy assault. The troop commander placed his men in position and assigned tasks.

'Initially, it's just common sense,' D says.

The explosion and rushed movement from the troops slamming themselves into the ground to lower their profile didn't rattle Sarbi.

She had a job to do.

Sarbi's job was to find any other unexploded IEDs. The enemy often buried a second bomb to take out the reaction force that went to the aid of the fallen soldiers.

Sergeant D unclipped the leash from his hip and told Sarbi to seek on.

'We searched a path back towards the terp [interpreter] and ANA soldier so the guys could get to them if they needed first aid, but they were already dead. We still had to recover them, so Sarbi and I searched a route for the guys to go in and pick them up,' he recalls. 'It was frightening, you'd be lying if you said it wasn't.'

Sergeant D and Sarbi treaded gently, searching for signs of roadside bombs. They established a path over which the soldiers would walk. The engineers followed with metal detectors to make sure Sarbi hadn't missed anything, hoping they didn't trigger another IED.

They followed strict track discipline. Veering off the identified and cleared path could be deadly.

Sarbi and D moved to search where the soldiers had taken fire positions, making sure IEDs had not been planted where they were laying up.

Forty-five minutes later, the commandos were on the move, back to base.

Back in Australia, the chief of the defence force, Air Chief Marshal Angus Houston, announced the incident via a press release.

'These deaths, on the same day we welcomed Signaller Sean McCarthy home, reinforce the danger faced by Australian, Afghan and International Security Assistance Force troops, and the local population in Afghanistan every day,' he said.

Sergeant D used the incident as a learning experience. *Keep a better eye out.*

The lesson came in handy later on an SAS patrol.

The dog handler and Sarbi were on a mission to search a string of suspected Taliban compounds outside Tarin Kot. The troops came across a mud brick building that looked 'a bit off'. The building wasn't on the list of intended targets or compounds but a number of locals ran off as soon as they saw the patrol moving into sight.

That reaction alone was suspicious.

The soldiers did a final weapons check and moved in, blasting the compound door open. They raced through, one at a time, covering each other's backs. The Afghan compounds—or *qualas*—are a series of rectangular or square buildings, often with one or two rooms, attached to each other.

Clear. Clear.

They secured the building and conducted an initial search. Once done, the SAS boys turned to Sergeant D and Sarbi.

'Off you go.'

Sergeant D went in through the door. Sarbi got straight down to business but within a minute, her handler noticed a shift in the dog's body language, a change so slight it went unnoticed by everyone else.

Sarbi didn't move into her passive response sit to indicate, but she paid extra attention to a section of the mud wall where some rocks had been moved. She returned to the spot, nostrils twitching. Sergeant D went in for a closer inspection. He scratched at the mud walls and found nothing. His training, however, told him otherwise.

'If someone places something somewhere it will leave what we call a disturbance—it could just be the scent of a person from being in the area,' he explains. 'When the dogs are finding things they will find the disturbance and it is up to us to recognise when it's an IED, or a weapon or something else. If it's not natural to the area it will get the dog's interest, and if there is an explosive with it, that's when they will indicate.'

D knew every muscle movement in Sarbi's body and was 100 per cent sure she was on to something. He just didn't know what. He called over an engineer with a metal detector and asked him to sweep the mine lab over the wall.

The detector gave off an electronic signal indicating metal. Sergeant D went in for a better look.

His pulse began to race. He dug a bit deeper into the wall, moving crude mud bricks weathered with age. Finally, he felt something. He pulled out communications equipment and a handful of mobile telephones, all with working SIM cards. The discovery was a major find.

'Good girl, Sarbs, good girl,' Sergeant D said, giving her a vigorous pat on her big black head.

The phones contained the phone numbers and names of local mid-level Taliban leaders. Some had text messages in the memory. The phones were passed to the electronic intelligence operators.

'The bears can do amazing things with those,' says Sergeant D.

SAS troopers are hard to impress. They are the best of the best with a reputation for getting things done on their own terms in their own time by their own methods. *Who dares wins.*

They are the masters of surveillance and reconnaissance, absolutely second to none. Yet the explosive detection dog had proven herself. She had spotted something they had missed. She had won them over.

'The SAS guys were really happy,' D says. 'They loved Sarbi after that.'

Chapter 16

BLACKHAWK DOWN

Sergeant D was not a superstitious man but he was starting to think he and his hound might have nine lives. He and Sarbi had survived a few near misses completely unscathed when those around them hadn't been so lucky, dogs included. Luck, like life, was measured in margins. It was well known that the Taliban and insurgents were targeting the explosive detection dogs. Canines play little part in Afghanistan culture, unless you include the barbaric practice of organised weekly dog fights on the holy day of prayer.

A year earlier, the high-tech electronic warfare experts had warned Sapper Pete Lawlis that the Doggies were in the enemy's sights and, in July, a British dog handler and his yellow Labrador retriever, Sasha, were shot dead on a patrol in the Helmand desert. 'They're a major asset,' said

Lance Corporal Ken Rowe prior to leaving the British FOB Inkerman in the Upper Sangin Valley, a few days before he was fatally shot. 'The soldiers love having them on patrol . . . and the Taliban don't.'

There was no point in asking Ares, the Greek god of war, why Sarbi was so lucky. But it might be time to rethink the dictum that cats are blessed with nine lives and apply that curious feline logic instead to canines, Sarbi especially. It couldn't hurt and, as it soon turned out, it wouldn't.

Under the cover of darkness in the very early hours of 11 August 2008, Sergeant D and Sarbi exited Camp Russell in a multi-vehicle mounted patrol to search a suspect compound outside of Tarin Kot. They had received their operation orders at an extensive briefing the night before and each man had precise knowledge of what was expected of him.

At the last minute and for no apparent reason, Sergeant D and Sarbi were redirected to the second Bushmaster in the convoy. D was initially allocated to the lead protected mobility vehicle that carried SAS Corporal Mark Donaldson, who would be manning a machine-gun and would become famous for his courage under fire three weeks hence in another patrol with Sarbi and Sergeant D. But this was the army; D's was not to question why.

The troop was heavily tooled up. D was armed with his M4, body armour, helmet, radio, side arm and other fighting equipment. His pack was stuffed with enough rations to keep him and Sarbi going for a couple of days, if need be. He tossed in a couple of chocolate bars, too, for energy— for him, not Sarbi. The journey in was expected to take a couple of hours, but no one could be sure what lay ahead. War is the sum of a thousand moving parts, any of which can go wrong.

The Bushmasters dropped off small SAS patrols at intervals along the route, to conduct surveillance. The clandestine units would ensure the locals were sound asleep and not gearing up for a night fight from well-concealed machine-gun nests or vantage points on higher ground.

As the Bushies got closer to their target, an urgent message came over the radio network.

'We've just been hit by an IED.'

The lead Bushmaster—'actually the vehicle that I was supposed to be in,' Sergeant D says—struck a roadside bomb packed with twenty kilograms of homemade explosives. Corporal Donaldson, a 29-year-old lean, muscled-up warrior from New South Wales who'd been in the SAS since 2004, was blown off the back of the vehicle and smashed hard into the ground. A second soldier was also blasted out of the Bushie. No one was killed and neither trooper had life-threatening injuries. Donaldson's injuries were minor; his mate's were considered serious. A combat medic treated and stabilised both men.

'One had a suspected back injury and the other was hurt as well,' Sergeant D says now. 'Two of the guys had to be airlifted out.'

The Bushmaster was a melted, twisted wreck but Donaldson said later: 'that thing saved my life'. The right rear wheel was blown off and the suspension destroyed. A Dutch recovery convoy was called in to collect the mangled metal. The vehicle was going nowhere under its own steam.

It was past midnight and an SAS commander radioed a nine-liner request for an air medical evacuation (AME). He ordered the patrols into position to provide security for the troops and incoming helicopter—an American Blackhawk that took off from Tarin Kot under Apache escort. The return flight should be about 30 minutes, if all went to plan.

The Australians relied on the American and Dutch helicopters in the absence of their own medevac choppers that, back then, weren't up to the task. The situation wasn't ideal and had caused serious angst the previous month when a Dutch doctor at the Tarin Kot hospital criticised the delay of a Dutch-US AME for SAS Signaller Sean McCarthy, who bled to death from major internal injuries sustained when his LRPV hit an IED. The medevac chopper was delayed because the crew refused to fly without an Apache gunship escort and McCarthy was pronounced dead when he reached the hospital, 113 minutes after the attack. The 25-year-old was standing in the middle of the LRPV and had copped the full force of the blast.

'He [McCarthy] was badly injured on both legs. However, he was alive for an hour. We will never know what might have been or what we could have done,' Lieutenant Colonel Ed van der Zee said.

An army reservist and trauma surgeon told journalist Jamie Walker it was critical that wounded soldiers reached hospital within the 'golden hour' when trauma treatment was most effective. But an official army inquiry later found the medevac procedures were not to blame for McCarthy's death.

Sergeant D and Sarbi slipped into their preset cadences of war. With D's weapon in action condition, locked and loaded, they searched the surrounding area and possible landing zone for IEDs, accompanied by the engineers with the mine lab metal detectors.

Sarbi worked well outdoors at night. Her eyes adjusted to the ambient light of the moon and the stars but her nose did all the work. Sergeant D, wearing night vision goggles that turned the landscape a spectral green, quietly urged her on. The team conducted a thorough open area search and Sarbi zig-zagged across the terrain, as sure-footed as a billy goat that danced precipitously up the craggy ledges of the mountains. Good to go. He recalled his trusted hound and gave the patch of rock-strewn dirt the all clear. A secure landing zone was established.

The wounded were set up in a safe spot for easy access to the landing zone, so the loadmaster could get them on to the Blackhawk as fast as possible and then give the pilot the signal to get the hell out of Dodge before they became a prized target for the enemy. The soldiers were deep in hostile territory, potentially surrounded by Taliban and insurgents in fortified compounds.

Sergeant D grabbed Sarbi and dropped down beside a Bushmaster close to the landing zone, waiting for the Blackhawk to roar in overhead. Sarbi lay prone next to her handler, alert to her surrounds. Her furry ears stood up in stereo, as flexible an antenna as any of the high-tech systems of war. She could hear the signature pitch of the Blackhawk engine in the distance. Sergeant D sensed she was on to something and soon after he heard rotors *thwomping* as the chopper drew close, its pitch changing as the pilot cut back power ready to flare in. As the helo descended, the Blackhawk's powerful rotors kicked up a huge cloud of dust, causing an instant brownout.

'He couldn't see so he took off again for another go,' Sergeant D says of the pilot.

Hound and handler were covered in a layer of the gritty reddish dust that ground its way into everything. D moved to the lee side of the Bushmaster with Sarbi to avoid another blast of Afghan earth.

The helo circled overhead just as they got into position. D knelt down, commanding his mutt to drop, and she sprawled on the ground as close to him as she could get, leaning on him equally for comfort and protection. 'Sarbi was fully aware something was going on but she reacted well,' he says now.

The chopper was coming in fast to avoid turning itself into a sitting duck. *Smash!* A crashing thud rang out as the Blackhawk smacked down with enormous force.

D popped up and saw the helo blades shear off with an unmistakable screeching metallic sound. The rotors tore through the air at breakneck speed, spinning with lethal force at head level.

Bloody hell!

'I'd only just ducked around the side of the Bushmaster and there's chopper blades flying everywhere,' he says. 'The boys out on sentry were getting them coming past 300 metres away.'

He ordered Sarbi to stay down, worried that the blades would slice her in half.

'Nine lives, *I know*,' he says with a grin.

Donaldson and the other wounded soldier were closer to the landing zone and made a run for it, trying to put some distance between them and the crashed chopper.

One of the crew on the ISAF medevac chopper was hurt. The Blackhawk, like the Bushmaster, was out of action. Sergeant D noted wryly to himself that it had landed flat, but—*no rotors, no flying*.

The patrol now had extra bodies to protect, one additional wounded, and another piece of damaged military hardware to watch over and keep safe from the enemy. At least the incoming medical crew that remained unhurt would help treat the wounded.

A second nine-liner medical evacuation was requested out of Kandahar, south of Tarin Kot, but it was grounded due to bad weather. The wounded were being treated at the crash scene and the troop was secure.

'If the injuries had been life-threatening there would have been assets deployed and the commanders on the ground would have taken a greater risk launching that aircraft out of Kandahar,' Defence spokesman Brigadier Brian Dawson said.

Sarbi, Sergeant D and the hard men from the SAS were static as they waited for the medevac and Bushmaster recovery convoy. None of the damaged machinery would be left behind in case the enemy exploited it.

The bright light of a summer's dawn had cracked the ink black night by the time a third rescue attempt was launched six hours later, using an American CH-47 Chinook helicopter from Kandahar. The weather had cleared and the massive tandem-rotored beast had been retasked to support the 'hard landing' incident, an Orwellian neologism used by the military brass to mean a crash.

'But then it gets even better,' Sergeant D recalls.

The element of surprise had been lost. Afghan villagers were milling around to check out the action, keeping a safe distance. As Sergeant D says, they weren't openly hostile, even if some of the troop suspected the locals had planted the IED.

Around 0700 hours, a Chinook roared in to fetch the Blackhawk with an escort of Apache gunships—just in case. All eyes were cast upward. The rotors, powered by the Chinook's enormous 714 engines, kicked up a sea of dust equal to a sandstorm but the loadmaster and crew finally manoeuvred the bird in place for the extraction. The wounded and Blackhawk crew were loaded on board as the rotors turned and burned. Next up: recover the downed aircraft.

'They went to pick up the Blackhawk and take it away but they accidentally rolled it on the side,' Sergeant D recalls with an amused shake of his head. 'So, not only did it bust off all its blades, but now it's rolled over as well. Eventually they worked it out and took it away.'

Finally, the Chinook had its payload on board and the wounded Australians and Blackhawk crew were flown to the ISAF medical centre at Tarin Kot. Donaldson was back in action the following day; his mate eventually returned to Australia for further medical treatment.

Back in Australia the incident made the headlines. The *Australian* newspaper published a story highly critical of the 'botched helicopter rescue' under the headline, 'Push for Diggers to get medivacs (sic) in Afghanistan'. Journalist Mark Dodd wrote 'three wounded Diggers waited six hours on the battlefield before being taken to hospital . . . in the second botched helicopter rescue of Australian troops in as many months'.

The *Sydney Morning Herald* quoted Defence Minister Joel Fitzgibbon saying 'a string of bad luck' caused the events and the Australian troopers were 'stuck' with the allied medevac. 'One, we are already overstretched. Second, our helicopters would have to be upgraded to deal with the modern-day threats which exist in a theatre like Afghanistan,' Fitzgibbon said.

The minister told the national broadsheet that the Rudd Labor government would consider sending its own specialised medical helicopters, with 100 specialist defence personnel, to support the Australian troops in Afghanistan the following year.

A year was a long time in a war zone.

Chapter 17

AMBUSHED

Soon after the sun came up on 2 September Sergeant D and Sarbi boarded a US Army Humvee at FOB Anaconda in the district of Khas Uruzgan for their next mission into bandit country. They were roughly 100 kilometres north-east of Tarin Kot, operating with two SAS patrols plus an explosive ordnance disposal engineer—twelve Australians in all—and a dozen US Special Forces soldiers and the same number again of Afghan National Army soldiers. They had been airlifted in by Chinooks several days earlier and had been conducting a series of in-and-out strategic patrols, mostly at night, in the region.

The Americans at the remote US firebase were down to skeleton staff and conducting offensive ops with limited numbers was near to impossible. A little help from their Aussie Special Forces counterparts wouldn't go astray.

The operations orders were to capture or kill key Taliban targets, route the enemy from the area and destroy IED facilitators. They were 'highly targeted operations against insurgent command infrastructure'. In other words, their task was to chop off the head of the insurgent snake and watch the body wither. The work was split between four patrols, working in pairs with allied partners. The previous night two SAS foot patrols were inserted by vehicle, and snipers and scouts climbed through the blackness to establish overwatch positions in the hills on the north. Nightfall gave them a primary advantage and freedom of movement. The second element of the task group, including Sergeant D and Sarbi, set off in a convoy of five Humvees at daybreak. Their task was to carry out compound searches in the small villages near Ana Kalay in Khas Uruzgan.

Sarbi was up for anything. She was travelling with a fellow four-legged companion, US Army K9 Jacko. The yellow Labrador retriever and his 35-year-old handler, Sergeant First Class Gregory Rodriguez, had arrived for their first tour of Afghanistan three months earlier. They were assigned to the K-9 unit of the 527th Military Police Company, 709th Military Police Battalion, Eighteenth Military Police Brigade in Ansbach, Germany. Like Sergeant D, Rodriguez, or Rod as he liked to be known, grew up with a deep affection for man's best friend. As a child he had a cocker spaniel that he trained as a hunting dog. One Valentine's Day, while he was based in Alaska with his first working dog, a narcotics sniffing hound, he presented his wife, Laura, with a red-headed doberman they named Ellie.

Rod had been a handler for seven years and had a reputation for being able to straighten out even the unruliest
of mutts. Difficult dogs were his speciality. 'He would tell
everyone, "I have the best job in the US Army",' says his
wife Laura.

The ebullient father of three was a firm believer in gaining in-depth field knowledge and trained Jacko on the latest
explosive finds, polishing processes and enhancing skills.
The hours spent together had paid dividends and their
mutual devotion was obvious to anyone who saw them.
'[Jacko] was Greg's best companion for the past couple of
years,' his wife said. 'He'd been sleeping with Greg every
night since they landed in Afghanistan.'

Sarbi and Jacko had trained together on base and Sergeant D rated Rod highly. 'Rod and his dog Jacko's methods
and drills were spot on, perfect,' he says now. 'Jacko was an
awesome dog, as well.'

Sergeant D welcomed the addition of another twin pair
of paws to the mission. Not that Sarbi and he weren't well
used to the cauldron intensity of working in Afghanistan
and rapid insertion overnight missions. They were. They
had their routines mapped out. When D was on piquet, he
left Sarbi tied to his pack, beside her canvas-covered foam
mattress. One pitch-black night, while D was on watch, a
troop commander observed Sarbi through his night vision
goggles. She was standing up, staring obsessively into the
darkness. He didn't know who was out there and worried
the unit was under attack.

The commander grabbed his rifle and went to inspect.

'He came out and checked and saw me on piquet,' recalls

Sergeant D. 'Sarbi was standing there waiting for me to come back. That's how loyal she is. She also had a habit of stealing people's beds when they went out on piquet.'

Smart dog, all right.

One captain from the SME said he came back from a routine guard watch to find Sarbi curled up inside his swag. He'd been gone two hours and felt guilty about booting her out of the cocoon she'd so obligingly kept warm. He turned over the scenario in his head, watching Sarbi snoozing for about fifteen minutes before the cold made him shift the hound over. 'It's great to have the dogs around; they make a difference,' he says.

The Special Forces soldiers exited FOB Anaconda feeling confident of the mission ahead. The previous day SAS patrols had successfully wiped out thirteen Taliban fighters who had been causing chaos in the area, including a regional commander. Commandos on a clandestine op two weeks before that had managed to sneak into Taliban leader Ahmad Shah's compound, in the heart of a safe haven, while he slept. They made a bloodless arrest without firing a single bullet. For good measure, they grabbed a couple of the Shah's surprised somnolent henchmen, too. All were now on their way to the US prison at Guantanamo Bay.

Success breeds success.

'The morning was pretty relaxed and calm and we had the snipers up in the over-watch positions as we came through [the villages] and did compound searches and checks,' recalls Sergeant D. 'Nothing too overt.'

Sarbi performed to her usual gold star standard. But the enemy didn't welcome their presence in the valley. The patrols had gone in to tease out the Taliban and insurgent fighters—poking an anthill with a stick—and the serial provocation worked.

'The enemy came in to ambush us but we had guys in other positions that were able to prevent them from coming to get us,' Sergeant D says now.

Seven Taliban were killed by the SAS boys working clandestinely in the hills. 'We had clobbered them in the preceding days and also had a very good success against them that morning,' recalled SAS Corporal Mark Donaldson, who infiltrated that morning and was ready for any show the enemy might put on.

The US-led operation was complete by early afternoon. FOB Anaconda was five kilometres away at the end of a narrow valley. A steep mountain ridge to the north dominated the valley and to the south was the heavily vegetated green belt, where the enemy lived and through which ran the pot-holed track that doubled as a road. The convoy was stretched out over about 300 to 400 metres, driving off the side of the road through the *dasht* that spread out about 400 metres between the spur and greenbelt.

The interpreter had intel that the roads were laced with IEDs so they went cross country, over terrain strewn with steep creek beds and sharp inclines. There was no cover, no trees, no big boulders, just rocky open ground. It was slower going and more difficult to navigate but as Sergeant D says, there's no point looking for a roadside bomb if another route exists. 'It's easier to avoid [an IED threat], otherwise you can tie yourself up for hours and be exposed to greater risk.'

The Humvees drove to a rendezvous point to collect two SAS patrols and head back to the firebase.

D and Sarbi were on the second Humvee. The Afghan interpreters had been picking up enemy chatter over the radio network all day but as the convoy moved west back to the FOB the traffic was becoming more excitable.

'They were saying they were going to hit us when our boys got to the vehicles but nothing happened and we moved off. Then we got more chatter, "yeah, we are going to hit them on the flat",' D recalls. 'We got a little bit of a pre-warning that something was going to happen.'

One of the insurgents went to speak but was told three times by his commander to shut up. 'The translator was translating that. *Shut up, shut up, shut up*,' D says. 'They were going to move when we closed on a compound.'

The convoy continued picking its way through the valley, avoiding the main route due to the threat of IEDs. More chatter was intercepted.

The vehicles harboured briefly. Soldiers performed a standard combat readiness check of weapons and gear, and calmly discussed tactics.

Sergeant D was sweating, but not from nerves. The temperature was in the mid to high 30s and he was fully kitted up. He was decked out in camouflage gear over a t-shirt, full body armour with ballistic plates, and webbing. He also wore protective Nomex gloves and ESS ballistic glasses to protect his eyes from shrapnel. He had a Camelbak filled with two litres of water on the back of his webbing and Peltors over a baseball cap. Sarbi's leash was attached to his hip with a rock climber's karabiner, good and secure.

His pack in the back of the Humvee had a day's worth of rations, and dry dog food and four litres of water for Sarbi.

Sergeant D's M4 was locked and loaded; ammo pouches velcroed on to his Molle webbing system. He was combat-ready.

The troop had decided that if the ambush came, they would leap out of the Humvee and take a combat position out of the line of fire on the protected side of the vehicles. Three of the heavily armed trucks had open trays at the back—like big utes—and a couple were enclosed vehicles that resembled armoured four wheel drives on steroids. The Australians rode on the exposed trays and, other than the machine-gunners in the turrets, were the most exposed. Three of the Humvees were crewed by Americans, the other two by ANA soldiers.

The convoy was westbound, driving into the sun. The air was charged; the soldiers were on alert and prepared.

Around 1500 hours, all hell broke loose.

Two of the lead Humvees rounded a raised knoll and were passing through a gully when mortars and RPGs exploded all around. The unmistakable sound of 7.62-millimetre machine-guns rang out as the bullets churned through the air, whizzing past and stitching into the ground, kicking up clouds of dust and dirt. Sergeant D spun around to see a rocket-propelled grenade land to the rear left of his vehicle, about twenty metres away. He flew off the truck with Sarbi as fast as he could. Out of the corner of his eye he could see his mates doing the same.

'Get out. Get out. Get out. Go. Go. Go.'

The convoy was hit by a wall of metal from weapons

fired by the enemy in hidden positions between 100 and 300 metres to the south in the green belt. The enemy was parallel to the row of vehicles. The lead cars copped the worst. They were in the kill zone. Soldiers bolted for cover on the right side of the trucks, away from the green belt, as bullets slammed into the metal on the other side, cracking like a stockman's whip. It happened so fast that the soldiers had no time to pinpoint the enemy, up to 200 heavily armed insurgents. Fear, if they felt it, would wait. Instinct took over. Training. TTPs. Whatever it takes.

'It was too instantaneous to stop and over-think it. You are just reacting and that all comes back to your training. That's done instinctively,' Sergeant D says.

Men ran for cover and manoeuvred into firing positions on the flanks, zeroing in on the enemy, a choreograph of synchronised teamwork and controlled aggression. Their superior weaponry gave them a significant advantage despite the overwhelming enemy numbers surrounding them. The joint patrol locked on the Taliban locations and opened fire, blasting them with everything they had.

The Americans identified a compound in the green belt and gave it a blast with the machine-guns.

The terps intercepted a Taliban commander's radio message.

'Kill them, kill them all.'

One of the SAS snipers took up a fire position to the rear of Sergeant D and Sarbi, searching for enemy targets through his scope. D scanned the rear.

'Covering my arse and making sure no one is coming up there,' he says.

Sporadic bullet rounds began walking in on the sniper to Sergeant D's rear, getting closer and closer. Ten metres. Seven metres. Five metres.

They've got us nailed, he thought.

'Mate, you better move,' Sergeant D shouted to the sniper.

Sarbi let loose with her own barrage and began barking at the gunfire, edging towards it in a stubborn defensive stance, as if to say *bring it on*. 'It's her coping strategy, barking was her release,' Sergeant D says now.

Sarbi was on a lead nearly two metres long, giving her handler room to manoeuvre without tripping over or getting tangled. She instinctively knew how to keep out of his way, and better yet, to stay low. Sarbi skipped around as bullets ripped into the hardened ground, turning rocks into razor sharp shards of stone. Sergeant D raced from one side of the Humvee to the other to avoid fire. Sarbi ran with him. He couldn't leave her sheltered under the truck because the drivers kept manoeuvring the vehicles to provide security and cover.

Instructions and target indications were bellowed over the radio network. Donaldson grabbed the 84-millimetre anti-armour rocket launcher and ran out to a flank and started pumping rockets into the engagement area. Self-assured and strong, Donno had won prizes for best shot and best at physical training in his platoon during his initial infantry training. He had also been hailed as the most outstanding soldier. He shot off seven well-placed rounds from the shoulder-fired weapon but drew return fire for his effort. A colleague bravely ran rockets out to him and Donno ran back to load up as well.

'Some of those were air burst as I was trying to rain the shrapnel down on where the fire seemed to be coming from. I used 66-millimetre rockets as well,' he said later. 'It's combat and it's war and you know, sometimes you don't know when someone's going to shoot at you.'

Sergeant D felt the *swoosh* of rockets flying by and the percussive waves of grenades tossed into the green belt.

About ten minutes into the firefight an American machine-gunner in the vehicle behind D and Sarbi was shot in the hand while standing in the turret. 'That's when we realised we were getting engaged from the rear as well,' Sergeant D says. Bullets were streaking through the air from the higher ground on the right rear flank. They were pincered, caught in a classic ambush. Tracers lit up the sky.

A non-commissioned SAS sergeant leapt up and took over the .50-calibre machine-gun.

Tat tat tat tat tat tat tat tat tat.

Known only as Sergeant H for operational security reasons, he let rip with a burst of fire while the convoy pushed on from the initial ambush position. The enemy's pre-ranged position was deadly accurate. A bullet exploded through his leg as he stood exposed in the Humvee.

H kept firing at the entrenched enemy until he was unable to stand any longer. He withdrew from the weapon, but he wasn't out of the fight. A replacement gunner took over and H continued to feed ammo to his replacement. As the firefight continued, more soldiers were wounded and loaded onto the truck. H helped treat them and keep them alive.

A Joint Terminal Attack Controller (JATC) called in

air support early but there were no aircraft on station and bombers had to be launched from elsewhere in the Middle East.

'The effect of the initiation [was] that the combined patrol suffered numerous casualties, completely lost the initiative and became immediately suppressed,' an official army citation for Donaldson later stated.

Sergeant D couldn't see the enemy. They had prepared well and dug in tight. But he could see the signature dust plumes kicked up by the Taliban mortars and RPGs and lasered in on the positions. Muzzle flashes that burst bright through the green also drew fire from the troopers' M4 rifles and machine-guns. D looked over and saw the Afghan Humvee further up the hill to the right, shooting across the front of the friendlies into the green belt. The ANA were not always known for their accuracy.

'We got them to move forward a bit so they weren't shooting so close to us,' he says. 'We had to maintain that and push them up . . . and get the convoy moving again.'

Two other American vehicles and the second ANA-manned Humvee were behind them. One roared down to support D's vehicle. The machine-gunner swept his .50-calibre on to the green and lit it up while the soldiers jockeyed for fire positions on the rear of the Humvee, pouring a wall of lead into the lush area.

The soldiers worked out that the initial coordinated contacts were launched from four points—two in front and one on each flank. The number of enemy fighters was a guess but it was estimated between 150 and 200. 'I honestly didn't think, "shit, there's a lot of fire coming down",' recalled Donno. 'It was more that we just had to fight back'.

The initial engagement lasted roughly twenty minutes, before the shooting died down and the vehicles were able to move. Not for long. They had got a few hundred metres when the intensity flared up again.

Thirty minutes into the battle, an American F-18 fighter roared over and dropped a five hundred pounder on the compound in the green belt where the ambush had been initiated. A massive explosion rumbled through the valley floor and a column of smoke rose through the air before flattening into a mushroom-shaped dust cloud. 'We didn't get any more fire from that point,' says Sergeant D.

The convoy moved forward in metres and the enemy ambush rolled with it. They were surrounded and outnumbered. Sergeant D, with Sarbi tethered to his hip, fought on the run, manoeuvring around the vehicles for safety. The soldiers were engaged on two levels—individual fights to stay alive and collectively to protect their mates. Controlled chaos.

D's heart rate was steady. He was clear-headed and calm, focused on the job, focused on keeping Sarbi safe and alive.

'It wasn't too bad,' he says now. 'I had done a lot of DAs [direct actions] and contacts into compounds. At that stage I'd been in the army twelve years . . . it's what we are trained for, and we are doing it with the SAS. These are professionals. The dogs react to how their handlers react and we react to the way the SAS react. They're calm. That feeds down to me.'

The F-18 fighter dropped a second bomb, which found

another target. The JTAC gave grid locations to the electronic warfare officer on the plane and the fighter swooped around for a series of strafing gun runs on the green belt. At some point during the battle British and US helicopters were called in and lit up the hillside, where the enemy were entrenched on the higher ground. But the insurgents kept firing.

'It's a funny thing, they were pretty staunch fighters. I don't know whether they were dug in or blasé to the aircraft, but every time the aircraft dropped a bomb or did a gun run . . . it just didn't seem to stop them firing. Generally, when the aircraft come overhead that slows things down a bit, but it didn't,' Donaldson said later.

An SAS JTAC spotted two Dutch Apache gunships escorting a Chinook into FOB Anaconda. The Apache helicopters are considered the premier attack choppers in the world. They come armed with unguided rockets, laser-guided Hellfire missiles, and a 30-millimetre chain gun under the nose that fires with deadly precision.

The air controller got on the comms to call in air support.

'We need your assistance as we're taking casualties,' the JTAC said.

The JTAC radioed target indications for the gunship pilots to launch their Hellfire rockets at the enemy positions, and marked the targets with bursts from the machine-guns. The Aussies relied on the Dutch for air support and logistical backup throughout the war on terror in southern Afghanistan. The precision-guided munitions could have ended the show in an instant or, at the very least, reduced the recalcitrant enemy force to a rump by taking out mortar positions and machine-gunners.

But, as Rob Maylor writes in his book, *SAS Sniper*, 'they wouldn't open up on the Taliban for fear they might draw some fire themselves'.

Sergeant D couldn't believe it. 'They stayed too high and said they couldn't see anything and left. Meantime, we are getting rounds and explosions all around us—but they said they couldn't see anything,' he recalls.

'They do have very tight rules of engagement but we needed all the help we could get,' Maylor said.

Two years later, after Maylor aired the coalition troops' frustration at the lack of air support from the Dutch Apaches, the Australian Defence Force contacted its counterpart in the Netherlands. The Dutch launched a review of the Apache response, or lack of it.

A spokesman for the Dutch minister of defence now says a Dutch Apache was used on three occasions to escort a medevac chopper safely to base. 'This helicopter was responsible to rush the wounded soldiers to a medical facility,' Marloes Visser says. 'In these missions the priority of the Apache helicopter is with the safe retrieval of the wounded, not in the battle on the ground.'

The Dutch Apache gunships responded to another call for direct air support but found the enemy contact had been broken and coalition forces were spread over a large distance. 'The Apache used its sensors to search the location for some kind of enemy activity. The activity which was observed was reported to the Forward Air Controller on the ground,' Visser says. 'Because the activities were not pointed out as hostile or [a] threat, the Forward Air Controller didn't ask for weapons to be deployed.'

And none were.

At one point an SAS trooper identified as G saw a mate go down in the kill zone, unable to move. Trooper G bolted out in the hail of bullets, grabbed his mate and carried him to a tray-backed Humvee. There was no room inside the cabin. G lifted his comrade onto the tray, using his own body as a shield. He put his mate down and kept him covered while he went back into fighting mode, engaging the enemy as he hovered over his comrade. It was a ballsy move. The enemy fire was intense. 'On several occasions, enemy bullets and RPG fragmentation struck his clothing and equipment,' Major General McOwan said later. Trooper G stayed in position. During a lull in the fighting, he applied life-saving first aid.

'This small example illustrated the mettle of the men that I command but we should never forget the quality of our adversary. They should never be underestimated. They are fearless and elusive, there are many of them and they are tough,' the Special Operations commander added.

The five Humvees stopped in a safe harbour position and medics treated the wounded but the enemy onslaught continued with deadly accuracy. Bullets and RPGs exploded all around. Donno ran across open kill zone to draw fire away from his fallen mates so they could get to safety. He'd seen them get shot and hit by RPG fragmentation and opened up his weapon.

'If you see them in trouble out there you go and help them out or you go and protect them, you give them covering fire so they can get back to where they need to,' he said later. 'It all comes back to the training. We train hard and we train hard for situations when, you know, when it does hit the fan.'

Donaldson's doggedness springs from his tragic family background. His father, Greg Donaldson, was a Vietnam War veteran who died of a heart attack in 1995. At the time, Donaldson was fifteen years old and a regular, sporty teenager growing up in the country town of Dorrigo in north-western New South Wales, the second of two sons. Three years later, his widowed mother, Bernadette, disappeared while planning a holiday to the Gold Coast. She has never been found and the NSW Police Service's Unsolved Homicides Team are still investigating her case. Donaldson, then studying at art school in Sydney, had no real direction in his life. The tragedy made him rethink his future.

'You look back on it now and think, "Well, did I process it?" I wasn't really sure if I did or didn't at the time,' Donaldson told radio interviewer Philip Clark. 'And when you're at that age and you're a young male, too, you think you know the world and you know everything and you can handle everything. But I think something like that comes along and I suppose, you know, if it doesn't kill you it only makes you stronger. I tend to just deal with it as best I could and just cracked on with life. Obviously, it affected me because it changed my whole career direction and my whole view on life. That was when I dropped out of art school and decided to chase what I thought were a bit more important things in life . . . I got interested in the military and wanting to give something back.'

And so Donaldson joined the Australian Army and has been giving something back ever since, particularly in Khas Uruzgan on 2 September 2008.

'This soldier deliberately exposed himself to enemy fire on several occasions in order to draw fire from those soldiers already wounded in the initial heavy fire,' Special Forces boss, Major General Tim McOwan, would later say of Donaldson.

But Donno reckons he was just doing his job, just like every other bloke out there.

A US Special Forces soldier was shot and lay wounded and exposed in the danger zone. Sergeant First Class Gregory Rodriguez ran out, providing cover, repeatedly putting himself in the line of fire to stop his colleague taking another bullet. Rod was known for his sense of duty and loyalty. His sister Lisa said later, 'He liked justice. If it wasn't right, he made it right.'

Rod was manoeuvring to protect his fellow soldier when an enemy fighter pulled the trigger. A bullet pierced Rodriguez's helmet. It was a fatal shot, the first and only fatality that day.

The Americans picked up Rod's body and put him in the back of a Humvee. Another soldier grabbed Jacko and secured the dog in the vehicle where he was safe. The pitiable dog would have felt lost and stranded, unsure of what had happened to his devoted master from whom he'd been inseparable for the past few months.

'Rod saved my life that day and ensured I would make it home,' wrote the Special Forces soldier he saved. 'After I had already been wounded . . . Rod on multiple occasions placed himself in harm's way to protect me and prevent me from being wounded again. Rod is truly a hero. He saved my life and gave his own protecting me.'

Rodriguez was the second dog handler killed in Afghanistan and the 501st American soldier to have lost his life fighting the war on terror in Iraq and Afghanistan.

At the base a few days later, the Americans placed Rod's rifle between his boots, wedged them together with sandbags, and put his helmet on the rifle butt. It was the traditional memorial for a fallen soldier. They hung Jacko's lead beside a photograph of Rod, crouched down next to his dog with his strong, tanned arm draped protectively over his mutt's dirt-covered furry shoulder. 'In loving memory,' it said.

'Jacko was running around looking for him,' Sergeant D recalls. 'He was running over to the boots and helmet and smelling them, looking for Rod.'

Jacko was retired from the US Army and adopted by the Rodriguez family.

'Jacko has bonded with our oldest son, Gregory Jr. He sleeps beside his bed, follows Gregory around, and waits by the door for Gregory to get home from school,' says Laura. 'We lost Jacko for a couple of days once and Gregory Jr was beside himself. The dog is a big part of our family and means a lot to us. We love being able to see him and take care of him.'

Before Rod left for Afghanistan, Laura asked her husband what he wanted her to do if anything happened to him, where he wanted to be buried. 'He told me Arlington, as he wanted to be among the best and the brave.'

On Monday, 22 September 2008, the United States flag was flown at half-mast in Rod's home state of Michigan to honour his sacrifice. The Democratic Governor, Jennifer M. Granholm, issued the order in accordance with federal law under the *Army Specialist Joseph P. Micks Federal Flag Code Amendment Act* of 2007. Every flag on official government buildings throughout the state and also on Michigan waterways was lowered. The star-spangled banners were raised to full-staff the following day.

Sergeant First Class Gregory Rodriguez is buried in the hallowed ground of Section 60 at Arlington National Cemetery, the final resting place of American soldiers killed in the Middle East.

Chapter 18

SAVING PRIVATE SARBI

Sergeant D and Sarbi were being pelted by an enemy machine-gun. They'd been in the valley near Ana Kalay for about an hour, give or take. Time has a way of contracting and expanding in the heat of battle. Men were going down all around, and those who could fought on.

Fire was raining down from four angles. The only way out of the ambushed valley was forward, but the enemy rolled along in tandem from their positions behind cover. The American trucks conducted a series of manoeuvres to protect the soldiers as they returned fire, running to whichever side of the Humvees taking less heat. Sergeant D and a few of the blokes worked out that a narrow V-triangle section at the rear of the truck provided the best cover for a few seconds, giving them time to return fire into the hottest enemy target, before metal started smacking into that side again. It was as if they were being chased around the Humvees by bullets.

Boom!

A rocket-propelled grenade exploded five metres away. Shrapnel spun through the air and ripped through Sergeant D's camouflage trousers, slicing into the back of his left knee and calf. There was no pain—'just a bit of a whack'—and he kept firing his M4.

The metal clip tethering Sarbi to D's body armour broke off in one clean snap, sliced in half by a piece of flying frag.

'Crap!' he yelled.

Sarbi whimpered and bolted from the blast effect, hit by a bit of hot frag. The robust dog headed for the road but didn't run off, her eyes fixed firmly on Sergeant D who kept her in his peripheral vision as he kept fighting, his finger on the trigger of his M4.

'A couple of the blokes got some frag in their backs and legs and bum,' he recalls. Sergeant D helped one to his feet and shepherded him to safety behind a nearby Humvee, providing covering fire as they moved.

Sarbi was now an open target for the Taliban. She was smaller, faster and more agile but she was at a distinct disadvantage—she couldn't hold a weapon and the Taliban saw value in targeting dogs. Sarbi ran along with the moving vehicles and ducked out of the line of fire when a heavy burst rang out, doing her best to avoid the wall of sound.

There was nothing her handler could do. Sergeant D calculated the risks in a heartbeat. It was pure chaos. He couldn't take a gamble on racing 50 metres across the open area being raked with weapons fire to grab Sarbi. If he risked his life for Sarbi and got wounded, he knew one of his mates would feel compelled to risk his life to save him. Brothers in arms. The coalition troops couldn't afford to lose another fighting body. The odds were stacked against Sergeant D—against Sarbi. He was gutted.

'Sarbi, come,' D yelled when he saw his beloved mongrel. She approached but a burst from the machine-gun on the vehicles repelled her.

Dogs have two responses when under pressure or when frightened—fight or flight. Sarbi was a fighter. The advanced training at the SME had prepared her for the noise of warfare and she was a combat-hardened war veteran. Sarbi had been exposed to gunfire in Afghanistan; she was familiar with the roar of aircraft and the rumble of engines. Some military working dogs had suffered a recognised canine version of Post Traumatic Stress Disorder, but not Sarbi. She rebounded from each deployment with no adverse side effects. She was a hardy hound and rarely frightened.

Sergeant D could see she was coping well, even without his constant instructions and encouragement. She cleverly, instinctively, distanced herself from the source of the explosions to avoid the percussive after-effects of the blasts. *Good girl, Sarbi.*

The Humvee got moving. Sergeant D was running on the right-hand side of the vehicle behind another SAS trooper. A few more men were on the left flank of the truck, firing into the green. Suddenly, the enemy on higher ground on the right let loose with a burst from the machine-gun. The soldier in front of D took a round in the rear end and calf. A third bullet blasted into the ejection port of his M4 and propelled it out of his hand. Another bullet ricocheted off the round and slammed into Sergeant D's hip with the force of a Mack truck, but it only left a massive bruise, not a permanent injury.

He thumped to the ground and returned fire. The other Digger who was injured crawled to the rear of the Humvee, taking cover under the back of the vehicle. When the bullets died down, Sergeant D crawled back to the Humvee, where he found the injured trooper's M4 and passed it back to him, but it was damaged and out of action. 'It can't work,' he says. 'The moving parts can't go backwards and forwards anymore.'

The trucks began rolling again. The soldier taking cover under the truck grabbed hold of the axle and was dragged along. D jumped up and sprinted after the Humvee, hammering his fist on the vehicle, shouting at the driver to slow down.

The truck jolted to a stop and the wounded soldier hobbled to the front of the Humvee and rode the rest of the way between the bullbar and the grill.

Sergeant D counted himself lucky.

'I only got the ricochet.'

Later in the hospital at Tarin Kot, medics found the bullet in his trouser pocket but it was too mangled for them to determine the gauge.

'Yeah, I've still got it,' D says. Blessed or just jammy he doesn't know. But one thing is for sure. The bullet had his name on it and he survived it. Nine lives.

Ninety minutes had passed. An SAS trooper was down,

shot through both legs, out of action. Sergeant D saw another Aussie. D thought he'd taken a hot cartridge from the rifle down his shirt but he'd been shot in the side. The bullet entered under one armpit and exited through the hip. He was lucky to be alive.

'We had to stop for a short while to patch him up and stabilise him before we could keep moving,' Sergeant D recalls. An EOD technician was also shot in the leg and took some frag in the hand. It was an armour-piercing round and it punched a neat hole through his thigh bone.

Explosions were booming, instructions were being shouted through the radio network, bullets streaked across the sky. The firefight was spread out over the *dasht* and casualties were mounting. Every soldier was fighting his own battle, going through his own unique experience and each has a story to tell of raw frontline action. Sergeant D was amazed he was still alive. Donno saw one Taliban jump up and launch an RPG from 50 metres away.

Machine-gun fire and RPGs were coming in thick and fast.

Four RPGs exploded around a Humvee that was surrounded by four SAS soldiers. Maylor felt the heat of the explosion as he was blasted through the air. 'I was hesitant to look at the injuries because I didn't want to know how bad the wounds were. I still wanted to keep on fighting even though I hadn't fired a shot,' he writes. 'As I lay on the deck I could see the bomb dog Sarbi through the dust. She was yelping and limping. Lucky for her I had been between her and the blast.'

Sergeant D kept calling for Sarbi to come and she did

the best she could. At least he could see her. She didn't seem too badly wounded. Her tail wasn't tucked under her hind legs in a show of fear or submission. She wasn't venturing into the green belt where the enemy were, either. Sarbi was determined to stay with the soldiers whose gear she recognised, whose voices she understood. D called and called, his throat parched from the heat and the fine dust.

The rolling ambush had gone two, two and a half, maybe three hours. The Aussies were taking serious casualties. The enemy swarm was relentless.

The Humvees began to speed up. Sergeant D had been running non-stop, dodging bullets and manoeuvring to whichever side of the truck was taking less fire. He kept shooting, wanting to give back as much and as hard as the coalition troops were copping. No mercy.

D and a couple of boys were trailing the Humvee on the safe side when it sped up to navigate a ditch, opening a gap two metres wide.

Whooosh.

'Holy shit,' D yelled in stereo with another bloke.

An RPG flew through the opening, narrowly missing the soldiers and the vehicle. It exploded 40 metres off to their right, sending another percussive wave rumbling through the valley.

'You can see it coming towards us, just a black blur,' D says. 'There was no time to do anything. If anyone had have been in the wrong position they wouldn't have been able to get out of the way. We were just lucky it went through that gap.'

Both soldiers swung around and returned fire to the point where they thought the RPG had come from.

'I knew there were about four or five Aussies down. That's pretty hard but they were all getting stabilised and getting on stretchers and on the vehicles, and we still had a job to do. We're still fighting for our lives,' he says.

The M240 heavy machine-gun on the truck was unarmed. Sergeant D began to climb up on the back of the Humvee to man the massive weapon. An Afghan interpreter was on the vehicle.

Two RPGs came in.

One exploded under the Humvee, tossing it up in the air. A second RPG had been set to air burst, and exploded over the vehicle, sending a cone of shrapnel down to the ground.

'The boys behind me thought we hit an IED because one blew up above the vehicle—an air burst—and one hit just under the vehicle,' Sergeant D says. 'That blew me off the truck and the interpreter rolled out seconds later.'

The trucks kept moving, oblivious to the lost human cargo.

The interpreter copped a hammering; half his face had been blown off. He lay exposed on the ground. Enemy rounds were zinging past, pinging up the dirt.

Donaldson was in the vehicle behind and saw the RPG explode. He watched Sergeant D and the terp get blown out. The terp was motionless on the ground.

No one gets left behind.

The wiry fella charged without regard for his own life into the line of fire, to certain death. He sprinted 80 metres through open ground raked by machine-guns and small arms, dodging bullets and RPGs to reach the wounded interpreter, who'd been working closely with the SAS boys for the last five days. Sergeant D was knocked around. He saw someone run out to the Afghan soldier but didn't know who it was.

The enemy bombardment 'was pretty heavy and pretty accurate. It was kicking all around us,' Donno said. 'I suppose it was like looking at a puddle of water in a heavy rainstorm and seeing all the droplets landing in the puddle of water. Imagine that, but being in the dirt and the dust—that's what it looks like.'

The interpreter was lying facedown in a pool of blood. Donaldson started by dragging him but the ground was too rocky. After fifteen metres, Donno scooped his arm under the terp and carried the wounded man back to safety. He gently put him on the back of a Humvee and began emergency medical treatment. Donaldson was a signaller, not a medic, but he knew enough to keep the man alive.

Adrenalin surged through Sergeant D's body. 'Just the right amount,' he says.

He forced himself up and chased the Humvee, from which he'd been blown off, but couldn't catch it. He was badly winded by the RPG blast. The dog handler ducked down towards the road and took cover in a culvert, trying to catch his breath. He was cut up and bleeding but, strangely, feeling no pain. At least, none to worry about.

Shrapnel frag had ripped into his left arm and shoulder, across his chest and on the inside of his right forearm, creating a latticework of injuries that would form permanent scars and leave frag in his body. Both legs were sliced from shrapnel. Bruises began to break out on his arms and burn marks from the red-hot metal seared his skin. The G-SHOCK watch he wore religiously on his left wrist had a few nicks in it but it had survived. Shrapnel had torn halfway into his Blackhawk webbing belt before coming to a stop.

He was alive. Sergeant D's body armour had saved him.

'I didn't really feel any pain but I knew I'd been hit in the face as well because I could feel all the blood on my lips,' he says. 'I ran my tongue around my teeth to see if they were still there and they were. I was happy about that.'

His pain threshold registered a four out of ten. 'It still wasn't too bad. I would have been working on adrenalin the whole time. My broken leg from the bike crash was much more painful.'

Sergeant D was still in the fight. He could feel bullets sluicing the ground around him. He popped off a few rounds towards the enemy and scanned the horizon for Sarbi. He has no idea how, but she was still in the vicinity. Sarbi was shadowing him, keeping track with the Humvees and tracing her handler's footsteps as he ran around the trucks, firing and taking cover. The tenacious mongrel hadn't given up. For all her handler knew she might have been thinking, *so what's happened to our search patterns?* Dogs love routines.

'Sarbi, come, come on girl, get over here,' D yelled, trying to coax her closer.

The courageous canine was running towards her handler, her body profile low to the ground, her senses heightened by the surround sound of war. She got to within five metres of D.

'C'mon, girl, c'mon Sarbs.'

One of the machine-gunners on a Humvee let rip with a blast from the 50-calibre and the percussion startled Sarbi. She turned and fled out of reach.

'It was the last time I saw Sarbi,' Sergeant D says now. He was crushed. She was so close.

The last American Humvee in the convoy was driving past and he had no choice but to run after it and jump on the open tray at the rear. The next vehicle was the Afghan unit and it was full and didn't have a rear tray. The US truck was his only way out of the valley. He legged it, sprinting as fast as he could.

What injuries?

D leapt up. The trooper who'd been shot through the legs was lying across-ways on a stretcher. He was in a bad way. Another injured bloke was laid up, too. Sergeant D faced out towards the back, still desperately searching for Sarbi. Another SAS trooper bolted up and jumped on but there was nowhere for him to sit. He landed with a thud on D's knee.

'Hey mate, you better not be enjoying this,' Sergeant D joked.

The wounded dog handler had an Araldite grip on the SAS bloke's webbing, so that he could lean out the truck and keep firing and fighting.

'He was sitting on my knee and I was holding him in the truck, gripping him by his webbing. He had my rifle and was shooting. That was when I first noticed my injuries—they started throbbing. The adrenalin was starting to wear off.'

Sergeant D distracted himself from his pain by focusing

on the worst-injured Aussie, whose eyes were starting to close. Not a good sign.

'Mate, look at me. What's going on?' D said whenever his eyes closed. Sergeant D wanted to keep him awake to prevent him going into shock. Later, back in the hospital, the injured soldier told Sergeant D that he wasn't slipping into unconsciousness when he closed his eyes.

'He just didn't want to look at me because my face was cut up and looked pretty horrible. I didn't know how bad it was,' D says now.

The convoy was picking up speed, bouncing across the terrain, heading for Anaconda. They were about 600 metres from the gates when one of the soldiers spotted Sarbi chasing the vehicles, following her handler. Sergeant D couldn't see her, but he yelled her name at the top of his voice, hoping she'd follow.

The convoy was roaring across the country. The men were firing out both sides of the truck and the rear trays of the trucks, Wild West-style, letting loose with their dwindling ammunition. They wouldn't have survived much longer without an ammo drop. *No point worrying about that now.*

The enemy maintained their offensive until the convoy was about 300 metres from the perimeter of the firebase, where soldiers were on full alert, manning every position to repel the encroaching insurgents.

The vehicles couldn't stop to get Sarbi, though every man wanted to. She was a soldier just like them, never to be left behind, but they had too many injured soldiers, some of them with life-threatening wounds. The wounded were the priority.

One American was dead and several were injured. The Afghan interpreter was fighting for his life. Nine of the twelve Australians on the operation were hit—one of them was also fighting for his life and five were seriously wounded.

'There was a mate of mine there who actually got shot in the head and he survived,' Donno said later. 'Seeing that, and realising he actually got a bullet through his head and he got up and kept fighting for the rest of us—that's how close it came for us there.'

The two SAS boys who weren't injured, including Donaldson, had bullet holes through their clothes and gear. 'That's how lucky we are,' he said.

Finally, with the sun settling behind the mountains, the convoy of Humvees raced through the gates at FOB Anaconda. Between 30 and 90 Taliban and insurgent fighters had been killed in the three-hour-long ambush that had stretched over four kilometres through the valley.

A medevac chopper arrived soon after, its rotors burning and turning. It was too dangerous to attempt a 'dust off' while the ambush was rolling. The crew was ready to pick up the most seriously wounded men and get them to the well-equipped field hospitals at Tarin Kot. The injured were laid out on stretchers for assessment and triage. The three most seriously wounded, including Rob Maylor and the young bloke Sergeant D had kept awake, were further stabilised and loaded on the chopper and flown out first.

One of the US medics gave D a shot of morphine with an autoinjector, but it had little effect.

'I think they might have put it into my notebook in my

trousers,' he says. An intravenous line was inserted and the pain that had been marshalling force began to subside.

An hour later, as blackness descended on the district of Khas Uruzgan, the medevac chopper made its second run from Anaconda to Tarin Kot with Sergeant D and two others on board. D was bound for an operating table at the Dutch-run hospital. As he was loaded up, someone clocked him in the forehead with the butt of an M4 rifle, leaving an instant bruise.

'I had to explain that one when I got to the hospital,' he says with a laugh.

In total, six of the nine wounded Australians were medevaced. Three were treated at the base and returned to action within days.

'This is the largest number of casualties suffered in a single contact since the Vietnam War,' the Australian Defence Force spokesman Brigadier Brian Dawson said in Canberra the following day.

The soldier with life-threatening injuries was flown to the high-tech combat hospital in Germany, where his family joined him. Three of Sergeant D's fellow wounded had returned to Australia for ongoing medical treatment within days of the ambush. The remaining five stayed in Afghanistan.

As Dawson said: 'It is important to note that the incident has not affected the operational tempo of the SOTG, which continues to be extremely effective in its ability to disrupt Taliban extremists' command and control processes and support structures.'

He also noted that Uruzgan remained a dangerous place, especially since the ISAF forces were fighting 'in areas which coalition soldiers have not been [in] before . . . They are moving and contesting [the Taliban] in their heartland areas and I think we can expect more heavy fighting.'

The following day, Prime Minister Kevin Rudd praised the soldiers and said they were 'engaged in a vital mission'. 'It's the men and women of the Australian Defence Force like those who put themselves in harm's way last night that are taking the fight to this enemy of us all.'

Yet nowhere in the official version of the battle was there any mention of EDD Sarbi—not that she'd been in the firefight or that she had gone missing after it was over. But word of the dog's MIA status spread quickly among the soldiers in Afghanistan and, in no time, was relayed to Australia.

Back in Sydney, the blokes at the SME were rocked by the news of Sarbi's disappearance. 'A lot of the guys did feel it,' said chief trainer Sergeant Damian Dunne. 'We class them as our best mates. It was devastating.'

Chapter 19

EDD SARBI MIA

Sarbi was listed as Missing in Action, the first Australian military working dog to be lost during an operation in Afghanistan. Sergeant D was stricken. But he reckoned his devoted mongrel would try to make her way back to the remote firebase. She had a nose trained to track familiar scents and a store of memories of familiar places. And, typically dog-like, she had an inbuilt GPS for direction. Stories abounded of extraordinarily dogged canines that had survived against the odds in the harshest of environments or had been lost for weeks, months and even years and miraculously found their way home—even after their two-legged families had moved.

An Australian cattle dog Sophie Tucker fell off a boat in shark-infested waters in north Queensland and swam five nautical miles to an uninhabited island and survived by hunting wild baby goats for four months before she was found. In 2007, an Iraqi desert dog with cut-off ears famously adopted a group of US Marines, who dubbed him Nubs for his missing lobes. The Marines were banned from keeping stray dogs as pets and left the dog at a remote fort when their fast-moving convoy moved to the Jordanian border 110 kilometres away. But Nubs wasn't one to obey official orders. He tracked down his beloved Marine, Major Brian Dennis, in a two-day odyssey across inhospitable, snowbound terrain. Dennis also defied orders to get rid of Nubs and began a mercy mission to repatriate the mutt back to the United States, where he now lives with the soft-hearted Marine. Nubs is a canine celebrity. He has appeared on American TV chat shows and a book has been written about him.

Sergeant D remembered a training session a month earlier, when the headstrong Sarbi picked up a scent and got lost in her olfactory world. He called her off, but she was out of hearing range and kept going, determined to find whatever odour the wind was delivering into her nostrils. D let her go, amused at her tenacity. Suddenly, Sarbi stopped. She realised she was on her own, without her trusted handler. She swung around, searching for the soldier, who was now a couple of hundred metres away, out of her line of sight and well beyond hearing range. She swivelled her head around one way—nothing—then the other way. Still nothing.

D could see Sarbi's uncertainty. *Oh no, where's my master?* He yelled her name at the top of his voice and waved his arms above his head, tossing a tennis ball in the air.

Sarbi began to retrace her tracks, looking around in circles for Sergeant D. Finally she tracked his voice.

Rafi and Sarbi as pups with brothers Marcelo (left) and Nic, at home in Bowral in November 2002. Rafi automatically gravitated to Marcelo and his sister, Gemma, and Sarbi loved snuggling on Nic's lap even when fully grown. (Courtesy Wendy Upjohn and family)

On 19 June 2005 Corporal Murray Young (left) from the Explosive Dog Detection Section adopted the much-loved Rafi and Sarbi (right) from the heavy-hearted Wendy and Carlos and kids. (Courtesy Wendy Upjohn and family)

There's no dispute about who reigns as Top Dog at the School of Military Engineering. As the sign declares, dogs and their handlers have right of way. (Courtesy Sandra Lee)

New recruit, EDD 436 Sarbi, easily identifiable by her zig-zag white blaze, breezed through her initial employment training at the EDD Section in Holsworthy, Sydney. (© Commonwealth of Australia)

Sergeant D shows the safest and most efficient way to carry the 27-kilogram Sarbi if she is injured on operations. He would also be fully armed and loaded with his backpack weighing more than 40 kilograms. (© Commonwealth of Australia)

Sarbi was a quick learner and easily mastered the intricacies of scent imprinting. She also added a few tricks to her professional repertoire, like shaking paws with Sergeant D for a job well done. (© Commonwealth of Australia)

Sapper Pete 'Lucy' Lawlis guides his nose-driven EDD Merlin at an Afghan market outside the wire at Tarin Kot in April 2007. The blue heeler cross was rescued from a pound in Queensland and nicknamed 'Tipdog'. (© Commonwealth of Australia)

EDD Nova, who survived an IED blast, sits on the floor of a Bushmaster en route to a search mission in Uruzgan. Notice how happy the hound looks. Work time is playtime for the dogs. (© Commonwealth of Australia)

Sarbi and Sergeant D were ready for action as soon as they landed in Afghanistan on their first tour together in 2007. (Courtesy Lyndell Brown and Charles Green)

Looking after the dogs' health is serious business and Sarbi was repeatedly checked for diseases during her deployments to Afghanistan. Her medical records were kept on computer by the US Army's veterinary corps. (© Commonwealth of Australia)

The four-legged soldiers like Nova have a high-tech wardrobe for going into battle including custom-made goggles, called Doggles, and 'puppy Peltors' to protect their ears. (© Commonwealth of Australia)

A heavily armed Sergeant D and his trusted Sarbi find some shade during an operation outside Tarin Kot in July 2007. Sarbi is wearing her stylish red booties to protect her paws from the heat. (© Commonwealth of Australia)

Pup-a-boo. Sarbi peers over the back of a US Army Humvee on which she frequently rode while on joint US, Australian and Afghan missions as part of SOTG7. (© Commonwealth of Australia)

Sergeant D (far left) helps lower Merlin's coffin into a grave at Camp Holland. The three-year-old blue heeler cross was accidentally killed on operations on 31 August 2007. Merlin was buried with a photograph of his mutt-mate, FloJo, to keep him company. (© Commonwealth of Australia)

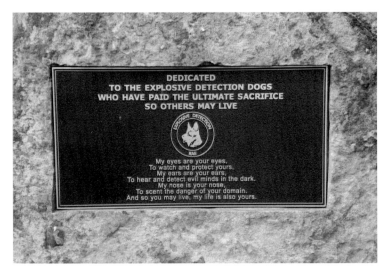

A poignant memorial was built at the School of Military Engineering in Holsworthy in 2007 to honour the dogs killed in Afghanistan since they were first deployed there in 2005, including Merlin, Razz, Andy, Nova and Herbie. (Courtesy Sandra Lee)

Explosive detection dogs Harry, Bundy and Tank sit behind a portrait of their fallen brothers in arms, Sapper Darren Smith and his dog, Herbie, who were killed by an IED on 7 June 2010. Fellow Sapper Jacob Moerland was also killed in the attack. (© Commonwealth of Australia)

In March 2009, EDD 435 Rafi (left) and his canine companions Aussie, Que and Mandy were presented with the War Dog Operational Medal for performing their duties in war conditions. Rafi died of snakebite later that year. (© Commonwealth of Australia)

The Doggies make the most of a break between operations to take a group photograph on a tank. (© Commonwealth of Australia)

Sarbi soaks her paws after a long, hot day on patrol sniffing for deadly weapons and lethal IEDs outside the wire. Sergeant D checked her for injuries and illness every day. (© Commonwealth of Australia)

It's a dog's life: Sarbi uses her handler's stomach as a pillow while having a snooze. The bond between the four-legged and two-legged soldiers is unbreakable. (© Commonwealth of Australia)

Sarbi meets Prime Minister Kevin Rudd and US General Stanley McChrystal at the SAS HQ in Camp Russell on 11 November 2009, the day her homecoming was announced. Defence Minister Senator John Faulkner and the Chief of the Defence Force Angus Houston look on. (© Commonwealth of Australia)

Sarbi trots across the flight line after hitching a ride back to Camp Holland from FOB Anaconda on a US Army CH-47 Chinook helicopter in October 2009. A US Special Forces soldier negotiated her return from the Taliban leader who 'dognapped' her after she went missing during a life-and-death battle on 2 September 2008.
(© Commonwealth of Australia)

When Sarbi returned to her fellow Diggers after MIA for thirteen months she was five kilograms heavier and a lot dirtier. Her first order of business was a bath, followed by a special meal before going on a doggie diet.
(© Commonwealth of Australia)

The Australian soldiers knew for sure they had found Sarbi when she obsessively began chasing her beloved tennis balls across the rock-strewn base, a habit formed when she was a puppy growing up in Bowral with her first loving family. (© Commonwealth of Australia)

Sarbi enjoys Christmas with her Aussie mates in 2009 and received gift-wrapped presents under the tree, as well as a meaty bone from Santa. (© Commonwealth of Australia)

Calling doggie Doctor Freud! Soldiers ham it up with Sarbi and put her through Return to Australian Psychological Screening while she waits to get the all clear to return home. (© Commonwealth of Australia)

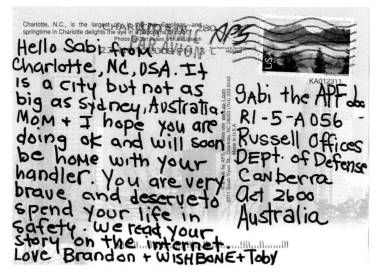

Hello Sabi from Charlotte, NC, USA. It is a city but not as big as Sydney, Australia. Mom + I hope you are doing ok and will soon be home with your handler. You are very brave and deserve to spend your life in safety. We read your story on the internet. Love Brandon + WISHBONE + Toby

Gabi the APF
RI-5-A056 -
Russell Offices
DEPT. of Defense
Canberra
Act 2600
Australia

Sarbi was an instant pupstar at Camp Holland after she returned from her missing months in Afghanistan and received postcards from dog lovers around the world wishing her well, not to mention a safe and speedy homecoming. (© Commonwealth of Australia)

In May 2010 Sergeant D, then on his third deployment to Afghanistan, walks Sarbi to a waiting RAAF C-130 Hercules at Tarin Kot to begin the first leg of her long but final journey home to Australia. She spent another six months in Dubai to meet quarantine conditions before arriving home in December. (© Commonwealth of Australia)

On 5 April 2011 the RSPCA awarded Sarbi the prestigious Purple Cross for outstanding service to humans. It was her third medal for wartime activities. Sarbi follows in the hoofsteps of Murphy, a donkey who ferried injured soldiers to safety in World War One. (Courtesy Sandra Lee)

Artists Lyndell Brown and Charles Green painted Sarbi and Sargeant D in 2010 after photographing them in Afghanistan in 2007. Oil on linen and measuring 31cm by 31cm, the portrait has toured Australia and now hangs in the Australian War Memorial in Canberra. (Courtesy Lyndell Brown and Charles Green)

'She came bolting over to me. It was almost as if she was saying, *I was busy searching, what happened?*' he says now.

Sergeant D hoped Sarbi would show the same tenacity now she was out in Khas Uruzgan on her own.

Before Sergeant D flew out of FOB Anaconda he asked his mates from the SAS and US Special Forces to keep an eye out for the black dog. Many of the soldiers were dog people with their own pets at home, and Sarbi had become a much-loved member of the team.

'Let me know as soon as you hear anything,' he said.

'No worries, mate.'

Some went one better. A couple of the guys went through Sergeant D's gear and left sweaty clothes at strategic points around the perimeter fence and front gates of Anaconda, hoping Sarbi would pick up D's scent and be lured back to base by her nose. The dog handler knew the Special Forces boys would have Sarbi's back. That is, if she was alive.

The next day Sergeant D was under the surgeon's knife at the Dutch-Australian hospital at Tarin Kot.

'They basically scrubbed me with a wire brush and pulled out all the frag and stitched me up,' he says now. 'The padre came around and gave me a medallion for healing. I'm not religious, but I still took it from him because it gave me something to focus on.'

The commanding officer of the Special Operations Task Group met with the wounded soldiers at Tarin Kot and the story of the battle made headlines back in Australia, though minus the drama of the ambush. The CO reported all nine of the injured men were faring well and 'morale is high'.

But Sergeant D was frustrated. He was itching to get back out there to find Sarbi. He'd received intel from the soldiers at Anaconda that his dog had been seen wandering outside the base. 'The Special Forces boys are awesome that way; they always have someone there to let you know what was going on,' he says.

A senior Australian military official said later that Sarbi had returned to the base she'd been calling home but the dog-averse Afghan guards had shooed her away.

The US Special Forces soldiers had developed a good relationship with the villagers in the Khas Uruzgan district, through a series of food-for-work and cash-for-work projects they'd been conducting with the US Agency for International Development (USAID). They also helped repair the key mosque in the district, and were building an irrigation canal with the locals. Hearts and minds. The goal was to empower the Afghan population and improve their lives while reducing their support for and reliance on the Taliban. The strengthening relationship had tangential benefits: it provided for *quid pro quo*. We help you, you help us. *Pashtunwali*.

Nine days after the ambush, covered in bruises and with a row of neatly stitched sutures holding his wounds together, Sergeant D and another soldier returned to FOB Anaconda on a mission. Recover Sarbi. The operation was strategic and methodical.

The US military intelligence staff recorded messages about Sarbi in Pashto and Dari and broadcast them over the public address system and local radio stations. They asked villagers to pass on any information they might have about the missing dog and gave instructions about how they could give her back. 'An Afghan version of a lost-and-found notice,' an Australian Defence spokesman said.

Conflicting intelligence filtered back. Sarbi had been sighted at one village, then another. Sarbi had been shot dead. But the information was rated as single source intelligence and therefore wasn't reliable; none of it could be adequately confirmed. The Afghan culture is an oral culture, and stories about Sarbi were passed from villager to villager as if in a game of Chinese whispers.

'It was pretty hard hearing all those things,' Sergeant D says now. 'But we couldn't act on it.'

Afghan police in the region reported that a local Taliban commander Mullah Hamdullah had Sarbi in his possession. It was a strong lead. Hamdullah, who was in his mid-thirties, was one of two or three Taliban leaders in the region and had been vying for power with another Afghan. Sarbi would be seen as a status symbol, a prize of war. According to a former Dutch diplomat and independent political analyst presently based in Kabul, Hamdullah was proud of his war booty and paraded her around.

Martine van Bijlert is fluent in Dari and has spent more than eleven years in various roles with government bodies and non-government organisations in Afghanistan, Iran and Pakistan. She meets regularly with Afghan people and has a good and open relationship with them. One of the tribal elders from the area had recently told her that Sarbi had taken refuge in a building after the bombs and rockets had stopped flying and the ambush was over. A local boy ventured out to gather spent cartridges from the firefight as soon as the coalition soldiers had left the bullet-strewn valley and the Taliban retreated from the area around Ana Kalay. The boy was rummaging around the building when he found Sarbi and took her home.

'As soon as Mullah Hamdullah heard about it—it was still the same day—he came and collected the dog,' van Bijlert says now. 'He took it and was very proud of it.'

Hamdullah's father had been arrested. The coalition forces used the local radio to spread the word that the old man would be released if the son returned Sarbi to the US firebase.

'It was not Hamdullah who tried to trade,' says van Bijlert.

But the Taliban commander rejected the dad-for-dog swap. 'I am not sure why,' she says. 'Maybe he wanted to show he was dominant and he didn't want to cave in.'

Or perhaps Hamdullah thought the highly trained explosive detection dog was more valuable to him than his father. It is possible he wanted to keep Sarbi to trade her at a later date when the stakes were higher. The Taliban knew that NATO troops did their best to retrieve equipment left on the battlefield or destroy it if that was not possible, not that the latter would befall Sarbi. Hamdullah might also have wanted to use Sarbi as collateral in the internecine world of tribal politics and Taliban power plays. Nothing would surprise in Afghanistan, where alliances shift as quickly as they form.

Eventually, Hamdullah's father was released but Sarbi's whereabouts remained a mystery.

Sergeant D says the SAS boys were keen to launch a search mission for the dog based on the intelligence, but the risks were too high. There was no telling why a bunch of hardened men, trained to fight wars in foreign lands, were willing to put their lives on the line to find a dog, but they were. Some things you just can't explain, like the bond between man and his best friend, like protecting your mates, like needing to finish a mission. Problem was, they just couldn't do it. The troopers were restricted by operation orders and rescuing a missing dog wasn't on them. It didn't matter how precious Sarbi was and how well she'd performed her duty. The brass simply would not risk the lives of their elite soldiers to find Sarbi.

The soldiers accepted the logic of war and understood the rationale behind it. But it still felt like a kick in the guts. So they did what resourceful Special Forces do. They adapted. Whenever they went out on patrol, they kept an eye out for Sarbi. They gathered intel, slowly, day by day, week by week.

Sergeant D spent ten exasperating days at Anaconda. Because of his injuries he was not permitted to leave the base. He hammered away at the intelligence to pinpoint Sarbi's location. He walked the boundaries of the firebase repeatedly, scanning the horizon with binoculars, searching to no avail. He bombarded his American mates as soon as they returned from patrols. They returned empty-handed. No news.

The dog handler returned to Tarin Kot in mid-September.

The herringbone of stitches was removed from his wounds. He was cleared to return to active duty. But he was without a dog and there were no free canines with which to work. Sergeant D was reassigned to the Persons Under Control (PUC) unit for the final ten weeks of his deployment. He conducted biometric assessments and processed suspected Taliban and insurgent captives who had been brought in by SOTG soldiers. He fingerprinted them and took iris scans and DNA samples. The PUCs were then either sent elsewhere for interrogation or freed to return to their homes. Sergeant D also did one final mission outside the wire on a combined Australian–British patrol.

Sergeant D missed Sarbi and his hands-on role as a dog handler. He kept his lines of communication open with the American Special Forces boys. He never lost faith she would be found.

'I was hopeful,' he says now. 'I always hoped that she was still out there because nothing definite had been said either way.'

But he was troubled by a niggling thought.

'It was always in the back of my mind that I would never see Sarbi again.'

Sarbi went missing in action on the cusp of winter, when sub-zero temperatures, snow and fierce blizzards did cruel things to the landscape and those who inhabited it. She had survived the initial contact and shrapnel wounds, dodged enemy weapons and terrain booby-trapped with lethal landmines and IEDs. But how would she survive beyond the razor-wire perimeter of the Australian base without the constant care and supervision of her handler? Sergeant D hoped like hell his beloved dog wouldn't suffer the same tragic fate as the three Australian explosive detection dogs who had been killed in action in Afghanistan. The deaths of those little Diggers, as they were dubbed, had been soul-destroying. He didn't dare think of what the Afghans might do to her.

Sergeant D returned to Australia on 13 November 2008. His deployment was complete but it felt hollow. Leaving Sarbi weighed heavily on him. This was the first time he had exited an operation without his four-legged partner. He was like a kid whose puppy had been taken away.

'I was pretty upset leaving Afghanistan,' he says.

On 16 January 2009 the ambush in Khas Uruzgan was back in the headlines, dominating the hungry beast of the news cycle.

SAS Corporal Mark Gregor Strang Donaldson was presented with the Victoria Cross for his courage under fire in Ana Kalay on 2 September 2008, during a dignified ceremony at Canberra's Government House, attended by his wife and young daughter. A retinue of SAS troopers decked out in civilian gear and wearing sunglasses to protect their identities crowded the back of the fancy room, quietly proud of their mate.

'You have cradled life in your arms and opened your heart to its meaning,' the Governor-General Quentin Bryce told him. 'By your doing and knowing, you will shoulder more than most. You are the finest example and inspiration.'

Donno was the first soldier to receive the prestigious medal since the Vietnam War; the ninety-seventh Australian awarded the highest recognition for gallantry under fire the country has to offer.

'I don't see myself as a hero, honestly,' he said after the pomp and ceremony was done. 'I still see myself as a soldier first and foremost. I'm a soldier. I'm trained to fight, that's what we do. It's instinct and it's natural. And you don't really think about it at the time. I just saw [the interpreter] there; I went over there and got him. That was it.'

No false modesty, no barely concealed sense of grandiosity. Just an honest bloke doing an honest, heroic job.

Later, when Donaldson was asked by a journalist how far he had sprinted across enemy ground, he replied with his trademark verbal continence: 'Oh, look, I don't know . . . You know, I didn't have a tape measure there.'

The newspapers and television stations hailed the modern day hero, who did his genuine best to deflect the attention and share the honour and glory with the mates who had fought with him in Khas Uruzgan. As Donaldson said, there were eleven other heroes on the mission.

But the media was missing a prized piece of the puzzle, the thirteenth hero.

Sarbi.

The military hierarchy still had not released the news of the explosive detection dog's disappearance. It was as if Sarbi had never existed. Behind the scenes, though, the hound had not been forgotten, especially by the tight-knit Special Forces community in Afghanistan. Always faithful, ever loyal, perpetually playful, Sarbi had gotten under their collective skins. The soldiers lived by the credo of never leaving a fallen comrade behind and their four-legged comrade was no different. If Sarbi was alive, they would find her. No matter how long it took. She might not have been on the official radar, but she was in their collective consciousness.

'Plans were prepared to retrieve her, should the situation allow,' a defence spokesman later confirmed.

*

Sergeant D had been teamed with a new dog, Tana. He was a dopey Lab, easily influenced by moods.

'You have to be the alpha dog, show him you're not worried or upset. With him, you can't get angry because he won't do anything,' D says now.

Tana is motivated by a hunt drive, not a retrieval drive. When he first deployed with his handler to Afghanistan in 2010, Tana caught five chickens during the deployment, including a couple of sickly birds. Hardly challenging. 'The Afghan soldiers had to pay the locals and then left the chickens for them,' he says.

Sergeant D suspects his expectations might be too high.

'The dogs have to be on the ball all the time. Tana can work well and he does work well, but he needs a lot of work to get him to the standard and a lot of work to keep him at the standard. I measure all dogs against Sarbi.'

Tana was no Sarbi.

Sergeant D still held a candle for his single-minded Newfie–Lab cross a year after she went MIA. Harder heads had given up on her, but he wouldn't hear of it.

Sergeant D was on a promotion course at the School of Military Engineering in October 2009 when he took a phone call from his old boss, Corporal Murray Young.

It was around midday Sydney time; 0700 hours in Tarin Kot where Young was then deployed with Rafi, who had already notched up a stint in the Solomon Islands and was proving as adroit at bomb detection as his sister.

'Mate, we think we've got Sarbi,' Young said. 'Have you got a picture you can email over?'

Sergeant D was ecstatic. Murray wouldn't be taking the

mickey. He had a vested interest in getting Sarbi back. D emailed a photograph of Sarbi to Camp Russell and waited for confirmation.

The early intelligence was right. The ever-resourceful pooch had used her canine charms and made a new home amid the Afghan people.

Mullah Hamdullah had had Sarbi since the ambush thirteen months earlier. She had made the best of her new surroundings, even though her Afghan existence could not have been more removed from the intense relationship she had with Sergeant D.

But for some unknown reason, Sarbi had worn thin her welcome. Afghan elders told Martine van Bijlert that Hamdullah had engaged a local *malek* to help him do a deal. A *malek* is a member of the community, viewed by many as a man of integrity and with a reputation for dealing with government officials. He was from a different tribe to Hamdullah and was not Taliban, says van Bijlert. The *malek* also served another function—NATO forces wouldn't arrest him as an enemy combatant.

Hamdullah dispatched the *malek* to Anaconda to propose a deal. Hamdullah would sell the dog for a fee. The princely sum of US$10,000 was rumoured. 'I don't think it's a fixed price tag. Again, it could be one of the different details,' says van Bijlert, who had been told about the doggie drama by locals.

The US soldiers told the *malek* the US army required proof of life to ensure the dog was Sarbi, the lost Australian explosive detection dog. The Americans have more than 300 of their own bomb-sniffing, tracker and sentry dogs in

Afghanistan. Many of the soldiers regard them as more reliable—and loving—than metal detectors.

US Special Forces don't mess around. They refused to exchange money until they saw the dog. Establishing proof of life was standard operating procedure in ransom and hostage situations, even a canine version.

The *malek* dutifully returned with a photograph of Sarbi on his mobile phone, and the Americans recognised her beautiful black face and white blaze. She looked pretty healthy, too. She hadn't gone hungry during her time in Khas Uruzgan, unlike the unkempt, half-starved mutts native to Afghanistan. Still, no deal. The US soldier told the *malek* to bring the dog.

The *malek* made good on his end of the deal and returned to Anaconda with Sarbi.

A US Special Forces soldier known as John noted she was in good condition—even though she hadn't been washed in a year. Sarbi was eager to please. Her ears pricked up, her front paws danced on the ground in excitement and her tongue hung at a lopsided angle from her mouth, anticipating contact. She flicked her snout up and tossed her head to the side as if to say, *throw the ball*.

John took the dog's demeanour as a sign of encouragement.

He gave Sarbi some commands in English, albeit with an American accent.

Pant, pant, pant, wag, wag, wag. Sarbi's body shook side to side from head to tail, wobbling with pure joy. This was a language she could understand.

The soldier tossed a tennis ball. Sarbi responded in an

instant. Her reaction was proof positive of her pedigree and provenance. She was the Aussie's MIA EDD—the missing-in-action explosive detection dog.

'Good girl,' John said, giving the canine warrior a pat.

He clipped a leash to her collar, handed the *malek* a small amount of money—not the promised $10,000 jackpot—and walked back inside the base with the dog. Coalition soldiers have access to discretionary sums of money for payment to locals, to settle grievances and right wrongs in accordance with accepted cultural practice.

'Hamdullah was not happy with how it turned out,' van Bijlert says now. 'The *malek* still owed him for getting the dog back cheaply.'

She believes the Taliban leader was killed in a coalition airstrike in 2010.

The Special Forces boys put Sarbi on a US Army CH-47 Chinook helo as soon as possible and she was flown to Camp Russell in Tarin Kot.

Corporal Young recognised Sarbi as soon as she leapt out of the chopper. This was home. Sarbi raced over the rocky airfield. Young nudged a tennis ball to her with his foot and Sarbi took it straight away. 'It's a game we used to play over and over during training,' he said. 'It's amazing, just incredible to have her back.'

Sarbi was a little greyer around the muzzle and she had gotten fat. Her extra bulk had nothing to do with the winter coat she was growing in, in preparation for another season in sub-zero temperatures. The mongrel usually weighed in at 27 kilograms but came home a very healthy 32 kilograms.

'Either they were feeding her very well or she was getting into their food stores,' Sergeant D says with a laugh. 'I'm thinking probably the second.'

Sarbi was sent to the United States Veterinary Corps in Kandahar to have her microchip scanned for verification and she received a full medical check-up. The American vets look after all the dogs in Afghanistan and boast one of the most sophisticated animal clinics in the country. They conducted doggie blood drives and stored all six canine blood types for emergencies in a high-tech operating theatre. 'When you know some of these dogs are saving others' lives you place a very high priority on caring for them,' said one US Army vet. 'And when you hear a story first hand about how the dog on your exam table saved others' lives by finding explosives planted on a vehicle or beneath it, it really validates [the dog's] importance in the war effort.'

The microchip in Sarbi's shoulder positively identified her as EDD 436, a member of the Australian Army, Royal Australian Engineers, School of Military Engineering, Explosive Detection Dog Section.

The American vets gave Sarbi the all clear. The greatest fear was that she'd contracted rabies, a common disease in Afghanistan, but she hadn't. Her pads were fine. No sign of coughs or worms or parasites, any of which would prevent her ultimate return to Australia.

Sarbi had defied the odds.

'I was over the moon,' Sergeant D recalls.

Sarbi received a hero's welcome at Camp Russell.

The black mutt got her first bath in a year. She was soaped up and got a good scrubbing while posing for the cameras. She lapped up the attention. Her shining coat now had the look and touch of black velvet. She was a prima donna dog. A box of tennis balls was brought out and Sarbi, true to form, was back in business, thundering across the rocky ground to fetch.

It was as if she'd never gone missing.

Chapter 20

MUTT MORALE

Sarbi was a high-octane shot of morale for the men and women at Camp Russell, a welcome distraction from the ever-present spectre of death and destruction beyond the wire. They could use a boost.

Five days before Sarbi returned to her army family, a fellow explosive detection dog, Nova, was killed. The two-year-old black and white mongrel died from injuries sustained in a car crash during a training exercise with her handler inside the base.

Nova had been adopted from an animal shelter on the Sunshine Coast in Queensland. The staff spotted the intelligent dog's obsession with balls and thought she would make a great bomb-sniffing hound for the army. Nova passed the initial trial and was shipped to Sydney for the EDD training course. Fully qualified, she joined the Townsville-based 3CER with her handler Sapper Rueben Griggs.

She was a popular and successful addition to the task force in Afghanistan. Her face was almost albino-white, topped with a black nose and translucent pink ears held aloft like wimples. The mutt had had a tough start in life and came to the army with a stumpy tail, the result of either a mishap at birth or accident along the way. Griggs carried a big red plastic bowl on operations and she rarely left his side. When riding in the back of the MAC troop transport truck she stood up, paws perched on Griggs's lap, while peering over the heads of soldiers, her nose in the wind and dust.

A month before Nova died, she starred in Operation Baz Panje, one of the largest air mobile missions in Uruzgan. The operation aimed to route the Taliban from the Mirabad Valley, where they had operated unchallenged for seven years. By then, the lightweight dog was battle-hardened. She had recently survived an IED blast while riding in the back of a Bushmaster with Griggs. Fellow engineer Sapper Tristen Westkamp from 3CER suffered a fractured jaw and cuts to his face and mouth. 'There was no noise, just the desert coming up to meet me,' Westkamp said. 'Afterwards we were dragged out by our Doggie, Sapper Rueben Griggs, who was in the back with his dog Nova. When I woke up I thought "What a rush". Now I have a lot of faith in the Bushmaster. Anything else and I would be dead.'

The regimental medical officer at Camp Russell put Nova down when it was determined she would not survive the injuries suffered in the accident. The soldiers were heartbroken. EDD 472 Nova was the fourth member of the Doggies killed in Afghanistan. The soldiers held a ceremony at the base and formed a guard of honour when her coffin was carried up the back of a RAAF Hercules for her return to Australia.

No wonder Sarbi lightened the load. She became the unofficial mascot in charge of morale as she padded around the sprawling forward operating base on her daily rounds. Soldiers hammed it up with her and Sarbi played along. She seemed to divine that her extra-curricular duties now included mood management and being extra cute. She roamed their offices and supervised soldiers at work. The cooks treated her with raw chicken necks and photographed her gnawing away as if she'd never been fed—a typical Labrador response to food.

Sarbi went through the mandatory Return To Australia Psychological Screening—known as an RTAPS debrief—in which she sprawled on a chaise longue, Freud-style, while a soldier took notes of what she had been through.

If only she could talk!

The question everyone wanted answered was how Sarbi had survived in such dramatically changed circumstances?

One can imagine her constantly in peril, sniffing out the explosives and weapons she had been trained to detect, staring patiently at her dangerous finds. She'd be wondering why her new 'handlers' weren't calling her off and telling her 'good girl, Sarbi, attagirl' and tossing her a tennis ball, like Sergeant D used to. Did her temporary owners even have a ball for her?

What did the local Afghans make of the intelligent dog

whose nose never stopped working? Did they ask her to do tasks for which she was never trained? Did they take her on missions with them? Had they tried to turn her against her comrades, her Australian Army family? Did she growl at their foreign dress, like she did when on patrol with her handler Sergeant D? Did she get on with the children? Where did she sleep? Was she moved from *quala* to *quala* by Hamdullah to keep her hidden from coalition forces? What mangy mutts did she play with?

The missing months prompted journalist Misha Schubert to speculate humorously that Sarbi had been on a top-secret undercover mission all along. 'You can see it now: Sabi (sic) swathed in the cornflower blue of an Afghan *burqa*, the only clue to her real identity a glimpse of paw beneath its crimped hem.'

There was no denying Sarbi's appeal. Her story reached the highest political office.

Australian Prime Minister Kevin Rudd flew into Camp Russell on 10 November 2009 with the Chief of the Australian Defence Force, Angus Houston, and the Minister for Defence, Senator John Faulkner. Travelling with them under a cone of silence was a small, hand picked media contingent including Katharine Murphy from *The Age* and veteran political reporter Malcolm Farr from the *Daily Telegraph*.

That night the dignitaries were guests of honour at an Australian-themed barbeque in Poppy's Bar, where the commanding officer handed out achievement awards to his troop and the prime minister presented the soldiers with a new coffee machine. Murphy thought the huge roll-out was for the prime minister but the Diggers assured her it was for the food. When VIPs come to town, the quality of the tucker improves markedly and while there's no beer, they make do with a substitute the Diggers dubbed 'Near Beer'.

With the presentation night under way, the commander called out each soldier's name. Each shuffled through the applauding group to the front of the recreation room, where they were handed a certificate in recognition of their performance.

'Private X,' the commander hollered.

X moved to the front. Salute.

'Thank you, Sir.'

The exercise was repeated with military efficiency for 'Private Y.' Salute.

'Thank you, Sir.' Handshake.

'Private Z.'

No movement.

'Private Z.'

Silence.

'*Private* Z,' the CO called, this time louder.

'Redraw,' a Digger up the back wisecracked.

'I will crack the jokes around here,' the CO retorted, to howls of laughter.

Says Farr, 'It was my favourite moment of the trip.'

The amiable event underscored the gravity of the meeting the next morning. Prime Minister Rudd and his cohorts were to meet with United States Army General Stanley McChrystal, the go-to man for fighting the Taliban and anti-coalition militia. It was a crucial time for the war. The outlook was depressing, as McChrystal had written in his recent appraisal to the president. 'Inadequate resources will likely result in failure. While the situation is serious, success is still achievable.' The general's singular mission was to fulfil President Obama's mantra of 'disrupt, dismantle and defeat' the enemy in Afghanistan.

EDD Sarbi had been doing just that as part of the Australian war effort.

Rudd had been briefed on the shaggy dog story and was taken by Sarbi's extraordinary tale. Why not introduce the four-legged top dog of war to her two-legged counterpart?

Rudd had it all worked out. After breakfast with the SAS troopers he led the general outside the mess tent to where Sarbi was sitting quietly beside her handler. McChrystal appeared slightly confused about meeting a dog, says Murphy. But, being part diplomat, part warrior, he played his role for international relations and knelt down to pet Sarbi. She accepted the attention with aplomb and greeted the stranger with a sniff and a lick. 'She showed no signs of stress,' wrote Katharine Murphy in *The Age*.

Rudd couldn't contain himself. Grinning widely, he hailed Sarbi as a 'loyal daughter of Australia' and said her return sent a significant message about the nation's contribution to the war in Afghanistan. '[It] may seem quite small, but in fact the symbolism is quite strong, and the symbolism of it is us out there doing a job. Sarbi is back home in one piece and she's a genuinely nice pooch, as well.'

Cameras moved in tight for their close-ups of Sarbi flanked by the prime minister and general. Shutters clicked and whirred. Farr and Murphy, seasoned journalists with decades of political reporting between them, understood the value of the story.

'There we were at this strategic moment of great import for the Americans who were at a key decision-making point with their policy on Afghanistan,' Murphy says now. 'It was a global moment of importance and we thought, "It will be all about the dog".'

She was right. They were on a winner.

The Australian newspapers fell in love with the hero hound and the public took her to heart. Sarbi's story went global. The pawparazzi was on her tail. The BBC in the United Kingdom focused on Sarbi's gritty canine survival. So did the Canadian national broadcaster and agencies across Europe and Asia. An EDD Sarbi fan page was established on Facebook and soon had more than 1000 friends, who left messages of support and adoration for the mutt. Sarbi received fan mail by the bagloads from people who had mistaken her wonder-dog status for an ability to read! A child from Charlotte in North Carolina sent a heartfelt postcard wishing Sarbi well. 'You are very brave and deserve to spend your life in safety. We read your story on the Internet. Love Brandon + Wishbone + Toby.'

Sarbi had become an instant part of the cultural conversation. She showed up on the social network website Twitter, as a member of a fictional panel for the ABC television current affairs show *Q&A*. Her fellow guests were Simone de Beauvoir, Winston Churchill, Hadrian and Leo Tolstoy. 'Churchill is drunk but in the morning Sarbi will still be a dog,' some wit tweeted.

At a well-attended press conference the following day, a journalist questioned the army's humanity in sending dogs to war. Later a Canberra commentator, with tongue firmly in cheek, asked if was appropriate that female dogs such as Sarbi were on the frontlines in combat. Another queried sardonically if Sarbi should be hailed a hero after, effectively, going absent without leave for thirteen months.

'Mythmaking aside, it's a great tale and the dog is cute,' Murphy says now. 'It also makes an incomprehensible conflict comprehensible. The power of the story was that it personalised and made a distant conflict have a heart and have meaning. It was pretty obvious that this was a dog with a great deal of meaning to these soldiers on the base. I don't think you can engineer or fake that. It was obvious there was a bond between the people at Camp Russell and Sarbi.'

When the news broke, SAS Corporal Donaldson was in London to meet Queen Elizabeth II at a biennial ceremony to honour recipients of the Victoria Cross and its civilian equivalent, the George Cross.

'Sarbi's the last piece of the puzzle,' he said, resplendent in full dress uniform. 'Having Sarbi back gives some closure for the handler and the rest of us that served with her in 2008. It's a fantastic morale-booster for the guys.'

Curiously, Sarbi's VIP status had even filtered back to the Afghan elders in Khas Uruzgan. One old man told Martine van Bijlert the story about Hamdullah's experience with the dog when he visited her in Kabul, where she had her headquarters. Other people in the region confirmed the details for her, even if some of the fine points differed.

The dignified elders were quietly amused that Sarbi, a dog, had had an audience with the prime minister of Australia. Not only the leader of a country, but also the most powerful military man in Afghanistan—a four-star general from the United States Army. Van Bijlert noted that one tried not to smile too broadly under his turban. 'It must have been a very high-ranking dog,' he said.

Chapter 21

PUPSTAR

Sarbi and Sergeant D were reunited in April 2010. The dog handler was back in Afghanistan with his new dog, Tana, attached to Special Operations Task Group 11. Sarbi recognised her handler immediately but, Sarbi being Sarbi, only had eyes for her tennis ball. Sergeant D also had a rival for Sarbi's affection. Like most food-obsessed Labs, she'd fallen in love with the soldier from the quartermaster stores—also dubbed the Q-ee by the soldiers—who had been feeding her. 'Fattening her with love,' says D. Food and tennis balls—nothing had changed, which told him Sarbi hadn't suffered any great trauma during her absence.

Sergeant D was on a mission to return Sarbi to peak fitness and get her back to work. He put the big girl on a diet and gave the Q-ee strict instructions to walk her twice a day whenever he and Tana were outside the wire on patrols.

Where possible, D took Sarbi on continuation training with Tana and trained the dogs together. 'No loss of skills despite not doing it for nineteen months. She is a natural,' he says. Dogs learn by example and those mutts that recognise the top dog defer to the dominant canine. Tana, an exuberant lumbering Lab with a short attention span, would learn a thing or two from Sarbi's experience.

Sarbi's popularity showed no sign of waning. She was a 'bone fide' pupstar. Visiting dignitaries lined up for photographs with the canny canine, who conned people into patting and feeding her with a simple pleading look from those beautiful eyes, crinkled brow and tilted head. Sometimes she'd sit politely, with one paw slightly raised in a pre-emptive shake. Who could deny that level of cuteness? Even the supremely coiffed Governor-General, Quentin Bryce, obliged Sarbi during a visit for the 2010 Anzac Day service at Tarin Kot. She tossed a tennis ball and knelt down in the dirt and dust of Afghanistan beside the mutt for the waiting cameras.

Sarbi was awarded the War Dog Operational Medal with Afghanistan Clasp and the Canine Service Medal to recognise five years of service. The Australian Defence Force Trackers and War Dogs Association presented the medals after gaining permission to strike the gongs for the canine warriors. Four other dogs were awarded the medals in Australia, including Rafi, who had, by now, completed his deployment and was back in Townsville with 1CER.

From May through August, Sarbi was the star attraction—in absentia—at the Australian War Memorial in Canberra. Her portrait hung in pride of place in the

Framing Conflict exhibition of war art by Lyndell Brown and Charles Green.

The most common question asked by adults and children alike was, 'when is Sarbi coming home?'

Sarbi's customs and quarantine import permit had expired during her lost months in Khas Uruzgan and her handler had to prove she was beyond reproach, health-wise. The Australian Quarantine and Inspection Service had strict veterinary and health criteria that had to be met before she was allowed home. The process was exacting and drawn out.

On 24 May, after attending an air-movements brief on the flight line at Tarin Kot, Sergeant D walked Sarbi across the rocky tarmac to load her on to a RAAF C-130 Hercules transport plane for the first leg of her journey home. He was sad to see her go. The sergeant had packed a travel box with five days' worth of food and all her official paperwork. She was bound for the United Arab Emirates—via Kanda-har and Kabul—for a six-month AQIS-mandated 'holiday' at the privately run Dubai Kennels and Cattery, a leading boarding facility and shipping operation in the UAE.

No expense was spared. Sarbi was housed in five-star luxury in her own air-conditioned kennel that led to an out-side run from where she could see her neighbours and watch the busy life of the kennels. She settled into the routine and the attentive staff exercised her three times a day, includ-ing an exclusive tennis session at noon. 'Yes, the tennis ball. Her love, her passion, her obsession—her everything!' says Sandra Popp, a senior animal handler at the kennels.

The staff didn't let Sarbi mix with the other dogs, having

been warned by the army that she wasn't overly fond of other canines, especially those she didn't know well. When it came to a hound hierarchy, Sarbi was at the very top of the chain of command!

Sarbi's star status guaranteed a long list of visitors including the Commander of Joint Task Force 633, Major General John Cantwell. Sometimes, six or seven people would show up at once wanting to see how the black mutt was getting on—all with cameras.

The six months flew by. On 8 December, Cantwell led Sarbi across the runway at the Australian Forces staging area in Kuwait, for the final leg of her Afghanistan odyssey. He wore combat fatigues. She wore a royal blue collar and an army green leash as she snuggled into her custom-built crate, opulently lined with blue carpet. Her name tag hung on the door.

Two years has passed since the explosive detection dog had left Australia as an anonymous military working dog. Now, Sarbi was returning as the country's most famous hound.

Sarbi arrived in Sydney on 10 December 2010 and spent the next month in quarantine. With a clean bill of health, she returned to the SME with Sergeant D on 9 January 2011, where she helped train new dog handlers.

Sarbi was awarded the prestigious RSPCA Australia Purple Cross at an outdoor ceremony at the Australian War Memorial in April 2011. The award recognises the deeds of animals that have shown outstanding service to humans, particularly if they've shown exceptional courage.

Sarbi was driven to Canberra for the ceremony with a

small entourage of Doggies, including Sergeant D, who was dressed in casual clothes to remain anonymous. He sat in the front row of the Australian War Memorial's sculpture garden beaming with obvious pride as Sarbi took centre stage in front of 200 Canberra school children who had been invited to the event. A posse of media had been marshalled off to one side, waiting to capture every delightful move Sarbi made. She had been given a bath for the occasion and was resplendent in the ceremonial jacket of the Incident Response Regiment. The emerald green satin coat was trimmed with white edging and emblazoned with the official regimental logo under which was embroidered the regiment's motto, To Protect. Sarbi's two square operational war medals were pinned over her left shoulder, adding to her dignified look and proof positive that she had fulfilled the credo of the IRR.

As the ceremony got underway Sarbi was still able to pull rank. The chief of the Australian Army, Lieutenant General Ken Gillespie, sat on the podium holding her leash while she sniffed the ground and focused on a leaf, no doubt wishing it was a tennis ball about to be tossed.

'I think there's no doubt that Sarbi has shown an incredible resilience and strength that should be recognised,' the RSPCA's national president Lynne Bradshaw told the crowd. 'By presenting this award to Sarbi, the RSPCA hopes to raise awareness of the role that animals play in war, the unquestioning and unwavering service to man.'

Bradshaw bent down to hang the Purple Cross around Sarbi's neck. On cue, the dog cheekily covered Bradshaw's face with licks and the children squealed with delight.

Only nine medals have been awarded to animals since the first RSPCA Australia Purple Cross was presented to a nine-year-old civilian silky terrier named Fizo in 1996. Two were backdated and awarded in honour of animals that have long since died. In all, seven have gone to civilian dogs that have saved people's lives or risked their own to protect human companions.

Fizo attacked and killed a deadly brown snake that was threatening young children and miraculously survived several snakebites himself. The other civilian dogs that have received the medal for loyalty and courage are Tank and Muck, Boots, Rockie, Wee Jock (who was acknowledged posthumously) and Anzac. The last dog, Anzac, is a tenacious, deaf, four-year-old blue heeler that almost knocked his owner's bedroom door down to alert her to a house fire, saving her life. Anzac subsequently defeated the strict 'no animals allowed' policy at Parliament House in New South Wales in 1997 when then Premier Bob Carr presented the medal to the mutt with plenty of moxie.

Sarbi is only the second animal to receive the Purple Cross for her actions in wartime.

She follows in the hoofsteps of Murphy, the donkey that ferried soldiers with leg wounds to safety at Gallipoli under the guidance of his Geordie handler, John Simpson Kirkpatrick. Simpson, as he is known in Australian legend, was an English merchant seaman who jumped ship in Queensland, dropped his last name and joined the Third Field Ambulance in the First World War.

Sarbi's former owner Wendy Upjohn and her children were delighted and relieved when their beloved pet made it home. They had followed her career with great interest, getting updates on her service whenever they could. 'I'm sure her early years in Bowral, with massive walks through the bush, tennis games with Rafi and that strong sense of belonging and family, helped give her the strength and resilience needed to survive against the odds,' Wendy says now.

The family had hoped to reclaim their beloved pet upon her retirement from the army but it wasn't to be. Sarbi will be repatriated to live with Sergeant D and his fiancée, Kira, in accordance with official policy. She'll also have a housemate, retired EDD Vegas.

The warm-hearted Upjohn readily accepted the decision and was horrified by the spin of a 'tug-of-love story' published in a Sydney newspaper under the headline 'Give back our hero dog'.

'Sarbi and Sergeant D had some amazing experiences together and lived through very tough times and situations that, fortunately, we can hardly begin to imagine. They have obviously forged a strong bond, survived extreme situations together, and we don't have the right to take that away now. For us it's enough knowing she won't be sent back to Afghanistan but allowed to retire gracefully.'

They will be reunited with the wonder dog of war once she has finished serving her country, and Sergeant D hopes Wendy and her children will become regular visitors.

Sarbi will not return to war or be deployed from Australia again. After tours of duty in Afghanistan and countless operations on Australian soil, she has served her country well enough.

The decision to retire Sarbi from frontline duties was

difficult. As Sergeant D says, she had a few good years left in her yet.

The army's most senior man didn't disagree. But Lieutenant General Gillespie, himself a dog owner, made the decision after considerable thought. He could see something powerful at work. This wasn't about the gossamer-thin threads of mythmaking or the burgeoning folk hero status of a conscripted four-legged soldier.

This was about something more intangible: the steely bond between human and hound.

As Gillespie says now, 'I don't think the Australian public would forgive me if anything happened to Sarbi.'

Epilogue

On a glorious Thursday in early March of 2009 four explosive detection dogs made history at the Gallipoli Barracks in Enoggera. Sarbi's brother Rafi and his canine companions Aussie, Que and Mandy, were presented with the highest military honour our four-legged warriors can receive in a dignified ceremony on the regimental parade grounds at the headquarters of the Magnificent Bastards of 2CER. All four dogs were presented with the War Dog Operational Medal for performing their duties in war conditions and Aussie, Que and Mandy received the Canine Service Medal for notching up five years of accumulated service.

Razz, the first dog to be killed by enemy action in Afghanistan, was honoured posthumously and his medals were presented to his handler, Corporal Craig Turnbull.

Rafi, Que, Aussie and Mandy were scrubbed up for the occasion and decked out in their finest ceremonial dress uniforms. They wore snappy signal-red satin jackets with royal blue trim adorned with the section's round logo. The words 'Explosive Detection' were embossed in gold across the top, and RAE along the bottom. A silhouette of a German shepherd sits proudly in the centre of the logo. The Commanding Officer of 2CER, Lieutenant Colonel Joel Dooley, did the honours and pinned the square medals on the dogs' jackets. EDD Mandy, a mixed mutt with a striking black and tan coat, stole the show when she sat down and shook the CO's big mitt, clearly proud of her achievement.

It was only the second time the medals, which are square to distinguish them from medals presented to their human counterparts, had been presented and the parade marked the first time the explosive detection dogs had attended their own ceremony. The year before in Perth, eleven dogs from the Australian Army and the RAAF who served in the Vietnam War were similarly honoured. That presentation may have been 34 years late but the significance and symbolism of the ceremony was all the greater for the delay.

That the current corps of canine warriors was even recognised was, in itself, a major achievement. The Australian Defence Force Trackers and War Dogs Association had fought a long, hard battle to have the medal struck for the military working dogs although it is still not an 'official' medal under the Australian Honours and Awards System of the Department of Defence. Under the *Defence Act 1903*, members of the Australian Defence Force are awarded medals for bravery, service overseas and long service but their canine counterparts are denied that honour.

The Australian Minister for Defence, Stephen Smith,

rejected the association's request to amend the Act to include a separate category for canine soldiers. At the time of writing, the ADFTWDA's president George Hulse was waiting on a response from the Leader of the Opposition, Tony Abbott, whom he asked to put up a Private Members Bill seeking to amend the Act to include 'canine members'. Hulse says the association does not want to diminish the great and brave efforts of the soldiers, or even equate the actions of the dogs with those of their human counterparts, but it does believe the dogs' duty should be recognised in a separate category.

No one would or could deny that the working military dogs had earned their honours. As Hulse points out, as well as Sarbi there have been several extraordinarily brave hounds that have performed above and beyond in Afghanistan with their two-legged counterparts, such as EDDs Gus and Storm. Storm is a tough dog and a top searcher. When the yellow Lab was first deployed to RTF1 in 2008, he discovered ammunition, explosives and mines hidden under a false floor in an abandoned village. He and his handler later survived an IED blast when the Bushmaster in which they were travelling hit an IED. Neither was hurt.

'Other high IED hitting dogs include Tank, Bundy, Bailey, Bolt, and Que,' Hulse says. Their handlers are, respectively, Sapper Brett Turley, Corporal John Cannon, Corporal Craig Turnbull, Sapper David Brown, Corporal Jim Hoy, Lance Corporal Andrew Sichter, and Sapper Ruebin Griggs.

Explosive detection dog Gus once detected an anti-personnel mine packed with 30 kilograms of high explosives buried on the side of a road. Had it detonated, it would have killed several soldiers travelling in vehicles behind them. Gus, a black and white kelpie cross, was teamed with Sapper Turley—Turls to his mates—in 2006 when no one else wanted him.

Like all Doggies, Gus and Turley were inseparable and even survived an IED explosion in 2008. They were en route to base after a four-hour patrol when their Bushmaster ran over a roadside bomb.

Fortunately, the Bushmaster took most of the blast. The front wheels of the vehicle were blown off, the remote control machine-gun dislodged, the windshield blasted out and exterior protective plates were damaged. One soldier suffered a broken leg. 'The remainder of us received shock over-blast effects and Gus, who had been lying on the floor of the Bushmaster, was blown from the floor to the ceiling and received some bruising,' Turley told Hulse in an interview for the Australian Defence Force Trackers and War Dogs Association (ADFTWDA) website.

Turley and Gus were medevaced to the US Army hospital at Kandahar and the highly trained medicos at the US Army Veterinary Corps clinic treated the dog. The American vets look after the working dogs of all the NATO and ISAF forces in Afghanistan. Each dog's records are kept on file and each hound has a patch of fur permanently shaved on the front leg just above the vein for urgent insertion of canulas in medical emergencies.

'We were both back on patrol duty at TK three days later,' Turley said. They returned to Australia after a nine-month-long deployment which included 100 days patrolling outside the wire.

On 26 June 2009, Gus and his fellow EDDs Jasmine, Sam, Scuba, Kylie and Mick became the second platoon of pooches awarded the War Dog Operational Medal and Canine Service Medal in a ceremony at Robertson Barracks in Darwin, where 1CER is based.

Tragically, Rafi, who survived two overseas deployments and everything the Taliban and anti-coalition militia could throw at him, died in 2009 soon after returning from Afghanistan. A venomous snake, type unknown, sank its fangs into him about the same time Sarbi was making headlines around the world.

Wendy Upjohn and her family were told Rafi was bitten during the night. Had he been bitten during the day, his handler would have been in a position to take immediate medical action and it is highly likely the dog would have survived. Rafi was seven years old and had been in the army a little more than four years.

In the years since EDDs Jasmine and Sam led the way for their canines-in-arms, five dogs have been killed in Afghanistan and at least two dozen have been deployed there. The courage and devotion of the hounds to their two-legged masters will never be forgotten.

On 7 June 2011, the Doggies were honoured with the inaugural Military Working Dog Day at the RAAF base at Amberley, 40 kilometres south-west of Brisbane in Queensland. The event was endorsed by the Chief of the ADF, Air Chief Marshal Angus Houston, and George Hulse hopes it will become an annual event.

The date was especially poignant as the event was held on the first anniversary of the deaths of Sapper Darren

James Smith and EDD Herbie who were killed in action in the Mirabad Valley in 2010. Sapper Jacob Moerland was also killed in the enemy assault.

Smith and Moerland were the first multiple fatalities suffered by the Australian Defence Force in a single operation since the Vietnam War, and the first deaths in 2010. Smith was the first Australian dog handler killed on the battlefield while working with his explosive detection dog.

Sapper Smith had been an EDD handler since 2006 and had worked with two other dogs—Mandy and Buster—before taking charge of Herbie. Smitty had also represented Australia on Exercise *Long Look* in the United Kingdom, where he met the Queen. He loved the work and his wife, Angela, said later he was determined to improve the dogs' 'training and conditions'. Smitty was on his first operational deployment with the First Mentoring Task Force (MTF-1). Herbie, designated EDD 476, was a three-year-old rescue mutt. He was a handsome black and white border collie–husky cross with a patchwork of fulvous markings over his eyes and on his snout, ears, chest and legs. Smith and Herbie were attached to Mentoring Team Alpha. Like all the Doggies, they had successfully detected weapons caches and IEDs in the three months they'd been in country. In early June they discovered a large IED before it could take out a number of soldiers.

Smith was a respected operator and instantly bonded with the men from Alpha, who were especially fond of Herbie. The mutt was treated like 'one of the boys . . . everyone looks after him. He's part of the family.'

No official studies have been done of the psychological

impact of the military working dogs on the personnel around whom they work, but when you listen to the soldiers talk about the hounds you realise that none, really, is needed. Just as it is impossible for dogs to reveal anything other than their true instincts when responding to the emotional emissions of humans, the same can be said for the soldiers when it comes to what the dogs mean to them.

'[It's] just great morale having [Herbie] around. Like you come back [from patrol] and you're in a shitty mood and then there's this dog,' one soldier said, not feeling the need to further limn the emotional bond between hound and human or the feel-good ripple effect of a four-legged warrior.

On the morning of 7 June 2010, Mentoring Team Alpha was en route to base after a successful dismounted patrol during which Herbie and Smith found a Pandora's box of weapons in a local village. The blokes were hot and covered in dust. They were still a couple of kilometres out from the remote patrol base and hard at work, concentrating on completing the mission.

Around 1100 hours Sapper Moerland spotted what he suspected was an IED. Moerland was regarded by his fellow Diggers as one of the hardest working members of Alpha and thought nothing of carrying a 40-kilogram pack when 20 kilograms would do. His troop commander once said, 'If only we had a troop full of Snowys we would be unstoppable.' He was known for his can-do fighting spirit, not to mention his extroverted personality, occasionally 'disturbing fashion sense' and a penchant for wearing aviator sunglasses. Moerland called for Smith and Herbie to take a look at the suspect item. Smith unleashed Herbie and told him to seek on. The well-trained dog went up and began sniffing. He stopped and stared, proving Moerland's hunch right. Herbie's response identified an improvised explosive device and Moerland and Smith put their drills into practice. Not for nothing did they wear the logo 'Engineers out front' on their shirts.

The two sappers and Herbie were at the IED when Taliban insurgents detonated the roadside bomb by remote control. The explosion was so loud it was heard by other patrols more than two and a half kilometres away.

'Even though it was one of many bangs that we heard, everybody knew that this one was especially ugly,' journalist Chris Masters said the following night.

The field medic raced in and performed battlefield treatment on Moerland, himself a combat first aider.

'Arterial bleeding,' came the call over the internal radio.

That message was followed by the words no soldiers want to hear.

'No vital signs.'

Sapper Jacob Moerland, nicknamed Snowy for the colour of his hair, was killed instantly. He was 21, engaged to be married and had been in the army for three years. It was the only job he ever wanted to do and he was proud to serve his country, his family said in a heartbreaking statement days later.

Within seconds another transmission was broadcast over the radio network.

'EDD deceased.'

Herbie was also killed by the massive IED.

Unbelievably, Smith survived the initial blast. Heroically, the first thing he did was try to get back to work.

'The first five minutes after it happened, Smith was trying to stand up and keep searching. He was trying to push everyone off him so he could keep doing his job,' Corporal Jeremy Pahl said later.

As Smith was being treated he spoke about his wife, Angela, and their two-year-old son, Mason. 'He basically said he loved his family and he doesn't regret anything. It was just amazing to know that this, this guy who honestly was, was in a bad way . . . everything that was going through his mind was family and friends.'

A nine-liner medical evacuation call was transmitted over the communications network and minutes later two American Blackhawks arrived from Tarin Kot. Smith and Moerland were rushed on to the helicopters and the birds took off in a cloud of dust.

The choppers were wheels down 38 minutes later. But it was too late. Sapper Smith died en route to the base hospital.

Jacob Moerland and Darren Smith were the twelfth and thirteenth soldiers killed in Afghanistan.

'Jacob and Darren were the epitome of the engineer motto "follow the sapper". They died as they lived, putting their own lives at risk to ensure the safety of their fellow soldiers,' said Major General John Cantwell, the commander of Joint Task Force 633, at a farewell ceremony at the JTF headquarters at Al Minhad Air Base in the United Arab Emirates. 'They truly are heroes who have paid the ultimate sacrifice in service not only to their nation, but also to those with them on that fateful patrol.'

Herbie was farewelled by fellow EDDs Harry, Bundy and Tank in a separate and poignant memorial service at Tarin Kot, where a photograph of the trusted dog and his handler was on display alongside the tattered remains of the dog's search harness, with 'Herbie' embroidered in black. Harry, a regal-looking golden retriever, and Bundy and Tank, two scrappy black mutts with loads of character and spunk, sat beside a portrait of Smitty and Herbie for an official photograph for the army photographer. The image is a striking yet tough reminder of the dangers the dogs and their handlers face in Afghanistan.

'At the end of the day, Herbie saved lives,' said Lieutenant Colonel John Carey, the commanding officer of 2CER. 'The Regiment and Army will miss him—he protected us on the field of battle. He is gone, but will never be forgotten.'

Herbie was cremated and his ashes returned to Australia and handed to Sapper Smith's wife, Angela.

'It's nice to finally leave them both to rest together. He was protecting Darren and he paid the ultimate sacrifice as well for Darren and the innocent people who could have been injured,' Angela Smith said. 'Darren was a very loving husband and father, an absolutely remarkable human being. He was very passionate about his job and understood the risks involved but he was the sort of man who always put others first and did his best for them whether it was his mates in the army or at home with his family and friends.'

The deaths of Sappers Moerland and Smith, and EDD Herbie, were a major blow to the battle-hardened Diggers at Camp Holland. The men's names would be added to a memorial for fallen soldiers, but there was nothing to commemorate the loss of the four-legged soldier who fought alongside them. The Australian contingent wanted to build a fitting tribute as a permanent reminder of the sacrifices made by the explosive detection dogs and their handlers and erect it at Merlin's Kennels, named in honour of the first of the five EDDs to be killed in Uruzgan.

The memorial project had an enormous impact on all personnel in Tarin Kot, not just the Doggies: the men and women deployed to Afghanistan understood its significance and appreciated its symbolism. The dogs are a much loved and respected element of the task force for many reasons, both professional and personal, and the brass decided to move the memorial to a busy corner of Poppy's Bar, the Australians' recreation area. There it would be passed by hundreds of coalition and Afghan soldiers every day, a constant reminder of the life-saving and dangerous work undertaken by the Doggies.

And so in early July 2011, a motley and lovable crew of thirteen canines then deployed with the Special Operations Task Group and the Mentoring Task Force in Afghanistan joined paws with their handlers and fellow soldiers for the official opening of the EDD and Handlers Memorial.

The memorial features a polished metal board with two images in silhouette, one of a hound standing at ease and the other of a handler kneeling on the ground and shaking his dog's paw, which was inspired by a photograph of EDD team, Raven and Sapper Nathan Cooper.

'I call the photo "the bond",' said Corporal John Cannon, an experienced Doggie who completed a nine-month deployment in Uruzgan in 2011. 'It symbolises the working partnership and mateship between dog and handler. There is a unique and special bond between the two—they are a team that shares the risks and puts their lives in each other's hands. These teams save lives every time they uncover an IED or a cache.'

Sapper Darren James Smith's name and service number are etched on a small plaque underneath the image of the handler and dog with his regiment—2nd Combat Engineer Regiment—and the date of his death, 7 June 2010. The heartbreakingly tender words, 'At rest from this world', are inscribed in black lettering. Beside Sapper Smith's plaque is another for EDD 476 Herbie, with the same date and regiment. A profound and apt tribute reads, 'Side by side through dust and snow'.

Plaques for the four doggies killed before Herbie hang vertically beneath the image of the dog standing solo, and each has the dog's date of death, regiment and a poignant inscription that underscores the bond between human and hound.

437 EDD Merlin, 31 Aug 2007, 3rd Combat Engineer Regiment: A true mate.

409 EDD Razz, 21 Sep 2007, Incident Response Regiment: Mate till the end.

452 EDD Andy, 23 Nov 2007, Incident Response Regiment: Duty done.

472 EDD Nova, 23 Oct 2009, 3rd Combat Engineer Regiment: Always first.

On 7 June 2012, the ADFTWDA and the RSPCA are due to unveil a Military and Service Working Dogs

National Monument at the new RSPCA shelter in Brisbane. Half of the monument will be dedicated to Sapper Darren Smith and Herbie.

EDD Merlin, whose body was buried at Merlin's Kennels in Camp Holland in 2007, was eventually repatriated to Australia as his handler Pete 'Lucy' Lawlis so desperately wanted. A lot of work and quiet but very determined diplomacy, orchestrated by Lawlis and other hard men dedicated to serving their country, went on behind the scenes to get the fallen four-legged Digger home to Australia, like his comrades. Merlin's remains are now buried under a tree in the backyard of the Lawlis family home in New South Wales. Pete 'Lucy' Lawlis has retired from the Australian Army.

Most of the dogs that returned from deployments to Afghanistan continue their dangerous work. A few have retired due to old age.

Sergeant D and the eight other soldiers wounded with him in the Taliban ambush in Khas Uruzgan on 2 September 2008, all returned to operational duty, though some have since retired from the army.

Small bits of shrapnel still work their way out of Sergeant D's body, a constant reminder of how close to death he came. A piece of RPG frag remains lodged behind his knee; the doctors fear removing it could be more dangerous than leaving it where it is. His body armour was sent for a series of comprehensive tests to determine how it saved his life. Sergeant D is just glad it did.

The seasoned soldier has a few souvenirs of his life-and-death battle with the Taliban. He kept the Nomex gloves he wore during the ambush and a bottle of shrapnel picked from his body by the surgeons in Afghanistan. The G-SHOCK watch he wore on his left wrist is still ticking, albeit with a few nicks in the hardware. In the aftermath of the ambush, Sergeant D had a new tattoo added to his collection of body art. The tattooist worried about drilling ink on scar tissue but the Doggie wasn't bothered about decorating the Taliban-caused disfigurement. A tribal tattoo now covers his left shoulder blade and creeps around and down his left arm, over the scars he scored in Khas Uruzgan. The new artwork complements the ferocious-looking dog he had inked on his bulging right bicep early in his army career, an image borrowed from the *Live to Ride* motorcycle magazine. Soldiers love their tatts.

In 2011, at the age of 35, Sergeant D deployed to the other side of the world for his fourth rotation in Afghanistan.

Sarbi was tucked up safely in the kennels at the SME in Holsworthy where the trusted nine-year-old had started her distinguished army career six years earlier. She is helping train new explosive detection dog handlers and setting a stellar example for the hounds while she waits for Sergeant D to return from his rotation. When he does, Sarbi will receive brand new rules of engagement.

Her next mission is to protect Sergeant D's fiancée, Kira, and Vegas, an older dog that, like her, is a retiree from one of the most dangerous and selfless jobs in the world.

If only they could talk.

Notes

PROLOGUE

p. ix   'snake-eating rebel'
        Kevin Connolly, 'McChrystal in the line of fire.' BBC Online, 22 June
        2010 <bbc.co.uk>

p. x   'big-ass meal'
        Toby Harden, 'Interview: General Stanley McChrystal', *The Telegraph*
        (UK) 23 March 2010, <telegraph.co.uk>

p. xi   'about right'
        Kevin Rudd, interview on *CNN*, 21 September 2009

p. xii   'red cards'
        Patrick Walters, 'US to urge for bigger role for Diggers—More Afghan
        for troops', *The Weekend Australian*, 22 August 2009

p. xii   'yak with youse all'
        Malcolm Farr, 'Rudd visits Diggers: PM's food for thought', *The Herald
        Sun*, 12 November 2009

CHAPTER 1

p. 3   'well-proportioned triumphs of modern hairdressing'
        Konrad Lorenz, *Man Meets Dog* (translated by Marjorie Kerr Wilson),
        Routledge Classics, London and New York, 1954, p. 89

CHAPTER 2

p. 13 'Here Lies and Watches Wagner's Russ'
Stanley Coren, *The Pawprints of History: Dogs and the Course of Human Events*, Free Press, New York, 2002, p. 112

p. 14 'Dogs! Must I be defeated by them . . .'
Stanley Coren, *The Pawprints of History*, p. 19

CHAPTER 3

p. 25 'play is serious business . . .'
Stanley Coren, *How to Speak Dog: Mastering the Art of Dog-Human Communication*, Free Press, New York, 2000, p. 148

References to how dogs move and respond were drawn from various books cited in the bibliography and more closely from Stanley Coren, *How To Speak Dog* and Alexandra Horowitz, *Inside of a Dog: What Dogs See, Smell, and Know*, Scribner, New York, 2009.

CHAPTER 4

p. 35 'there is no domestic animal which has . . .'
Konrad Lorenz, *Man Meets Dog* (translated by Marjorie Kerr Wilson), Routledge Classics, London and New York, 1954, p ix

p. 37 'human companionship has become . . .'
Alexandra Horowitz, *Inside of a Dog*, p. 64

CHAPTER 5

Much of the material about canine–human communication, how many words dogs can be taught, and the story of the boastful German dog trainer is drawn from Stanley Coren, *How to Speak Dog* (particularly Chapter 3) and Stanley Coren, *Why We Love The Dogs We Do: How To Find The Dog That Matches Your Personality*, Fireside, New York, 1998.

p. 44 'Emotions allow each of us . . .'
Patricia B. McConnell, *For The Love of A Dog: Understanding Emotions in You and Your Dog,* Ballantine Books, New York, 2007, p. 11

CHAPTER 6

p. 47   'The RSPCA dog is like the Aussie soldier . . .'
Susan Oldroyd, *Army: The Soldiers' Newspaper* <www.defence.gov.au/news/armynews/editions/1077/topstories/story07.htm>

p. 49   '. . . 40,000 horses . . .'
M is for Mate: Animals in Wartime from Ajax to Zep, Department of Veterans' Affairs and The Australian War Memorial, Canberra, 2009, p. 16

p. 49   'One messenger dog, working with the Fourth Division Signal Company . . .'
M is for Mate, p. 8

The story about the three-dollar mongrel liberated from death row is told by an Australian Vietnam War veteran and dog handler, Peter Haran, *Trackers: The Untold Story of the Australian Dogs of War*, New Holland, Chatswood, NSW, 2000.

For more on the early days of the Australian war dogs and for stories about the longest serving Australian canine veterans of the Vietnam War—Marcus, Caesar and Tiber—see Peter Haran, *Trackers*. Also see the 'Combat Profiles' section on the website for the Australian Defence Force Trackers and War Dogs Association (ADFTWDA) <www.aussiewardogs.org/node/83>

CHAPTER 7

p. 66   '[Their capabilities] cannot be replicated by man or machine . . .'
'Herbie Finally Home to Rest', Australian Government, Department of Defence, press release, 30 June 2010

p. 66   'The best technology for sniffing . . .'
Grace Jean, 'Building Miniature "Noses" to Sniff Explosives', *National Defense* (US), business and technology magazine of the National Defense Industrial Association (NDIA), October 2007

p. 66   'We trust these dogs more than metal detectors . . .'
Jason Gutierrez, 'Dogs of War Save Lives in Afghanistan', *Discovery News*, American Free Press, 28 January 2010 <DiscoveryNews.com>

p. 66   'They are the only weapon system . . .'
Michael G. Lemish, *War Dogs: A History of Loyalty and Heroism*, Potomac Books, Dulles VA, 2008, p. 197

p. 67   '. . . up to 25,000'
      Meg Purtell, 'Sniffer Dogs', *Stateline*, ABC Television, 14 March 2008

p. 68   '. . . such as ammonium nitrate . . .'
      Alan Cullison and Yaroslav Trofimov, 'Karzai Bans Ingredient of Taliban's Roadside Bombs', *The Wall Street Journal*, 3 February 2010

p. 68   'like sticking two total strangers . . .'
      Corrine Boer, 'Dogs of War', *Army: The Soldier's Newspaper*, 15 May 2008

p. 70   '. . . make their own leashes . . .'
      Australian Sapper, Head of Corps, Royal Australian Engineers, Moorebank NSW, 2010 edition, p. 52

Corrine Boer tells the story of the dominant golden retriever named Mandy in the above article, 'Dogs of War'.

p. 77   '. . . Dookie and Jane . . .'
      Andrew Pierce, 'Hug for Queen Elizabeth's first corgi', *The Telegraph* (UK), 1 October 2007 <www.telegraph.co.uk>

CHAPTER 8

Material on the history of dogs in war was drawn from works cited in the text and also by the following authors (in alphabetical order):

John C. Burnam, *A Soldier's Best Friend: Scout Dogs and Their Handlers in the Vietnam War*, Union Square Press, New York, 2008

Stanley Coren, *The Pawprints of History: Dogs and the Course of Human Events*, Free Press, New York, 2002

Brian Dennis, Kirby Larson, Mary Nethery, *Nubs: The True Story of a Mutt, a Marine and a Miracle*, Little, Brown and Company, London, 2009

Tracy L. English, *The Quiet Americans: A History of Military Working Dogs*, Office of History, Lackland Air Force Base, Lackland TX <www.lackland.af.mil/shared/media/document/AFD-061212-027.pdf>

Michael G. Lemish, *War Dogs: A History of Loyalty and Heroism*, Potomac Books, Dulles VA, 2008

Frances E. Ruffin, *Dog Heroes: Military Dogs*, Bearport Publishing, New York, 2007

p. 79   'Attila the Hun relied on dogs . . .'
      Lemish, *War Dogs*, p. 3

p. 80   '. . . more than 19,000 family pets . . .'
Frances E. Ruffin, *Dog Heroes*, p. 13

p. 81   '. . . air assault was a 30,000 foot leap . . .'
Rebecca Frankel, 'War Dog', *Foreign Policy*, 4 May 2011

For one story about Sasha Rufus and Target, see the press release issued by charity organisation *Hope For The Warriors* titled 'Army Guardsman reunites with lifesaving Afghani dogs', 2010 <www.robertscause.org/hope_warriors_article_july10.pdf>

p. 82   'they were our babies'
'Rufus, Target and Sasha save US soldiers', *The Oprah Winfrey Show*, Harpo Productions, 4 October 2010

p. 82   'I think we underestimate . . .'
'UK Army Dog may have died of a broken heart', Fox News, 10 March 2011 <www.foxnews.com/world/2011/03/10/uk-army-dog-died-broken-heart-1606316739>

p. 84   '. . . read human gestures and behaviour . . .'
Randi Kaye, *Anderson Cooper 360*, CNN, 18 November 2010

p. 85   'By the end of 2011 . . .'
Emily Moser and Michael McCulloch, 'Canine scent detection of human cancers: A review of methods and accuracy', *Journal of Veterinary Behavior* [US], Vol. 5, No. 3, May/June 2010

p. 86   'Early successes with canine scent detection . . .'
Moser and McCulloch, 'Canine scent detection'

p. 86   'It may well be that, someday in the future . . .'
Stanley Coren, *How To Speak Dog*, p. 185

p. 87   'We often refer to our dogs . . .'
Sandra Lee, 'What's up, dog?, Sunday Magazine, *The Sunday Herald Sun*, 17 July 2009

p. 87   'Trakr came to a sudden stop . . .'
Genelle Guzman-McMillan, *Angel In The Rubble*, Inspired Living/Allen & Unwin, Sydney, 2011, p. 104

p. 88   'There is some anecdotal evidence . . .'
Sandra Lee, 'What's up, dog?'

p. 89   'community centre bulletin board'
Alexandra Horowitz, *Inside of a Dog*

p. 89   '... "read the headlines" ...'
Stanley Coren, *How To Speak Dog, Mastering The Art Of Dog–Human Communication*, Free Press, New York, 2000 p. 186

CHAPTER 9

p. 97   '... an estimated $90,000'
Max Blenkin, 'Dog Killed on Afghan Duty', *The Age*, 6 September 2007

p. 97   '$40,000 a year ...'
'Along with a troop surge in Afghanistan, a dog surge: along with a dog surge, a food dilemma', *The Los Angeles Times*, 25 January 2010

p. 97   'highly specialized piece of equipment'
Adrienne Killingsworth, 'Military working dogs: A tribute to Ardy', US Army, 11 May 2010 <www.army.mil/article/38878>

p. 97   'engineer stores'
Peter Haran, *Trackers*, p. 57

CHAPTER 10

Material about terrorists using violence against non-combatants was drawn from Jessica Stern, *The Ultimate Terrorists*, Harvard University Press, Cambridge MA, 1999

p. 101 'More than 4500 athletes from 71 countries ...'
Michael Tafe, 'Precinct Security Planning: Lessons Learnt—Melbourne 2006 Commonwealth Games', Speech delivered at the *Mass Transport, Mass Gathering and Precinct Security Conference*, 8 November 2007

p. 102 'Soldiers from the IRR ...' *Connections*, Defence, Science and Technology Organisation, May 2006

p. 105 '... *dukhi and dushman* ...'
Sandra Lee, *18 Hours: The True Story of an SAS War Hero*, Harper-Collins, Pymble NSW, 2006, p. 143

p. 107 'By 23 September . . .'
'Australian Special Forces conduction Operations in Afghanistan', Australian Government, Department of Defence media release, MECC 230/05, 23 September 2005

p. 107 '. . . pushing 70 kilometres north . . .'
Major General Michael Hindmarsh, Australian Government, Department of Defence press conference, Canberra, 27 September 2006

p. 108 'It was akin to poking an ant bed with a stick'
Major General Michael Hindmarsh, press conference 2006

p. 108 'And more dangerous than anything . . .'
Major General Michael Hindmarsh, press conference 2006

p. 109 'it is a distortion to use the word Taliban . . .'
Bing West, *The Wrong War: Grit, Strategy, and the Way Out of Afghanistan*, Random House, New York, 2011, pp. 7–8

p. 109 'wanted to make life difficult'
Presentation of the Military Order of William to Captain Marco Kroon, Ministry of Defence of the Netherlands, Directorate of Information and Communication, The Hague, 29 May 2009

p. 109 'The threat is ever-present . . .'
Paul McGeough, 'SAS combatants strike deep into Taliban heartland', *Sydney Morning Herald*, 27 September 2005

p. 109 'There were about 80 IED incidents . . .'
'ADP Prepared for Improvised Explosive Device Threat', Australian Government, Department of Defence media release, MECC 141/06, 29 June 2006

p. 110 'becoming more technical and constantly updated . . .'
Major General Michael Hindmarsh, press conference 2006

p. 110 '. . . were trained to mitigate the threat of IEDs. Every EOD . . .'
'Canberra cancelled robot unit for bombs', Department of Defence response to article by Mark Dodd, *The Australian*, 6 November 2007

p. 110 'The work of the Counter IED Task Force . . .'
'ADF prepared for improvised explosive device threat', Australian Government, Department of Defence media release, MECC 141/06, 29 June 2006

For more on the first deployment to Afghanistan of Explosive Detection Dogs Sam and Jasmine, visit the website of The Australian Defence Force Trackers and War Dog Association (ADFT WDA) <www. aussiewardogs.org>

p. 112 'He's your best friend, he's your best mate . . .'
Catherine Ellis, 'Sniffer Dogs', *Behind The News*, 1 April 2008 <abc. com.au>

p. 112 'You need to be able to tell when your dog has found . . .'
Catherine Ellis, 'Sniffer Dogs'

p. 112 'I found this part of the deployment really hard.'
George Hulse, *Interviews with War Dog Operatives*, Series 4, Profile 4— Afghanistan, Corporal John Cannon—Royal Australian Engineers <www.aussiewardogs.org/downloads/Cpl%20John%20Cannon.pdf >

CHAPTER 11

p. 114 'Weekly reviews of the latest information and intelligence . . .'
Australian Sapper, 2007 edition, p. 27

p. 116 'The US Army had lost 103 U.S. soldiers to IEDs.'
Anthony Cordesman and Emma Davies, *Iraq's Insurgency and the Road to Civil Conflict*, Centre for Strategic and International Studies, Washington DC, 2008, p. 698

p. 117 '. . . sent them to the Combined Explosives Exploitation Centre in Kandahar . . .' Haydn Barlow, 'Wired For Action', *Army: The Soldiers' Newspaper*, 20 September 2007

p. 117 'a mini arms race . . .'
Russell Maddalena, Australian Government, Department of Defence press conference, Canberra, 10 May 2007

p. 117 'He studied the Australians' rules of engagement . . .'
'Australian soldiers kill truck driver', 26 July 2007 <news.com.au>

p. 117 '. . . the first Standard Operating Procedure of the task force . . .'
Australian Sapper, 2007 edition, p. 9

p. 118 'in the conservative south . . .'
Sarah Chayes, *The Punishment of Virtue: Inside Afghanistan After the Taliban*, Penguin, New York, 2006, p. 233

p. 118 'The need to secure revenge . . .'
Mohammad Yousaf and Mark Adkin, *Afghanistan, The Bear Trap: The Defeat of a Superpower*, Casemate, Haverton PA, 1991, 2001, p. 34

p. 119 'Pashtun history is filled with heroes . . .'
Owais Tohid and Scott Baldauf, *The Christian Science Monitor*, 25 June 2004

p. 119 'betraying each other on a daily basis'
Anonymous, *Hunting al-Qaeda: A Take-No-Prisoners Account of Terror, Adventure, and Disillusionment*, Zenith Press, Minneapolis MN, 2005

p. 125 'It's an incredible story of hope . . .'
Kelly Ryan, 'Plea to save hero dog from Afghan war', *The Herald Sun*, 20 May 2010

CHAPTER 12

p. 126 'a dusty shit-hole'
Paul McGeough, 'SAS combatants strike deep into Taliban heartland', *Sydney Morning Herald*, 27 September 2005

p. 127 '. . . established by a United States Marine Expeditionary Unit . . .'
Global Security.org, *Forward Operating Base Ripley / Kamp Holland* <www.globalsecurity.org/military/facility/fob_ripley.htm>

p. 128 'Stay with your weapon, always'
Al Green, 'Home Sweet Home, The Special Operations Task Group's first days at Camp Russell', *Army: The Soldiers' Newspaper*, n.d. 2005

p. 128 'We must outsmart those who want . . .'
Haydn Barlow, 'RTF2 takes the reins', *Army: The Soldiers' Newspaper*, 3 May 2007

p. 130 '. . . there was no mobile telephone coverage . . .'
'The Dutch Engagement in Uruzgan, 2006–2010: A Socio-political Assessment', The Liaison Office (independent Afghan NGO), August 2010 <www.tlo-afghanistan.org>

p. 130 'Only 10 per cent of males in the province were literate.'
Progress in Afghanistan Since 2001, Australian Government, Department of Defence Fact Sheet <www.defence.gov.au/op/afghanistan/info/factsheet.htm>

p. 131 'IEDs are made of five main components . . .'
Russell Maddalena, Australian Government, Department of Defence press conference, Canberra, 10 May 2007

p. 131 'The Chief of Defence Angus Houston confirmed . . .'
Australian Government, Department of Defence press conference, Canberra, 9 June 2008

p. 131 'The explosive shockwaves of the blast . . .'
Russell Maddalena, Department of Defence press conference, Canberra, 10 May 2007

p. 132 'Twenty-six-year-old Smith, dubbed Smitty'
Australian Sapper, 2010 edition, p. 52

CHAPTER 13

p. 136 'bloodiest year'
Thomas H. Johnson, 'On The Edge of the Big Muddy: The Taliban Resurgence in Afghanistan', *China and Eurasia Forum Quarterly*, Vol. 5, No. 2, 2007

p. 136 '. . . one recorded case of a suicide bomber in Afghanistan.'
Seth Jones, *In The Graveyard of Empires*. W.W. Norton and Co., New York, 2009, p. 207

Material on the number of suicide attacks was drawn from Pamela Constable, 'Gates visits Kabul, cites rise in cross-border attacks', *The Washington Post*, 17 January 2007 and Seth Jones, *In the Graveyard of Empires*.

p. 137 'IEDs killed 492 civilians and injured at least 700 more.'
Thomas H. Johnson, 'On the Edge of the Big Muddy'

p. 137 'but it also suffered 90 fatalities . . .'
Bruce Riedel, 'Al-Qaeda Strikes Back', *Foreign Affairs*, May/June, 2007

p. 137 'retribution against "collaborators" neutralised . . .'
Barnett R. Rubin, 'Saving Afghanistan', *Foreign Affairs*, January/February 2007

p. 137 '. . . the Taliban relies on . . .'
Thomas H. Johnson, 'The Taliban Insurgency and an Analysis of *Shabnamah* (Night Letters)', *Small Wars and Insurgencies*, Vol. 18, No. 3, 317–44, September 2007

p. 137 'A bullet to the head is all it takes . . .'
Seth Jones, *In the Graveyard of Empires*, p. 227

p. 137 'death threats to intimidate and terrorise'
Special Operations commander Major General Tim McOwan, 'Update on Special Operations in Afghanistan', Australian Government, Department of Defence press conference, 11 December 2008

p. 137 'has become ever more daring and deadly . . .'
Bruce Riedel, 'Al-Qaeda Strikes Back'

p. 137 'striking . . . at the heart of the Taliban strength'
Major General Michael Hindmarsh, Australian Government, Department of Defence press conference, Canberra, 27 September 2006

p. 138 'the heavy lifting'
Brendan Nicholson, 'NATO Failure Endangering Australian Forces', *The Age*, 27 November 2007

p. 142 'The situational awareness of the RTF patrol . . .'
'RTF Soldier Slightly wounded in Failed Uruzgan Suicide Attack' Australian Government, Department of Defence media release, MECC 120/07, 4 May 2007

CHAPTER 14

p. 148 'there is a distinct possibility of casualties . . .'
'Australia to Double Afghan Force', BBC, 10 April 2007 <bbc.co.uk>

p. 151 '. . . manning a MAG58 . . .'
'Afghanistan, D Coy Op Slipper', 1 RAR: The First Battalion Association <www.firstbattalionassociation1rar.org.au/info.php?id=13>

p. 151 'Two afghan nationals were also wounded . . .'
'RTF Soldier Slightly Wounded in Failed Uruzgan Suicide Attack', Australian Government, Department of Defence media release, MECC 120/07, 4 May 2007

p. 153 '. . . restoration work in a ten-hour "backyard blitz" . . .'
Kieran Jackel, 'Australian and Afghan Sappers Deliver Magical Effect to Talani School', *Australian Sapper*, 2007 edition, p. 14

p. 155 '. . . Merlin was the first explosive detection dog . . .'
'Army Sniffer Dog Merlin Killed in Accident', *The Daily Telegraph*, 5 September 2007

p. 158 'A top EDD and very intelligent . . .'
'Canines Round Up Medals', Australian Government, Department of Defence media release, 6 March 2009

p. 158 'We spend every minute with the dog . . .'
Kelvin Healey, 'Our Troops Declare in Dogs We Trust', *The Advertiser*, 22 June 2009

p. 159 '. . . SAS Signalman Martin 'Jock' Wallace became the first Australian soldier . . .'
Sandra Lee, *18 Hours: The True Story of an SAS War Hero*, HarperCollins; Pymble NSW, 2006, p. 1

p. 159 '. . . insurgents had failed to capture the base . . .'
Nick Allen, *Embedded with the World's Armies in Afghanistan*, Spellmount, Stroud UK, 2010, p. 84

Material about the 120-plus commandos of 4RAR with whom Sergeant D and Sarbi were on patrol was drawn from Rob Maylor and Robert Macklin, *SAS Sniper: The World of an Elite Australian Marksman*, Hachette, Sydney, 2010.

p. 160 '. . . detonating two Russian anti-tank mines stacked . . .'
Rob Maylor and Robert Macklin, *SAS Sniper*, p. 246

p. 160 'Their wounds were assessed as slight . . .'
'Explosive Detection Dog Killed by Taliban Roadside Bomb', Australian Government, Department of Defence media release, CPA 330/07, 24 September 2007

p. 160 'as close to "one shot, one kill" as you can get'
Sean Naylor, 'Air Force Policy left ground troops high and dry', *Army Times* [US], 30 September 2002

p. 161 'It was a huge bomb and poor Razz . . .'
Josh Bavas, 'Vaporised war dog receives posthumous medal', ABC, 5 March 2009 <abc.net.au>

p. 162 'It was pretty harsh, but he saved my life . . .'
Kelvin Healey, 'Our Troops Declare in Dogs We Trust', *The Advertiser*, 22 June 2009

p. 162 'A bad experience, but better than one of our soldiers.'
Josh Bavas, 'Vaporised war dog receives posthumous medal'

p. 162 '. . . In dogs we trust.'
Kelvin Healey, 'Diggers in danger put trust in dogs', *The Herald Sun*, 21 June 2009

p. 164 'All of a sudden half the countryside was being shot at . . .'
Rob Maylor and Robert Macklin, *SAS Sniper*, p. 251

p. 164 'If the blast didn't kill them the shrapnel would have.'
Rob Maylor and Robert Macklin, *SAS Sniper*, p. 252

p. 165 'In this case, the dogs have paid the ultimate sacrifice . . .'
'Explosive Detection Dogs to Be Honoured', Australian Government, Department of Defence media release, CPA 336/072, 6 September 2007

CHAPTER 15

p. 167 'We will find you . . .'
Major General Tim McOwan, Australian Government, Department of Defence, press conference, Canberra, 11 December 2008

p. 168 'Afghanistan's deadly double whammy'
Tom Hyland, 'Afghanistan's deadly Double Whammy', *The Sunday Age*, 22 June 2008

p. 168 'misplaced and even counterproductive'
Tom Hyland, 'Hearts and Minds Not Won', *The Sunday Age*, 22 June 2008

p. 168 '. . . died from a single shot . . .'
D. K. Connery, *Inquiry Officer's Report Into The Death of Lance Corporal Jason Paul Marks and the Wounding of Australian Soldiers in Afghanistan on 27 April 2008 (Marks Inquiry)*, unclassified, 3 June 2008

p. 169 '. . . Private Luke James Worsley died . . .'
P.J. Short, *Inquiry Officer's Report Into The Death of 8265028 Pte L.J. Worsley in Afghanistan on 23 Nov 07*, unclassified, 18 December 2007

p. 169 '. . . SAS Sergeant Matthew Locke was shot . . .'
S.G. Durward, *Inquiry Officer's Report Into The Death of 8229246 Sergeant M.R. Locke In Afghanistan on 25 Oct 07*, unclassified, 22 January 2008

p. 169 'He was one of these guys . . .'
Brendan Nicholson, 'You Think I'm Brave? Meet My Mates: Ben Roberts-Smith', *The Australian*, 23 April 2011

p. 169 '. . . absolutely loved the army . . .'
Heath Gilmore, 'We Said Our Brave Son was Invincible', *The Sydney Morning Herald*, 28 October 2007

p. 169 'In October 2007, David Pearce . . .'
S.G. Durward, *Inquiry Officer's Report Into The Death of 8298024 Tpr D.R. Pearce and Injury to [unnamed] in Afghanistan on 8 Oct 07*, unclassified, 22 Jan 08

p. 170 'The enemy . . . [is] aggressively targeting . . .'
US Department of Defense, news briefing, 24 June 2008

p. 170 'They're burning schools . . .'
US Department of Defense, news briefing, 24 June 2008

p. 170 'The people that they're killing . . .'
US Department of Defense, news briefing, 5 September 2008

p. 173 'I'll wait for your nine potatoes . . .'
Bing West, *The Wrong War*, p. 8

p. 173 'once outside the wire . . .'
Special Operations commander Major General Tim McOwan, 'Update on Special Operations in Afghanistan', Australian Government, Department of Defence press conference, Canberra, 11 December 2008

p. 176 'These deaths, on the same day we welcomed . . .'
Air Chief Marshal Angus Houston, 'Australian Troops Assist Improvised Explosive Device Victims', Australian Government, Department of Defence media release, MECC 230/08, 16 July 2008

CHAPTER 16

p. 179 'They're a major asset . . .'
Sean Rayment, 'British Soldier and his faithful friend die side-by-side in Afghanistan', *The Telegraph* (UK), 27 July 2008

p. 180 '. . . SAS Corporal Mark Donaldson . . .'
Rob Maylor and Robert Macklin, *SAS Sniper*, p. 267

p. 181 'We've just been hit by an IED.'
Rob Maylor and Robert Macklin, SAS Sniper, p. 267

p. 181 'that thing saved my life'
Mark Dodd, 'VC Hero Tires of PR and Goes Back to Afghanistan', The
Australian, 23 July 2010

Material about the death of SAS Signaller Sean McCarthy was drawn from
various Australian Government Department of Defence press releases and the
official unclassified Inquiry Officer's report on Signaller McCarthy's death of
August 2008, as well as other references cited.

p. 182 'He [McCarthy] was badly injured on both legs.'
Jamie Walker, 'Botched Medivac as Digger in Afghanistan lay dying',
The Australian, 26 July 2008

p. 182 'the "golden hour" . . .'
Jamie Walker, 'Botched Medivac as Digger in Afghanistan lay dying'

p. 185 '. . . due to bad weather.'
'SOTG Soldiers Wounded in Uruzgan IED Blast' Australian Government,
Department of Defence media release, MSPA 255/08, 12 August 2008

p. 185 'If the injuries had been life-threatening . . .'
Sarah Smiles, 'Injured Soldiers Wait Six Hours', The Age, 13 August
2008

p. 185 '. . . a third rescue attempt was attempted six hours later . . .'
Mark Dodd, 'Push For Diggers To Get Medivacs in Afghanistan', The
Australian, 13 August 2008

p. 187 'botched helicopter rescue'
Mark Dodd, 'Push For Diggers to Get Medivacs in Afghanistan', The
Australian, 13 August 2008

p. 187 'a string of bad luck'
Philip Coorey, 'Forces Stuck with Borrowed Choppers', The Sydney
Morning Herald, 13 August 2008

p. 187 '. . . specialised medical helicopters . . .'
Mark Dodd, 'Push For Diggers to Get Medivacs in Afghanistan'

CHAPTER 17

The reconstruction of the ambush has been drawn from Sergeant D's recollections of the day and from various sources cited below and in the bibliography. There were twelve Australians and each fought his own battle that day. Each saw different action and has a unique perspective.

p. 189 'highly targeted operations against insurgent . . .'
Major General Tim McOwan, Australian Government, Department of Defence, press conference, Canberra, 11 December 2008

p. 190 '[Jacko] was Greg's best companion . . .'
Mark Ranzenberger, 'Rodriguez to be buried in Arlington', *The Morning Sun*, 8 September 2008

p. 191 '. . . had successfully wiped out thirteen . . .'
Major General Tim McOwan, 11 December 2008

p. 191 '. . . sneak into Taliban leader Ahmad Shah's compound . . .'
Major General Tim McOwan, 11 December 2008

p. 192 'We had clobbered them . . .'
Peter Pedersen, 'Recock and Refigure, Trooper Mark Donaldson, VC, speaks', *Wartime: Official Magazine of the Australian War Memorial*, Issue 46, 2009, p.14

p. 195 'Kill them, kill them all.'
Rob Maylor and Robert Macklin, SAS *Sniper*, p. 285

p. 197 'Some of those were air burst . . .'
Peter Pedersen, 'Recock and Refigure, Trooper Mark Donaldson, VC, speaks', p.13

p. 197 'It's combat and it's war . . .'
Howard Gipps, *A Current Affair*, Nine Network, 16 January 2009

p. 197 'A non-commissioned SAS sergeant leapt up . . .'
Major General Tim McOwan, 11 December 2008

p. 198 'The effect of the initiation . . .'
'Australian Army Awarded the Victoria Cross for Trooper Mark Gregor Donaldson' [official citation], Australian Government, Department of Defence, 16 January 2009

p. 198 'I honestly didn't think . . .'
Mark Donaldson, 'For Most Conspicuous Acts of Gallantry', *Defence*, Issue 1, 2009

p. 200 'It's a funny thing, they were pretty staunch . . .'
Philip Clark, *Summer Radio*, ABC702 Radio, 14 January 2011

p. 200 'We need your assistance . . .'
Rob Maylor and Robert Macklin, SAS *Sniper*, p. 288

p. 201 'They do have very tight rules . . .'
Ian McPhedran, 'Dutch left soldiers for dead in Afghanistan', *The Daily Telegraph*, 22 October 2010

p. 202 '. . . using his own body as a shield.'
Major General Tim McOwan, 11 December 2008

p. 202 'On several occasions, enemy bullets . . .'
Major General Tim McOwan, 11 December 2008

p. 202 'If you see them in trouble out there . . .'
Howard Gipps, *A Current Affair*

p. 203 'It all comes back to the training.'
Howard Gipps, *A Current Affair*

p. 203 'You look back on it now and think . . .'
Philip Clark, *Summer Radio*

p. 204 'This soldier deliberately exposed himself . . .'
Major General Tim McOwan, 11 December 2008

p. 204 'He liked justice. If it wasn't right . . .'
'Gregory A Rodriguez', *The Detroit News*, 6 September 2008

p. 205 '. . . the 501st American soldier to have lost his life . . .'
Mark Berman, 'A Loyal Soldier Is Mourned', *The Washington Post*, 16 September 2008

p. 205 'He told me Arlington . . .'
Mark Ranzenberger, 'Rodriguez to be buried in Arlington', *The Morning Sun*, 8 September 2008

CHAPTER 18

p. 211 'I was hesitant to look . . .'
Rob Maylor and Robert Macklin, SAS *Sniper*, p, 294

p. 214 'was pretty heavy and pretty accurate . . .'
Howard Gipps, *A Current Affair*

p. 214 'I suppose it was like looking at a puddle . . .'
Philip Clark, *Summer Radio*

p. 216 'There was a mate of mine . . .'
Philip Clark, *Summer Radio*

p. 218 'That's how lucky we are . . .'
Peter Harvey, 'Our Valient Few', *60 Minutes*, Nine Network, 24 April 2009

p. 219 'This is the largest number of casualties . . .'
Jonathan Pearlman, 'Nine Australian soldiers hurt in Taliban ambush,'
The Sydney Morning Herald, 4 September 2009

p. 219 'It is important to note . . .'
'Special operations Task Group soldiers Wounded in Afghanistan
Update', Australian Government, Department of Defence press
release, MSPA 295/08, 10 September 2008

p. 220 'in areas in which coalition soldiers . . .'
Mark Colvin, 'Australian soldiers wounded in Afghanistan', *PM*,
3 September 2008

p. 220 'engaged in a vital mission'
Mark Colvin, 'Australian soldiers wounded in Afghanistan'

p. 220 'A lot of the guys did feel it'
Jessica Johnston, 'Sarbi the Army wonder dog found safe in Afghanistan', *Perth Now*, 12 November 2009 <www.perthnow.com.au>

CHAPTER 19

p. 223 'morale is high'
'Special operations Task Group soldiers wounded in Afghanistan
Update', Australian Government, Department of Defence press
release, MSPA 295/08, 10 September 2008

p. 224 '. . . Afghan guards had shooed her away.'
Mark Dodd, 'Long-lost sniffer dog returns to duty with fellow Diggers',
The Australian, 13 November 2009

p. 224 '. . . developed a good relationship with the villagers . . .'
Anna K. Perry, 'Reconstruction efforts spawn hope in Southern
Afghanistan', *US Federal News Service*, US Army Special Operations
Command press release, 10 September 2008

p. 225 'An Afghan version of a lost-and-found notice . . .'
'Rescue plan for Digger dog', *The Australian*, 8 June 2010

p. 229 'You have cradled life in your arms . . .'
Ian McPhedran, 'Training was key to survival', *The Daily Telegraph*,
17 January 2009

p. 229 'I don't see myself as a hero, honestly . . .'
Mark Dodd, 'VC winner Mark Donaldson drew enemy fire, saved a mate
and fought on', *The Australian*, 17 January 2009. See also, Ian McPhedran, 'Nation salutes a true war hero', *The Daily Telegraph*, 17 January 2009

p. 230 'Oh, look, I don't know . . .'
Howard Gipps, *A Current Affair*

p. 230 'Plans were prepared to retrieve her . . .'
'Rescue plan for Digger dog', *The Australian*, 8 June 2010

p. 234 'It's a game we used to play . . .'
'Paws in the War: How Sabi [sic] the bomb dog's on the ball', *The Sydney Morning Herald*, 13 November 2009

p. 235 'When you know some of these dogs . . .'
'Keeping Our Four-Legged Forces Healthy,' Seattle Kennel Club
<www.seattlekennelclub.org>

CHAPTER 20

p. 237 'The staff spotted the intelligent . . .'
Bianca Clare, 'Furry friend killed in conflict', *The Sunshine Coast Daily*,
29 October 2009

p. 238 'There was no noise . . .'
Ian McPhedran, 'Scars, scares and death in Afghanistan', *The Daily
Telegraph*, 15 August 2009

p. 240   'You can see it now . . .'
         Misha Schubert, 'Sniffing around the real Sabi [sic] story', *The Age*,
         13 November 2009

p. 242   'Inadequate resources will likely result . . .'
         Stanley McChrystal, *Comisaf's Initial Assessment*, report to Robert M.
         Gates, US Secretary of Defense, 30 August 2009

p. 242   'She showed no signs of stress . . .'
         Katharine Murphy 'Sabi [sic] come home—Dog's year in the desert',
         The Age, 13 November 2009

p. 242   'loyal daughter of Australia'
         'Bomb Dog Sabi [sic] back on duty', *The Daily Telegraph*, 12 November
         2009

p. 242   'It may seem quite small, but in fact . . .'
         Brendan Trembath, 'Handler never gave up on lost army dog,' *PM*,
         ABC Radio, 12 November 2009

p. 243   'Churchill is drunk . . .'
         Amanda Meade, 'The Diary', *The Australian*, 16 November 2009

p. 244   'Sarbi's the last piece of the puzzle . . .'
         Mark Dodd, 'Long-lost sniffer dog returns to duty with fellow Diggers',
         The Australian, 13 November 2009

CHAPTER 21

Information about the RSPCA Australia Purple Cross was drawn from the
RSPCA's website. <http://www.rspca.org.au/what-we-do/awards/rspca-purple-
cross-award.html>

The author also attended the Purple Cross presentation ceremony for Sarbi at
the Australian War Memorial on 5 April 2011.

p. 251   'Murphy, the donkey that ferried soldiers . . .'
         'Kirkpatrick, John Simpson (1892–1915)' *Australian War Memorial*
         <www.awm.gov.au/Encyclopedia/spatrick.asp>

p. 252   'Give back our hero dog'
         Ian McPhedran, 'Give back our hero dog', *The Daily Telegraph*,
         22 November 2010

EPILOGUE

p. 257 'The remainder of us received shock over-blast effects . . .'
George Hulse, ADFT WDA, *Interviews with War Dog Operatives*, Series 4, Profile 3—Afghanistan: Sapper Brett Turley—Royal Australian Engineers <www.aussiewardogs.org/node/98>

p. 257 'We were both back on patrol duty . . .'
George Hulse, ADFT WDA, *Interviews with War Dog Operatives*

p. 259 '. . . the first multiple fatalities suffered . . .'
'Two Australian Soldiers killed by bomb on first tour of Afghanistan', *The Age*, 8 June 2010

p. 259 'training and conditions'
'Sapper Darren Smith, one of two soldiers killed in Afghanistan, is laid to rest', *The Courier Mail*, 20 June 2010

p. 259 '. . . one of the boys . . . everyone looks after him . . .'
Chris Masters, 'A Careful War', *Four Corners*, ABC TV, 12 July 2010

p. 260 '[It's] just great morale . . .'
Chris Masters, 'A Careful War'

p. 260 '. . . regarded by his fellow Diggers as one . . .'
Chris Masters, 'A Careful War'

p. 260 'If only we had a troop full of Snowys . . .'
'Sapper obituaries, Lest We Forget', *Australian Sapper*, 2010, p. 52

p. 260 'disturbing fashion sense'
'Sapper obituaries, Lest We Forget', p. 52

p. 261 'Even though it was one of many bangs that we heard . . .'
Leigh Sales, 'Defence mourning after tremendous loss', *Lateline*, ABC TV, 8 June 2010

p. 262 'The first five minutes after it happened . . .'
Chris Masters, 'A Careful War'

p. 262 'Jacob and Darren were the epitome . . .'
'Fallen Australian Soldiers commence final journey', Australian Government, Department of Defence press release, MECC 214/10, 10 June 2010

p. 263 'At the end of the day, Herbie saved lives . . .'
'Herbie Finally Home To Rest In Peace', Australian Government, Department of Defence press release, 30 June 2010

p. 263 'It's nice to finally leave them both to rest together.'
'Herbie Finally Home To Rest In Peace'

p. 263 'He was very passionate about his job . . .'
Ian McPhedran, 'Diggers Darren Smith and Jacob Moerland killed in Taliban bomb trap', *The Daily Telegraph*, 9 June 2010

p. 264 'I call the photo "the bond" . . .'
'A memorial for Australia's Explosive Detection Dogs killed in action in Afghanistan', Australian Government, Department of Defence news release, 5 July 2011

Bibliography

BOOKS

Nick Allen, *Embedded with the World's Armies in Afghanistan*, Spellmount, Stroud UK, 2010

Anonymous, *Hunting al-Qaeda: A Take-No-Prisoners Account of Terror, Adventure, and Disillusionment*, Zenith Press, Minneapolis MN, 2005

John C. Burnam, *A Soldier's Best Friend: Scout Dogs and Their Handlers in the Vietnam War*, Union Square Press, New York, 2008

Shane Bryant with Tony Park, *War Dogs, An Australian and His Dog Go To War in Afghanistan*, Pan Macmillan Australia, Sydney, 2010

Sarah Chayes, *The Punishment of Virtue: Inside Afghanistan After the Taliban*, Penguin, New York, 2006

Anthony Cordesman and Emma Davies, *Iraq's Insurgency and the Road to Civil Conflict*, Centre for Strategic and International Studies, Washington DC, 2008

Stanley Coren, *How to Speak Dog: Mastering the Art of Dog–Human Communication*, Free Press, New York, 2000

——*The Pawprints of History: Dogs and the Course of Human Events*, Free Press, New York, 2002

——*Why We Love the Dogs We Do: How to Find the Dog That Matches Your Personality*, Fireside, New York, 1998

Brian Dennis, Kirby Larson, Mary Nethery, *Nubs: The True Story of a Mutt, a Marine and a Miracle*, Little, Brown and Company, London, 2009

Tracy L. English, *The Quiet Americans: A History of Military Working Dogs*, Office of History, Lackland Air Force Base, Lackland TX <www.lackland. af.mil/shared/media/document/AFD-061212-027.pdf>

David W. Gaier, *Guidelines for Roving Security Inspections in Public Venues Using Explosives Detection Dogs*, American Society of Civil Engineers, 2010

Genelle Guzman-McMillan, *Angel in the Rubble*, Inspired Living/Allen & Unwin, Sydney, 2011

Sandra Lee, *18 Hours: The True Story of an SAS War Hero*, HarperCollins, Pymble NSW, 2006

Michael G. Lemish, *War Dogs: A History of Loyalty and Heroism*, Potomac Books, Dulles VA, 2008

M is for Mate: Animals in Wartime from Ajax to Zep, Department of Veterans' Affairs and The Australian War Memorial, Canberra, 2009

Peter Haran, *Trackers: The Untold Story of the Australian Dogs of War*, New Holland, Chatswood, NSW, 2000

Alexandra Horowitz, *Inside of a Dog: What Dogs See, Smell, and Know*, Scribner, New York, 2009

Seth Jones, *In the Graveyard of Empires*, W.W. Norton and Co., New York, 2009

Konrad Lorenz, *Man Meets Dog* (translated by Marjorie Kerr Wilson), Routledge Classics, London and New York, 1954

Rob Maylor and Robert Macklin, *SAS Sniper: The World of an Elite Australian Marksman*, Hachette, Sydney, 2010

Patricia B. McConnell, *For the Love of A Dog: Understanding Emotions in You and Your Dog*, Ballantine Books, New York, 2007

Frances E. Ruffin, *Dog Heroes: Military Dogs*, Bearport Publishing, New York, 2007

Jessica Stern, *The Ultimate Terrorists*, Harvard University Press, Cambridge MA, 1999

——*Terror in the Name of God*, Ecco, New York, 2004

Stephen Tanner, *Afghanistan: A Military History from Alexander the Great to the Fall of the Taliban*, Da Capo Press, New York, 2002

Bing West, *The Wrong War: Grit, Strategy, and the Way Out of Afghanistan*, Random House, New York, 2011

Mohammad Yousaf and Mark Adkin, *Afghanistan, The Bear Trap: The Defeat of a Superpower*, Casemate, Haverton PA, 1991, 2001

ARTICLES

'Dutch to review SAS claims', AAP, 22 October 2010

'Three soldiers still in a serious condition', AAP, 4 September 2008

'Service honours bomb detection dog', <ABCnews.net.au> 27 June 2010

Fisnik Abrashi, '2 NATO troops killed in Afghanistan', AP, 15 August 2008

Shahid Afsar, Chris Samples, Thomas Wood, 'The Taliban, An Organizational Analysis', Military Review, May–June 2008

'Aussie troops kill 150 Taliban fighters', The Age, 12 September 2006

'Army dog Nova killed in Afghanistan', The Age, 26 October 2009

'Two Australian Soldiers killed by bomb on first tour of Afghanistan', The Age, 8 June 2010 <www.theage.com.au>

Cathy Alexander, 'VC winner is Young Aussie of the year', The Sydney Morning Herald, 25 January 2010

'Tagged for action, Counter-terrorism capability unveiled', Army: The Soldiers' Newspaper, 2002

'Missing military dog found in Afghanistan after 14 months', Associated Press, 12 November 2009

'Diggers in Afghan gun battle', The Australian, 9 July 2007

'Medals bestowed on fallen soldiers Jacob Moreland (sic) and Darren Smith', The Australian, 13 June 2010

'Rescue plan for Digger dog', The Australian, 8 June 2010

Australian Sapper, 2007 edition

Australian Sapper, 2008 edition

Australian Sapper, 2009 edition

Australian Sapper, 2010 edition

Australian Sapper, Head of Corps, Royal Australian Engineers, Moorebank NSW, 2010 edition, p. 52

Lois Baker, 'Pet dog or cat controls blood pressure better than ACE inhibitor', newswise.com 11 August 1999

Haydn Barlow, 'RTF2 takes the reins', Army: The Soldiers' Newspaper, 3 May 2007

—— 'Wired For Action', Army: The Soldiers' Newspaper, 20 September 2007

Josh Bavas, 'Vaporised war Dog Receives posthumous Medal', <abc.net.au> 5 March 2009

'Australia to Double Afghan Force', BBC, <bbc.co.uk> 10 April 2007

'Dead soldier Liam Tasker and Army dog return home', BBC, <bbc.co.uk> 10 March 2011

'Dog lost in Afghan battle returns', BBC, <bbc.co.uk> 12 November 2009

Mark Berman, 'A Loyal Soldier Is Mourned, MP Sergeant from Michigan was killed in Afghanistan', *The Washington Post*, 16 September 2008

Max Blenkin, 'Aussie soldier braves Taliban fire to rescue Afghan', AAP, 11 December 2008

Max Blenkin, 'Dog Killed on Afghan Duty', *The Age*, 6 September 2007

Max Blenkin, 'IEDs pose highest risk to Aust troops in Afghanistan', AAP, 9 October 2007

'Bomb-sniffing dog back after year lost in Afghanistan', <www.cbc.ca/news> 12 November 2009

Corrine Boer, 'Dogs of War', *Army: The Soldier's Newspaper*, 15 May 2008

—— 'Razz dies saving his mates' lives', *Army: The Soldier's Newspaper*, 4 October 2007

Elbert Chu, 'The Bulletproof dog that stormed Bin Laden's lair', <www.fastcompany.com> 16 May 2011

Bianca Clare, 'Furry friend killed in conflict', *The Sunshine Coast Daily*, 29 October 2009

Philip Clark, *Summer Radio*, ABC702 Radio, 14 January 2011

Tom Coghlan, 'Combat dogs take to the skies for secret missions in Afghanistan', *The Times* [UK], 16 March 2010

Mark Colvin, 'Australian soldiers wounded in Afghanistan', *PM*, 3 September 2008

Kevin Connolly, 'McChrystal in the line of fire.' BBC Online, 22 June 2010 <bbc.co.uk>

Pamela Constable, 'Gates visits Kabul, cites rise in cross-border attacks', *The Washington Post*, 17 January 2007

Philip Coorey, 'Forces Stuck with Borrowed Choppers', *The Sydney Morning Herald*, 13 August 2008

'Sapper Darren Smith, one of two soldiers killed in Afghanistan, is laid to rest', *The Courier Mail*, 20 June 2010

Alan Cullison and Yaroslav Trofimov, 'Karzai Bans Ingredient of Taliban's Roadside Bombs', *The Wall Street Journal*, 3 February 2010

'Army Sniffer Dog Merlin Killed in Accident', *The Daily Telegraph*, 5 September 2007

'Aussie bomb detection dog's remains to come home', *The Daily Telegraph*, 15 June 2010

'Aussie war dog will be home for Christmas', *The Daily Telegraph*, 25 October 2010

'Bomb Dog Sabi [sic] back on duty', *The Daily Telegraph*, 12 November 2009

Thomas L. Day, 'Rare IED success: MRAPs cut U.S. death rate in Afghanistan', *McClatchy Newspapers*, 19 January 2010

Mark Derr, 'Darwin's dogs; celebrating the bicentennial of the father of evolution', <*thebark*.com> 27 February, 2009

'Gregory A Rodriguez', *The Detroit News*, 6 September 2008

Mark Dodd, 'Aussie special forces crush Taliban leaders in Afghanistan', *The Australian*, 12 December 2008

——'Blast kills second bomb dog', *The Australian*, 25 September 2007

—— 'Long-lost sniffer dog returns to duty with fellow Diggers', *The Australian*, 13 November 2009

——'Push For Diggers To Get Medivacs in Afghanistan', *The Australian*, 13 August 2008

——'VC Hero Tires of PR and Goes Back to Afghanistan', *The Australian*, 23 July 2010

——'VC winner Mark Donaldson drew enemy fire, saved a mate and fought on', *The Australian*, 17 January 2009

Mark Donaldson, 'For Most Conspicuous Acts of Gallantry', *Defence*, Issue 1, 2009

Mark Dunn, 'Fallen soldier Matthew Locke told: no armour', *The Daily Telegraph*, 1 November 2007

Damian Dunne, 'Our digger dogs', *That's Life!*, Issue 16, 22 April 2009

Catherine Ellis, 'Sniffer Dogs', *Behind the News*, 1 April 2008 <abc.com.au>

Malcolm Farr, 'Rudd's long haul promise to fight Afghan terrorists', *The Daily Telegraph*, 12 November 2009

——'Rudd visits Diggers: PM's food for thought', *The Herald Sun*, 12 November 2009

——'Rudd's secret visit; PM shares ceremony with Diggers in Afghanistan', *The Daily Telegraph*, 12 November 2009

——'Rudd in war for long haul', *The Australian*, 12 November 2009

John Ferguson and Malcolm Farr, 'Digger dog beats Taliban', *The Herald Sun*, 13 November 2009

'UK Army Dog may have died of a broken heart', *Fox News*, <www.foxnews.com/world/2011/03/10/uk-army-dog-died-broken-heart-1606316739> 10 March 2011

Rebecca Frankel, 'War Dog', *Foreign Policy*, 4 May 2011

Meghan Galer, Donna Magid and Les Folio, 'Radiology corner; Gun shot wound to the chest of a military working dog', *Military Medicine Radiology Corner*, Volume 174, June 2009

Heath Gilmore, 'We Said Our Brave Son was Invincible', *The Sydney Morning Herald*, <smh.com.au> 28 October 2007

Howard Gipps, *A Current Affair*, Nine Network, 16 January 2009

Global Security.org, Forward Operating Base Ripley / Kamp Holland <www.globalsecurity.org/military/facility/fob_ripley.htm>

Anand Gopal, 'Taliban wages war on aid groups', *The Christian Science Monitor*, 15 August 2008

Stephen Graham, 'US-led coalition: Warplanes kill 33 militants in eastern Afghanistan', *AP*, 1 July 2008

Al Green, 'Home Sweet Home, The Special Operations Task Group's first days at Camp Russell', *Army: The Soldiers' Newspaper*

Jason Gutierrez, 'Dogs of War Save Lives in Afghanistan', *Discovery News*, American Free Press, 28 January 2010 <DiscoveryNews.com>

Toby Harden, 'Interview: General Stanley McChrystal', *The Telegraph* (UK) <telegraph.co.uk> 23 March 2010

Gardiner Harris, 'A Bin Laden hunter on four legs', *The New York Times*, 4 May 2011

Peter Harvey, 'Our Valiant Few', *60 Minutes*, Nine Network, 24 April 2009

Michael Hastings, 'The Runaway General', *Rolling Stone magazine*, 22 June 2010

Kelvin Healey, 'Our Troops Declare in Dogs We Trust', *The Advertiser*, 22 June 2009

Joe Hirsh and Cynthia R. Fagen, 'Hero's welcome home for dogs of war', *The New York Post*, 30 July 2010

'Our Sappers today—what are our Sappers faced with in the Middle East?',

Holdfast, The Official Newsletter of the Vietnam Tunnel Rats Association Inc Number 14 February 2009

George Hulse, *Interviews with War Dog Operatives*, Series 4, Profile 4— Afghanistan, Corporal John Cannon—Royal Australian Engineers <www. aussiewardogs.org/downloads/Cpl%20John%20Cannon.pdf >

——'EDD 476 Herbie KIA 07 June 2010', *Australian Defence Force Trackers and War Dogs Association*, 12 June 2010

Tom Hyland, 'A very high-ranking mutt inspires a shaggy dog tale', *The Age*, 20 December 2009

——'Afghanistan's deadly Double Whammy', *The Sunday Age*, 22 June 2008

——'Aussie soldiers fire on civilians', *The Age*, 29 July 2007

——'Hearts and Minds Not Won', *The Sunday Age*, 22 June 2008

——'How the ADF kept saga of Sabi the wonder dog on a tight leash', *The Age*, 15 November 2009

Geoff Hutchison, 'The Secret is out – meet Australia's most decorated soldier', *Mornings with Geoff Hutchison*, Perth720 ABC Radio, 24 January 2011

Kieran Jackel, 'Australian and Afghan Sappers Deliver Magical Effect to Talani School', *Australian Sapper*, 2007 edition

Grace Jean, 'Building Miniature "Noses" to Sniff Explosives', *National Defense* (US), business and technology magazine of the National Defense Industrial Association (NDIA), October 2007

James Jeffrey, 'Strewth! Rudd dogs it for Sabi [sic]', *The Australian*, 13 November 2009

Ed Johnson, 'Gates wants NATO to reorganize [sic] Afghanistan Mission, update 1', <www.bloomberg.com> 12 December 2007

Thomas H. Johnson, 'On The Edge of the Big Muddy: The Taliban Resurgence in Afghanistan', *China and Eurasia Forum Quarterly*, Vol. 5, No. 2, 2007

——'The Taliban insurgency and an analysis of Shabnamah (night letters)', *Small Wars and Insurgencies*, Vol. 18, No. 3, September 2007

Jessica Johnston, 'PM gets a taste of Afghanistan', *The Townsville Bulletin*, 13 November 2009

——'Sarbi the Army wonder dog found safe in Afghanistan', *Perth Now*, <www.perthnow.com.au> 12 November 2009

Randi Kaye, *Anderson Cooper 360*, CNN, 18 November 2010

Colin H. Kahl, 'How we fight', *Foreign Affairs*, November/December 2006

Adrienne Killingsworth, 'Military working dogs: A tribute to Ardy', US Army, <www.army.mil/article/38878> 11 May 2010

Kahli Lynam, 'Canine heroes – man's best friend on the frontlines', *Queensland RSL News*, Autumn 2009

Sandra Lee, 'What's up, dog?' *Sunday magazine*, *The Sunday Herald Sun*, 17 July 2009

'Along with a troop surge in Afghanistan, a dog surge: along with a dog surge, a food dilemma', *The Los Angeles Times*, 25 January 2010

Chris Masters, 'A Careful War', *Four Corners*, ABC TV, 12 July 2010

——'Forward Base Afghanistan', *Four Corners*, ABC TV, 2 July 2007

——'Journalist Chris Masters recalls the moment Aussie troops lost two mates', *The Herald Sun*, 7 June 2010

——'Trouble at the gate', *Australia Network News* (provided by the ABC Asia Pacific News Centre) 11 June 2010

Aaron Matzkows, 'Doggies' style on Op Anode', *Army: The Soldiers' Newspaper*, June 2006

Steve Meacham, 'Welcome home, Sarbi, trusty dog of war', *The Sydney Morning Herald*, 11 January 2011

Amanda Meade, 'The Diary', *The Australian*, 16 November 2009

Paul McGeough, 'SAS combatants strike deep into Taliban heartland', *Sydney Morning Herald*, 27 September 2005

David McLennan, 'Locke will not be forgotten: commander', *The Canberra Times*, 30 October 2007

Ian McPhedran, 'Australian soldiers left for dead in Afghanistan by Dutch Apache helicopters', *The Courier Mail*, 21 October 2010

—— 'Battle salute for Diggers', *The Advertiser*, 28 September 2006

—— 'Diggers Darren Smith and Jacob Moerland killed in Taliban bomb trap', *The Daily Telegraph*, 9 June 2010

—— 'Dutch Left soldiers for dead in Afghanistan', *The Daily Telegraph*, 22 October 2010

—— 'How Diggers are risking all for mates', *The Daily Telegraph*, 12 December 2008

—— 'Sabi [sic] the wonder dog awarded two medals, but may never be able to come home to Australia', *The Herald Sun*, 9 February 2010

—— 'Sarbi heading back into the fray', *The Daily Telegraph*, 10 January 2011

—— 'Training was key to survival', *The Daily Telegraph*, 17 January 2009

—— 'Nation salutes a true war hero', *The Daily Telegraph*, 17 January 2009

—— 'Scars, scares and death in Afghanistan', *The Daily Telegraph*, 15 August 2009

——'Give back our hero dog', *The Daily Telegraph*, 22 November 2010

Alastair McPherson, 'Paws for reflection', *Army: The Soldiers' Newspaper*, 19 March 2009

—— 'Nose on the line', *Army: The Soldiers' Newspaper*, 18 March 2010

Donna Miles, 'Military working dogs', *American Forces Press Service*, 3 September 2004

Emily Moser and Michael McCulloch, 'Canine scent detection of human cancers: A review of methods and accuracy', *Journal of Veterinary Behavior*, Vol. 5, No. 3, May/June 2010

Katharine Murphy 'Sabi [sic] come home—Dog's year in the desert', *The Age*, 13 November 2009

—— 'We're in Afghanistan for long haul, PM tells troops', *The Age*, 12 November 2009

Katharine Murphy and Sally Pryor, 'PM amid dust and Diggers', *The Canberra Times*, 12 November 2009

Yuko Narushima, 'Soldier's feat the stuff of Australian legend', *The Sydney Morning Herald*, 17 January 2009

'When a dog is truly a man's best friend', *National Dog—The Ringleader Way*, Volume 12 Number 10

'The bloodhound's amazing sense of smell', *Nature* <pbs.org> January 2006

Sean Naylor, 'Air Force Policy left ground troops high and dry', *Army Times* [US], 30 September 2002

'Army dog picks up scent', *National Dog Magazine*, April 10 2010

'Australian soldiers kill truck driver', <news.com.au> 26 July 2007

'PM Kevin Rudd visits troops in Afghanistan on way to India', <news.com.au> 12 November 2009

'Brave dog remembered', <news.com.au> 6 July 2010

Brendan Nicholson, 'NATO Failure Endangering Australian Forces', *The Age*, 27 November 2007

——'You Think I'm Brave? Meet My Mates: Ben Roberts-Smith', *The Australian*, 23 April 2011

Susan Oldroyd, 'Explosive canines', *Army: The Soldiers' Newspaper* <www.defence.gov.au/news/armynews/editions/1077/topstories/story07.htm>

Will Pavia, 'Afghanistan war hero dog Target mistakenly put down by US pound', *The Australian*, 17 November 2010

Jonathan Pearlman, 'Alliance rescue did not fail signalman,' *The Sydney Morning Herald*, 27 August 2008

——'Nine Australian soldiers hurt in Taliban ambush,' *The Sydney Morning Herald*, 4 September 2009

Peter Pedersen, 'Recock and Refigure, Trooper Mark Donaldson, VC, speaks', *Wartime: Official Magazine of the Australian War Memorial*, Issue 46, 2009

Andrew Pierce, 'Hug for Queen Elizabeth's first corgi', *The Telegraph* (UK), <www.telegraph.co.uk> 1 October 2007

Meg Purtell, 'Sniffer Dogs', *Stateline*, ABC Television, 14 March 2008

Braden Quartermaine, 'Heroes tell of frontline hell', *The Sunday Times*, 3 December 2006

Sean Rayment, 'British Soldier and his faithful friend die side-by-side in Afghanistan', *The Telegraph* (UK), 27 July 2008

Mark Ranzenberger, 'Rodriguez to be buried in Arlington', *The Morning Sun*, 8 September 2008

Bruce Riedel, 'al-Qaeda Strikes Back', *Foreign Affairs*, May/June, 2007

Georgina Robinson, 'Ninth Australian soldier killed in Afghanistan', *WAtoday.com.au* 17 March 2009

Barnett R. Rubin, 'Saving Afghanistan', *Foreign Affairs*, January/February 2007

Kevin Rudd, interview on *CNN*, 21 September 2009

Kelly Ryan, 'Plea to save hero dog from Afghan war', *The Herald Sun*, 20 May 2010

Leigh Sales, 'Defence mourning after tremendous loss', *Lateline*, ABC TV, 8 June 2010

Misha Schubert, 'Sniffing around the real Sabi [sic] story', *The Age*, 13 November 2009

Richard Shears, 'Sabi [sic], the real story— how Aussie bomb dog was rescued from the Taliban', *The Daily Telegraph*, 26 December 2009

Sarah Smiles, 'Injured Soldiers Wait Six Hours', *The Age*, 13 August 2008

Britt Smith, 'Bomb dog Sarbi reunited with handler', *The Sydney Morning Herald*, 10 January 2011

Tony Stephens, 'Engraved in history, the bravery of No 97', *The Sydney Morning Herald*, 17 January 2009

Jason Straziuso, 'Official: 9 US troops killed in Afghanistan', *AP*, 13 July 2008

Jan E. Szulejko, Michael McCulloch, Jennifer Jackson, Dwight L. McKee, Jim C. Walker and Touradj Solouki, 'Evidence for cancer biomarkers in exhaled breath', *IEEE Sensors Journal*, Vol. 10, No. 1, January 2010

'Paws in the War: How Sabi [sic] the bomb dog's on the ball', *The Sydney Morning Herald*, 13 November 2009

Owais Tohid and Scott Baldauf, *The Christian Science Monitor*, 25 June 2004

Brendan Trembath, 'Handler never gave up on lost army dog,' *PM*, ABC Radio, 12 November 2009

'Tribute for Sergeant Matthew Locke', *Defence Magazine*, 2007

'True warrior receives Victoria Cross', *The Herald Sun*, 23 January 2011

Lanai Vasak, 'Just doing my job, says VC winner Mark Donaldson', *The Australian*, 4 January 2010

Jamie Walker, 'Botched Medivac as Digger in Afghanistan lay dying', *The Australian*, 26 July 2008

Patrick Walters, 'US to urge for bigger role for Diggers—More Afghan for troops', *The Weekend Australian*, 22 August 2009

—— 'Afghanistan test looms for leader', *The Weekend Australian*, 22 August 2009

'Homemade Bombs Basic But Deadly', <*TheWest.com.au*>, 28 June 2010

'Rufus, Target and Sasha save US soldiers', *The Oprah Winfrey Show*, Harpo Productions, 4 October 2010

Phillip Williams, 'SAS Trooper gets VC from Queen', *Radio Australia*, ABC Radio, 11 November 2009

GOVERNMENT PRESS RELEASES/MEDIA RELEASES/ PRESS CONFERENCES/REPORTS

Progress in Afghanistan Since 2001, Australian Government, Department of Defence Fact Sheet <www.defence.gov.au/op/afghanistan/info/factsheet.htm>

'Special Forces to Deploy to Afghanistan', Australian Government, Department of Defence media release, 113/05, 13 July 2005

Robert Hill, 'Press conference with Prime Minister John Howard, Parliament House Canberra', Transcript, 13 July 2005

——'Interview with Tracy Grimshaw, *Today Show*, Melbourne', Transcript, 14 July 2005

'Australian Special Forces conduction Operations in Afghanistan', Australian Government, Department of Defence media release, MECC 230/05, 23 September 2005

'Afghan Veterans Welcomed Home', Australian Government, Department of Defence media release, MECC 45/06, 4 March 2006

'ADF Prepared for Improvised Explosive Device Threat', Australian Government, Department of Defence media release, MECC 141/06, 29 June 2006

'Afghanistan Veterans Welcomed Home— Soldiers' Gallantry Honoured', Australian Government, Department of Defence media release, MECC 337/06, 2 December 2006

'RTF Soldier Slightly wounded in Failed Uruzgan Suicide Attack' Australian Government, Department of Defence media release MECC 120/07, 4 May 2007

'Dutch Attacked in Afghanistan', Australian Government, Department of Defence media release, MECC 161/07, 16 June 2007

'Shooting Incident In Afghanistan', Australian Government, Department of Defence media release, MECC214/07, 25 July 2007

'RTF mourns Merlin', Australian Government, Department of Defence media release, MECC 282/07, 5 September 2007

'Explosive Detection Dogs to Be Honoured', Australian Government, Department of Defence media release, CPA 336/072, 6 September 2007

'SOTG Soldiers Wounded in Uruzgan Attack', Australian Government, Department of Defence media release, MECC 301/07, 14 September 2007

'Explosive Detection Dog Killed by Taliban Roadside Bomb' Australian Government, Department of Defence media release, MSPA 330/07, 27 September 2007

'Diggers Defeat Taliban Attack in Heavy Fighting' Australian Government, Department of Defence media release, MECC 338/07, 24 September 2007

'Name released of SASR Trooper', Australian Government, Department of Defence, media release, CPA 400/07, 26 October 2007

'Sergeant Matthew Locke', Australian Government, Department of Defence media release, October 2007

'Sergeant Locke Returns Home', Australian Government, Department of Defence media release, MECC 408/07, 31 October 2007

'Canberra cancelled robot unit for bombs', Department of Defence response to article by Mark Dodd, *The Australian*, 6 November 2007

'Afghanistan soldiers mourn Andy', Australian Government, Department of Defence media release, MSPA 454/07, 25 November 2007

'Soldiers Wounded in Improved Explosive Device Attack in Afghanistan', Australian Government, Department of Defence media release, MECC 209/08, 8 July 2008

'Special Operations Soldier Killed— Three Wounded', Australian Government, Department of Defence media release, MSPA 211/08, 9 July 2008

'Aero-Medical Evacuation of Signaller Sean McCarthy', Australian Government, Department of Defence media release, MECC 244/08, 26 July 2008

'Senior Taliban Extremist Commander Captured by Australian Special Forces', Australian Government, Department of Defence media release, MSPA 253/08, 10 August 2008

'SOTG Soldiers Wounded in Uruzgan IED Blast' Australian Government, Department of Defence media release, MSPA 255/08, 12 August 2008

'Special operations Task Group soldiers Wounded in Afghanistan', Australian Government, Department of Defence press release, MSPA 284/08, 3 September 2008

'Special operations Task Group soldiers Wounded in Afghanistan - Update', Australian Government, Department of Defence press release, MSPA 290/08, 5 September 2008

'Special operations Task Group soldiers Wounded in Afghanistan Update', Australian Government, Department of Defence press release, MSPA 295/08, 10 September 2008

'Australian Army Awarded the Victoria Cross for Trooper Mark Gregor Donaldson' [official citation], Australian Government, Department of Defence, 16 January 2009

'The Chief of The Defence Force Salutes Trooper Mark Donaldson, VC', Australian Government, Department of Defence media release, MECC 19/09, 16 January 2009

'Canines round up medals', Australian Government, Department of Defence Image Gallery, January 2009

'Farewell ceremony for Explosive Detection Dog Nova', Australian Government, Department of Defence Image Gallery, 26 October 2009

'Sabi (sic) The Special Forces Dog Laps It Up', Australian Government, Department of Defence Speech, MECC 425/09, 9 December 2009

'Release of the inquiry officer report into the death of Private Benjamin Ranaudo', Australian Government, Department of Defence Speech, MSPA 91217/09, 17 December 2009

'Biography—Sapper Darren James Smith', Australian Government, Department of Defence press release, 8 June 2010

Fallen Australian Soldiers commence final journey', Australian Government, Department of Defence press release, MECC 214/10, 10 June 2010

'Herbie Finally Home to Rest', Australian Government, Department of Defence, press release, 30 June 2010

Major General Michael Hindmarsh, Australian Government, Department of Defence press conference, Canberra, 27 September 2006

The Chief of Defence Air Marshal Angus Houston, Australian Government, Department of Defence press conference, Canberra, Transcript, 9 June 2008

'Australian Troops Assist Improvised Explosive Device Victims', Australian Government, Department of Defence media release, MECC 230/08, 16 July 2008

'Canines Round Up Medals', Australian Government, Department of Defence media release, 6 March 2009

'MRTF-2 Mourns Nova', Australian Government, Department of Defence media release MECC 366/09, 26 October 2009

'Australian Dog Returns Home After a Year in the Afghan Wilderness', Australian Government, Department of Defence media release, MECC 386/09, 12 November 2009

'Battle casualties— AFG', Australian Government, Department of Defence, 23 December 2010

'Sarbi returns to her regiment', Australian Government, Department of Defence, defence news, 11 January 2011

'Australian Army Awarded the Victoria Cross for Australia Corporal Benjamin Roberts-Smith, VC, MG, Citation, Australian Government, Department of Defence, 23 January 2011

'The Chief of the Defence Force congratulates Corporal Benjamin Roberts-Smith, VC, MG, Australian Government, Department of Defence media release MECC 20/11, 23 January 2011

'A memorial for Australia's explosive detection dogs killed in action in Afghanistan', Australian Government, Department of Defence news release, 5 July 2011

Brigadier Brian Dawson, 'Media Doorstop for Return of Explosive Detection Dog Sabi (sic)', Australian Government, Department of Defence, Speech, MSPA 91112/09, 12 November 2009

Brigadier Brian Dawson, Australian Government, Department of Defence press conference, Canberra, 13 November 2009 (via <http://blogs.abc.net.au/files/brigadier-brian-dawson-press-conf-edit.mp3>)

'ADF Operations update— questions and answers', Australian Government, Department of Defence, Transcript, MECC 70221/07, 22 February 2007

Gus Gilmore, 'ADF Operations Update', Australian Government, Department of Defence, Transcript, MECC 7051/07, 10 May 2007

Russell Maddalena, Australian Government, Department of Defence press conference, Canberra, 10 May 2007

Lieutenant General Ken Gillespie, 'Announcement of the Inquiry Findings Into Operational Incidents in Afghanistan in 2007', Australian Government, Department of Defence, Transcript, MECC 80512/08, 12 May 2008

Air Chief Marshal Angus Houston, 'Media Conference By The Chief of Defence Force, Air Chief Marshal Angus Houston, Regarding the Death of an Australian Soldier in Southern Afghanistan', Australian Government, Department of Defence, Transcript, MSPA 80428/08, 28 April 2008

Air Chief Marshal Angus Houston, 'Media Conference By The Chief of Defence Force Regarding the Death of an Australian Soldier in Afghanistan', Australian Government, Department of Defence, Speech, MSPA 80709/08, 9 July 2008

Lieutenant General David Hurley, 'Media Conference By the Vice Chief of the Defence Force Announcement Re: Findings into the Death of An Australian Soldier in Afghanistan and Claims of Mistreatment of Detainees', Australian Government, Department of Defence, Speech, MSPA 80829/08, 29 August 2008

Major General Tim McOwan, 'Update on Special Operations in Afghanistan', Australian Government, Department of Defence press conference, 11 December 2008

'The Other Side of the COIN; 1st Reconstruction Task Force Operations and Observations', Lieutenant Colonel Mick Ryan

Official unclassified Inquiry Officer's report on Signaller McCarthy's death of August 2008

Kevin Rudd, 'Prime Minister Transcript of press conference New Delhi', Prime Minister of Australia, 12 November 2009

Stephen Smith, Australian Minister for Foreign Affairs and Trade, Ministerial statement, 'Afghanistan and Pakistan', 18 August 2009

P.J. Short, 'Inquiry Officer's Report Into The Death of 8265028 Pte L.J. Worsley in Afghanistan on 23 Nov 07, unclassified', 18 December 2007

S.G. Durward, 'Inquiry Officer's Report Into The Death of 8229246 Sergeant M.R. Locke In Afghanistan on 25 Oct 07, unclassified', 22 January 2008

S.G. Durward, 'Inquiry Officer's Report Into The Death of 8298024 Tpr D.R. Pearce and Injury to [unnamed] in Afghanistan on 8 Oct 07, unclassified', 22 Jan 08

D. K. Connery, 'Inquiry Officer's Report Into The Death of Lance Corporal Jason Paul Marks and the Wounding of Australian Soldiers in Afghanistan on 27 April 2008 (Marks Inquiry), unclassified', 3 June 2008

D. K. Connery, 'Inquiry Officer's Report Into The Death of Signaller S.P. McCarthy in Afghanistan on 8 Jul 08, unclassified', August 2008

US Department of Defense, 'news briefing with Maj. Gen. Schloesser from Afghanistan', 24 June 2008

US Department of Defense, news briefing, 5 September 2008

Michigan Governor Jennifer M. Graham press release, 'Flags to be flown half-staff on Sept 19, 22, for servicemen killed while on active duty in Afghanistan', 17 September 2008

Anna K. Perry, 'Reconstruction efforts spawn hope in Southern Afghanistan', *US Federal News Service*, US Army Special Operations Command press release, 10 September 2008

Stanley McChrystal, *Comisaf's Initial Assessment*, report to Robert M. Gates, US Secretary of Defense, 30 August 2009

'Afghanistan, D Coy Op Slipper', 1 RAR: The First Battalion Association <www.firstbattalionassociation1rar.org.au/info.php?id=13>

'The Dutch Engagement in Uruzgan, 2006–2010: A Socio-political Assessment', The Liaison Office (independent Afghan NGO), <www.tlo-afghanistan.org> August 2010

Connections, Defence, Science and Technology Organisation, May 2006

Presentation of the Military Order of William to Captain Marco Kroon,

Ministry of Defence of the Netherlands, Directorate of Information and Communication, The Hague, 29 May 2009

Michael Tafe, 'Precinct Security Planning: Lessons Learnt—Melbourne 2006 Commonwealth Games', Speech delivered at the *Mass Transport, Mass Gathering and Precinct Security Conference*, 8 November 2007

WEBSITES

The Afghanistan Analysts Network <http://aan-afghanistan.com/index. asp?id=47>

The Australian Defence Force Trackers and War Dogs Association (ADFT-WDA) <www.aussiewardogs.org>

Australian Government Department of Defence <www.defence.gov.au>

Australian Government Department of Defence, EDD Sarbi's homepage <http://www.defence.gov.au/sarbi/index.htm>

The Australian War Memorial <http://awm.gov.au>

'Keeping Our Four-Legged Forces Healthy,' Seattle Kennel Club <www. seattlekennelclub.org>

Hope For The Warriors titled 'Army Guardsman reunites with lifesaving Afghani dogs', 2010 <www.robertscause.org/hope_warriors_article_july10.pdf>

International Security Assistance Force (ISAF), Afghanistan <http://www. isaf.nato.int/>

Pets For Patriots, Bring Loyalty Home charity organisation (US) <http://www. petsforpatriots.org>

The Last Post Association Ieper, <http://www.lastpost.be/en/index/index/slug/ home>

The Royal Society for the Prevention of Cruelty to Animals, Australia <http:// www.rspca.org.au>

Acknowledgements

First and foremost, sincere thanks to Sergeant D. Unfortunately, because of his ongoing role in the Australian Army, he cannot be identified but he deserves recognition—and, arguably, a medal—for his actions under fire on 2 September 2008. He was wounded and kept fighting. The self-possessed Doggie gave generously of his time and talked me through dog training, battle strategy and tactics. He also taught me how to get a recalcitrant hound—mine—to shake paws in less than ten minutes. Sergeant D is a first-rate dog handler, a very fine soldier, and a truly decent Australian. Our nation is richer for his service. So are the Doggies.

I would also like to thank the beautiful, big-hearted Wendy Upjohn and her wonderful and talented children Gemma, Nic and Marcelo. They shared their beloved pets with the Australian public and did so with stellar intentions, if very heavy hearts. As a family, they raised two adorable pups and watched over them lovingly for three years, during which Sarbi and Rafi were prepared for a life of action, adventure and proud public service.

And to Sarbi, if she could read, *woof!* What a girl!

The Special Operations Command is especially protective of operational, security and tactical matters and, as such, the Army's highest command did not want Sarbi's story told. Fortunately, I had a secret weapon—a former Duntroon graduate and retired Royal Australian Artillery Officer who believed in the project and helped persuade the most senior brass they should, too. Thank you, Robert Joske. I have enormous respect for your style of 'golf diplomacy'.

Thanks, also, to the former Chief of Army, Lieutenant General Ken Gillespie (retired), who ultimately gave the green light and opened the door to the internal workings of the Explosive Detection Dog Section. Thanks must go to Sergeant D's chain of command at the Incident Response Regiment, who welcomed me to their headquarters and gave the Doggie valuable time off to speak with me.

Huge gratitude goes to the truly professional Miss Rebecca Constance at Army headquarters, who made things run smoothly. Many thanks for your assistance and permission to use the wonderful photographs of Sarbi taken by an army of Army photographers.

Profound thanks to those who shared their personal and professional insights with me: Rick Einstein, Pete 'Lucy' Lawlis, Lyndell Brown, Charles Green, Laura Rodriguez in the United States, Martine Van Bijlert and Alison Rhind in Afghanistan, Sandra Popp and Todd Carson in Dubai, British dog handler Paul Bunker, and Michael McCulloch.

Thanks, too, to the supportive and helpful staff in the art and photographic departments at the Australian War Memorial, and the researchers at the Australian Prime Ministers Centre.

In reconstructing the ambush in Khas Uruzgan, I relied on Sergeant D's personal accounts and recollections, and drew on the many resources listed in the bibliography and cited throughout the book and endnotes. Each soldier has his own unique recollections and experiences, as is to be expected with the chaos and urgency of fighting to stay alive, and may recall things differently. Any errors, however inadvertent, are mine.

To read more about the history of military working dogs in the Australian Army I highly recommend the website of the Australian Defence Force Trackers and War Dogs Association. I owe enormous thanks to the association's president, Lieutenant Colonel George Hulse, RAE, (retired) who explained the Doggies' early history and generously gave me permission to use his combat profile interviews.

Thanks to journalists Robert Carmody, Malcolm Farr, Tom Hyland and Katharine Murphy for your witty insights and assistance. Who said journalism was a dog-eat-dog world?

As ever, enormous thanks to my very good friend and super-sharp agent Selwa Anthony, another devoted dog lover.

Thanks to the great team at Allen & Unwin: publisher Rebecca Kaiser whose enthusiasm for the book was always encouraging, editor Ann Lennox whose patience and attention to detail proved a boon to the manuscript, and copyeditor Nicola Robinson who made valuable suggestions.

Eternal thanks to Linda Smith; a first-rate editor, dear friend, and a wonderful sounding board, simply bursting with ideas, all of them good.

Thanks also to my great supportive mates who pointed out interesting dog stories along the way; Ron Cutler, Miranda Devine, Sharon Krum (one of the finest authors I know—double check on that!), and Janine Perrett.

Mutt mates get a woof for providing houndish inspiration and for being physical and behavioural lab rats: our girl, Seisia, of course, and Jake (big blind red mutt), Biggles (fearless rodent-slaying mutt), Bridie (pedigree), Charlie Girl (princess pedigree), Cooper (goofy pedigree), Dizzy (Staffie), Murphy (lovable oodle mutt), Toohey (a fine-looking, agoraphobic rescue hound) and the ultimate top dog, Zinny, a 17-year-old blue heeler.

My ever-supportive, dog-loving dad, Dixie Lee, deserves a very special mention. He married a beautiful woman, Valda May, whose love of dogs became a family trait. Dogs were a part of my family before I was. Our first family dog was a magnificent mongrel, as have been the three that followed, Ruffles, Zak and Jake. The first, Poncie (named after an Hawaiian actor), arrived about ten months before I did, just as my brother Gavin began crawling. There is a photograph to prove it. My father gives it pride of place, on the kitchen bench in the same house to which that first pup would return. The photograph features my mother, beaming from ear to ear, crawling after a litter of pups trying to choose which mutt she and her baby boy will take home. The choice was made for her: by the pup. He chose my brother. Whenever I look at that photograph now, with my mother gone seventeen long years and decades too soon, her face lit like sunlight as she gently herds the pups, I pinpoint where my dog lover-ness came from. It is genetic.

Final thanks must go to another mad dog lover, JP Clemence. I am fortunate to have a wonderful husband who makes me laugh and who agreed to upturn our lives and take in our own rescue hound, Seisia. She was a fearful and starved pup covered with mange when our neighbour, Chris Hooke, thankfully and heroically plucked her from a tiny town called Seisia in Cape York. We are even more thankful that he couldn't keep her.

Seisia is a black mutt of unknown pedigree(s) and age. She has a grey muzzle, a white zig-zag blaze on her chest and was undeniably naughty the first time I met her. But when she disobediently leapt up on me and raced around with a mouthful of toilet paper, I was hooked. It is almost as if a subsonic ripple of energy (or was it love?) had passed from me to her and back again. I am never happier than with husband and hound.

Sandra Lee
Sydney, 2011